D1033983

Culture on Tour

Edward M. Bruner

Culture on Tour

Ethnographies of Travel

The
University
of Chicago
Press

*Chicago and
London*

Edward M. Bruner is professor emeritus of anthropology and criticism and interpretive theory at the University of Illinois, Urbana-Champaign. His publications include *The Anthropology of Experience*, edited with Victor W. Turner (1986), and *International Tourism: Identity and Change*, edited with Marie-Françoise Lanfant and John B. Allcock (1995).

The University of Chicago Press, Chicago 60637
The University of Chicago Press, Ltd., London

Printed in the United States of America

14 13 12 11 10 09 08 07 06 05 1 2 3 4 5

ISBN: 0-226-07762-4 (cloth)

ISBN: 0-226-07763-2 (paper)

Library of Congress Cataloging-in-Publication Data

Bruner, Edward M.
Culture on tour : ethnographies of travel / Edward M. Bruner.
p. cm.
Includes bibliographical references and index.
ISBN 0-226-07762-4 (cloth : alk. paper)—ISBN 0-226-07763-2 (pbk. : alk. paper)
1. Heritage tourism. 2. Culture—Semiotic models.
I. Title.
G156.5.H47B78 2004
306.4'819—dc22

2004007653

♾ The paper used in this publication meets the minimum requirements of the American National Standard for Information Sciences—Permanence of Paper for Printed Library Materials, ANSI Z39.48-1992.

To Cookie

CONTENTS

ILLUSTRATIONS

Introduction
Travel Stories Told and Retold

I LEARNED ABOUT the importance of narrative in tourism and the differences between a touristic and an ethnographic sensibility in 1987, while serving as an academic lecturer on an upscale group tour to Indonesia (E. Bruner 1995). The tourists were almost all college-educated professional or upper-middle-class Americans. Their average age was about fifty, and they were experienced travelers. Almost all had been on previous tours, many with the same tour company.

The trip was a turning point in my thinking about tourism, although my tour guide–lecturer role turned into a personal disaster. I had done years of ethnographic research in Indonesia, spoke the language (Bahasa Indonesia), had published and taught courses on the country, and had been recruited for the job of tour guide–lecturer because of my area expertise. My assignment was to present formal lectures on Indonesian peoples and places, as well as to participate on the tour, answer the tourists' questions, and give on-site explanations of what they were seeing.

It was an ideal situation for me as an ethnographer because it enabled me to study tourism from the inside, as I was there all the time, participating, observing, talking, traveling, eating, and sightseeing with the tourists who were my object of study. I was an attentive listener, always available to hear their reactions to and understandings of the sites presented to them on the tour itinerary. I told the tourists I was an anthropologist specializing in Indonesia and that I had an interest in tourism, but I did not stress that I was studying them. There was a delicious ambiguity in my dual role: I was an anthropologist but also, in effect, one of the tourists, my professional self but also one of them. I was enjoying the tourists but simultaneously observing them, and

I was providing the tourists with the very interpretations that I was studying (see chapter 7).

Was I a closet ethnographer on tour, or a closet tourist doing ethnography? Is Sidney Mintz correct, that "we are all tourists" (1977, 59)? It was similar to being a native anthropologist doing research on my own culture, a culture of travel and tourism, but always striving to maintain some distance so I could return home to write about my experiences. Whatever else may be said of my tour guide role, it had the one overwhelming advantage of allowing me to be the closest I could come to studying tourism from an ethnographic perspective, by actually being there on tour within the tour group.[1]

My difficulties began with Lisa (a pseudonym), the owner of the New York–based tour company that had hired me. I had worked for her agency in 1986, and she rehired me for the same three-week Indonesian tour in 1987.[2] The main difference between the two years was that in 1986 I was completely in charge, whereas Lisa decided to come on the 1987 tour herself because Indonesia was a relatively new country for her agency, which offered tours to many other areas of the world. On the second day of the tour in Jakarta, we had gone to the port, to the National Museum, and to visit other attractions. Because I had been to these sites many times, I began to photograph the tourists photographing the Indonesians. At the end of the day, Lisa told me to stop taking photographs of the tourists as it made them uncomfortable. My hope had been to discuss with the tourists how the Indonesians might feel being photographed by the members of an American tour group,[3] as the tourists never asked the Indonesians for their permission. My aim was to induce some reflexivity and awareness of tourism itself, to ask the tourists to examine their own subject position, but it was not to be. Lisa was clearly in charge.

Later on, as I describe more fully in chapter 7, the tour group moved to the central Javanese city of Yogyakarta to the home of Princess Hadinegoro for a private supper and to witness the Ramayana ballet, a performance based on an old Hindu epic (see Hughes-Freeland 1993). The characters in the dance drama wore elaborate, colorful costumes and flamboyant masks, and their movements were precise and controlled. In 1986 we had seen the same performance in the home of the princess. On that earlier occasion, without Lisa present, after the dance formally ended I had asked the tourists to remain in their seats and had requested that the performers come in their street clothes to meet with the tourists and to talk about their daily lives. A young married Javanese couple, for example, were students at the local Gadja Mada University, one a history major and the other in the dance program. The tourists asked questions, I translated, group photographs were taken, and the discussion was lively.

My objective was to take the performers out of their roles in the timeless Hindu past, with its stereotypic costumes and formal body movements, and to present them as modern Indonesians living in the present. I wanted to deconstruct the Ramayana ballet and the experience of being "guests" in the home of a Javanese princess, and to show that the entire event was constructed for tourism. Ballet was not a Javanese genre, I stated, and the Ramayana version was created in 1961 as a tourist performance (Seminar Sendra Tari Ramayana Nasional 1970), and further, the princess had group tours to her home twenty nights a month. The so-called guests were actually paying customers in a restaurant with a floor show.

On that occasion in 1986, the tourists were so interested in my analysis that a few days later it precipitated my presentation of a two-hour seminar on the concept of authenticity, held in a hotel meeting room in Bali. These educated tourists were not hesitant to disagree with me and they expressed their own views. They were not interested, they said, in "authenticity," but only in a good show. In 1987 Lisa would not permit the dialogue between the performers and the tourists. She prevented me from presenting my understanding of the evening, informed everyone that the event was over, and declared that it was time for the tourists to return to the hotel. The tensions between Lisa and me escalated.

In Bali, I had arranged in advance for a private performance of a Balinese frog dance, which the tourists enjoyed. On the bus I described the history of the frog dance in Bali, explaining that although it appeared traditional, it had in fact been devised in 1970 specifically for tourists, as was the case with many Balinese dances. The *kecak* (the monkey dance) and the current version of the famous *barong* performance had been created for foreign visitors in conjunction with Western choreographers. I described how in the 1930s Western avant-garde intellectuals—Walter Spies, Margaret Mead, Gregory Bateson, and others—had had a profound effect on Balinese arts (H. Geertz 1994; Jacknis 1988), but I explained that change is inherent in all cultures, and that the dances were still quintessentially "Balinese."

My objective was to engage the tourists in a dialogue in which they would think more deeply about such concepts as tradition, culture, and representation. I wanted them to become more reflexive about their touristic experiences. I had more to say, but once again Lisa stepped in. She asked what the frog dance was before 1970 (it had not existed) and effectively silenced me. Soon after, Lisa informed me that I was not being an adequate tour guide, and although I stayed with the group for the remainder of the 1987 tour, she, in effect, fired me.[4]

What was the basis of the conflict between Lisa and me? I see it as a confrontation between two metanarratives, two tourist stories, two competing tales about cultural tourism that parallel in remarkable fashion historical developments within anthropology as a discipline, changes in modes of ethnographic practice, and developments in the evolution of my own career as a cultural anthropologist. The late 1980s were also a time when tourism was emerging as an economic engine in the development of postcolonial societies.

To cut to the heart of the matter, Lisa's master tourist tale, one shared widely within the tourism industry, was to take tourist performances as representations of an authentic culture that were to be accepted as given and to remain essentially unexamined. The Javanese and Balinese dance dramas, and all cultural performances, were to be viewed as replicas of life in the ethnographic present, static, timeless, without history, without agency, without context. My narrative, which I had hoped to share with the tourists, was to examine tourist attractions not for what they were assumed to represent, but for what they actually were. Basically, the conflict between Lisa and me was over which story should be told and who had the right to tell it. Lisa's tourist tale was not reflexive in any respect, whether with regard to the tourists, to the cultural displays and performances, or to tourism more generally.

Performances for tourists have local histories, change over time, and are constructed specifically to be marketed and sold to an audience. My objective was to analyze them not as simulacra but as contemporary rituals offered in a particular political and touristic context, in order to understand the mechanisms of production, the artifices of display, and the contemporary meanings not only for the tourists but also for the performers, the producers, the agents, and all those involved in the touristic presentation.

In Java I introduced native voices and initiated dialogues between the Javanese and the tourists and between the anthropologist and the tourists, rather than speaking with a monological voice-over as the authoritative academic lecturer who would silence both the Indonesians and the tourists. It is the way I teach my anthropology students at the University of Illinois. I do not lecture in a manner that silences my students, but try to challenge them, to precipitate dialogue and debate, and I carried this over to tourism. What I had not counted on was the presence of Lisa, with her power as the owner of the tour agency and intention of presenting her story on her tour. Lisa had wanted an anthropologist who was a 1930s realist ethnographer, not one who was beginning a journey to postmodernism,[5] not one who, from her point of view, was ruining her tour by deconstructing one tourist attraction after another. I saw Lisa, and tourism generally, as chasing anthropology's discarded discourse, presenting cultures as functionally integrated homogeneous entities outside of time, space, and history.

It is not simply that Lisa's vision of tourism was to present frontstage Indonesian attractions whereas I took the tourists backstage, a distinction made famous by Dean MacCannell's pioneering work on staged authenticity (1976, 91–107). MacCannell has a series of fronts displayed to the tourists, based on "show," "mystification," and "a little lie" (1976, 93), but for him there is always a real and true at the very back. His frontstage-backstage distinction, as he clearly states (105), is based on the problem of authenticity and on what he perceives to be the touristic quest for authenticity (see Olsen 2002). Rather, my position is that authenticity is a red herring, to be examined only when the tourists, the locals, or the producers themselves use the term. The research in this book is an effort to move beyond such limiting binaries as authentic-inauthentic, true-false, real-show, back-front. I take the exact opposite approach, analyzing all of the tourist productions I encounter in Indonesia, Africa, and elsewhere for what they are in themselves: authentic—that is, authentic tourist productions that are worthy subjects of serious anthropological inquiry.

I do not look behind, beneath, or beyond anything. I reject concepts such as simulacra that are so privileged by some postmodern scholars (Eco 1986; Baudrillard 1983), in part because what is presented in tourism is new culture constructed specifically for a tourist audience. There is no simulacrum because there is no original. Performances for tourists arise, of course, from within the local cultural matrix, but all performances are "new" in that the context, the audience, and the times are continually changing (E. Bruner 1984b; 1986a). To put it another way, performance is constitutive.[6]

It must be said in fairness that MacCannell's work in 1976 was based on the structuralism then so dominant in the social sciences, which fundamentally looked beneath the surface to an assumed real underlying structure. The frontstage-backstage distinction in the study of tourism focuses on a given people and asks who are the real Balinese or the real Maasai behind the show. I not only reject this deep structuralism, but examine tourist productions within their larger historical, economic, and political context and study the very particularistic local setting within which they are displayed. It is how ethnographers study culture.

I certainly understood Lisa's perspective. She had a business to run and had advertised the trip as an educational tour, an opportunity to see Indonesia from an anthropologist's point of view, which added an aura of authority. The problem was that she had selected the wrong anthropologist as I had already moved away from a classical, objectivist ethnography to a more reflexive, processual, critical interpretive mode. I had been doing this kind of anthropology in the 1980s in my other writings (E. Bruner, ed., 1984; Turner and Bruner 1986) and had continued it in tourism studies.

Ethnography, at the time, was engaged in critical self-examination (Clifford and Marcus 1986; Marcus and Fischer 1986). If scholars were to be featured on educational tours, I wanted to invite the tourists into my anthropological world, with all its turmoil and debates, with the expectation that they would gain a better understanding of how contemporary ethnographers actually worked and thought. They would profit, I believed, by a reflexive examination of themselves in their role as tourists and of how the tourism industry was presenting the world. My method was what Johannes Fabian (1990) or Barbara Kirshenblatt-Gimblett (in Franklin 2001, 215) would call a performative rather than an informative mode of ethnography in that it was reflexive and ironic. I thought of myself as doing "interventional tourism," or "reflexive tourism," to disrupt the tourists' understanding of their travel experience. Indeed, a major objective of anthropology as a discipline is to teach our students and the public to think through their biases, egocentrisms, and taken-for-granted beliefs. Margaret Mead and Oscar Lewis were among those who brought anthropology to a wider audience with the objective of inducing reflexivity about American culture. I believed that within an interventional frame the tourists would learn more about contemporary Indonesia, have an active rather than a passive role, and begin to think about tourism as a mode of learning about other cultures. I rejected stereotypic conceptions of the country, the tourist, the performer, and the anthropologist.

What I eventually learned—to my regret—was that tourists, even those on educational tours, do not really want an ethnographic perspective. I took the 1987 tour group to a Balinese temple festival, a performance by Balinese for Balinese. We arrived at ten o'clock in the morning, too early we found, and we had to wait until shortly after noon before the ritual began. In Bali starting times are always uncertain. It was hot, and the tourists were impatient. Balinese temple festivals, however, are an ethnographer's nirvana—women dancing as if in trance; priests sprinkling holy water; fantastic *barong* and *rangda* masks being assembled for a procession around the temple grounds; incense burning; gamelan playing; offerings of flowers and fruit being regally presented to the gods; odors, sounds, and colors coming from everywhere—everything happening at once, a postmodern pastiche.

Just as the festival was developing, it was announced to the tourists that it was time for lunch and everyone was to return to the bus. I protested, explaining that to see such a Hindu temple ritual was a rare opportunity, that each temple held its festival only once a year, and that anthropologists in these circumstances just hang out and observe. As they were moving toward the air conditioned bus I pleaded with the tourists to remain to see this dazzling ceremony until one tourist said, "But we have seen it."

My efforts in 1986 and 1987 at being an interventional tourist guide to promote an ethnographic understanding were dashed. It was not what the tourists wanted, for after all, they were on vacation, it was time for lunch, and they had an afternoon itinerary. It was a sobering experience for me, and I did not attempt interventional tourism again but used other methodologies in my continuing efforts to understand how tourists travel. The phrase "but we have seen it" still haunts me; it is a vivid reminder of the disparity between touristic and ethnographic ways of seeing.

My Approach

This book explores cultural tourism in Africa, the United States, the Middle East, and Indonesia. It offers a multisited ethnographic analysis of local tourist productions, ranging from safari tours in Kenya, a slave castle in Ghana, and an Abraham Lincoln heritage site in Illinois, to a mountain fortress in Israel, dance dramas in Bali, and an ethnic theme park in Jakarta. My mobile approach is consistent with how tourists travel, from one country and site to another. The photographs in the book replicate how most tourists "see" the Other, through the lens of a camera. The studies were done over a twenty-year period of research, and although there were shifts in my thinking and in the nature of tourism during that time, my theoretical framework remained fairly consistent. I conceive of the work as a single intellectual project that analyzes tourist performances not as representations, metaphors, texts, or simulacra of something located elsewhere, but as social practice to be studied in its own right, grounded by the methods of ethnography. This is taking tourism seriously.

Tourism is a mystifying subject because being a tourist is deprecated by almost everyone. Even tourists themselves belittle tourism as it connotes something commercial, tacky, and superficial (Culler 1981). Those on the Indonesian trip were proud that they had their own academic lecturer, a differentiating status symbol as well as a marketing tool. It set them apart from those other travelers, who, they said, were mere tourists because they didn't even have their own professors.[7] From an ethnographic perspective the anxiety about tourism is especially acute, given that bad ethnography is labeled as touristic, that travel writing is central to the early history of anthropology, and that tourism performs outmoded ethnography. Anthropology as a scientific discipline is dependent upon its being distinguished from tourism (Crick 1995). Over the years, ethnographers have gone to great lengths to differentiate their accounts from those provided by missionaries, explorers, colonialists, travel writers, journalists, and, now, tourists (Stocking 1985; E. Bruner 1989; Clifford 1997a). Yet the similarities are disturbing as so many others journey temporarily to distant lands, observe and experience, and return home with stories about their encounters.

The problem these days is compounded as ethnographers usually find tourists and backpackers wherever they do fieldwork—they are now in competition for the same space (chapter 7). Tourists appear at our cherished field sites as intrusive country cousins, or as Clifford Geertz (1996) put it, "messing up the neighborhood." They are found wandering around, taking photographs, and seeking travel stories, but most often they are left out of professional monographs and articles. The result is publications that are reminiscent of 1920s ethnographic accounts that omitted any reference to the colonial governments around them and produced fantasy ethnography, which anthropologists call writing in the "ethnographic present," a mode now restaged in tourist productions. The contemporary omission of tourists is a similar phenomenon, a purposeful ignoring of that which is present but that ethnography finds embarrassing or threatening to its privileged position.[8] This ethnographic practice might be called writing in the "touristic nonpresent." We anthropologists are repeating the sins of our ancestors.

Whatever may or may not have been achieved in the 1986 and 1987 tours to Indonesia, a processual, constructivist, and performative perspective that views culture as emergent was gaining momentum within the discipline, and it is employed systematically in all of the analyses of tourist productions in this book. Although my first general statements of this position appeared in E. Bruner 1984b and 1986a, my previous studies reflected it (e.g., E. Bruner 1973a).

As an anthropology graduate student at the University of Chicago in the early 1950s, I worked in the realist ethnographic mode of the era, but nevertheless, there were continuities between those efforts and my later work, up to the present. In my dissertation I studied Native Americans: why and how they changed (E. Bruner 1955, 1961), why some aspects of culture changed more than others (E. Bruner 1956a), and why some Indian peoples remained on the reservation while others left (E. Bruner 1956b). In 1957 I initiated fieldwork in an Indonesian village among the Toba Batak of Sumatra, studying change and kinship, but after six months, because a regional revolution threatened full-scale warfare in those Southeast Asian mountain villages, I moved to the coastal city of Medan and changed my project to an examination of the processes of urbanization among urban Batak. I returned to Indonesia in 1969 as political unrest diminished, traveled to Sumatra in the early 1970s, and revisited the Toba Batak village of my earlier fieldwork in 1997 (chapter 9). Throughout this time my research questions remained the same—how and why Toba Batak culture had changed, how the social system worked, and what the interactions were among village and urban Batak (E. Bruner 1961, 1963, 1972, 1973b, 1974a, 1984a).

In this all too brief discussion of fifty years of empirical ethnography, what is constant is a focus on encounters, change, movement, mobility, and process. I have been fascinated by interactions between Native Americans on the reservation and those who have left, between Toba Batak from the village and those from the city, and later between tourists and indigenous people in the developing world. To me, cultures were never fixed, enclosed units or homogeneous, integrated entities. I learned at Chicago from reading George Herbert Mead and by working with the symbolic interactionist Herbert Blumer that persons have active selves and select among alternative courses of action. I discussed the developing concept of cultural performance with Milton Singer at Chicago in the 1950s, but I came to more deeply appreciate the power of a performative perspective by working with Barbara Kirshenblatt-Gimblett in 1983–1984, as we led a group of American students on a study-abroad program.[9] Over a full academic year, working together, we visited Kobe, Bali, Benares, Nairobi, Cairo, and Jerusalem, studying cultural performances. Although we were scholars, an anthropologist and a folklorist, we came to realize that we were, in effect, traveling as tourists: we were in each place for a short time, learning about indigenous culture but also about tourist attractions, interacting with a mix of other ethnographers and travelers, tourists, and locals (Franklin 2001, 212). In this cauldron, we were inevitably led to reflect on the nature of travel, tourism, and the ethnographic enterprise.

With a rereading of Marx in the early 1980s, I more deeply appreciated the role of conflict in social life and the contested nature of all cultures. My theoretical position, constructivism, which sees culture as emergent, was inherent in symbolic interactionism and also in the early Marx and Engels (1947). It enhanced my reading of Wilhelm Dilthey, introduced to me by Victor Turner, and of Mikhail Bakhtin (chapter 6), for whom language and culture are always evolving. I read Bakhtin, Roland Barthes, Jacques Derrida, and Michel Foucault, and I studied other streams of European thought by participating in the faculty reading group of the Unit for Criticism and Interpretive Theory at the University of Illinois.[10] It was in the reading group that I developed my continuing interest in narrativity (E. Bruner 1986b; E. Bruner, ed., 1984).

Thus, there was a temporal and theoretical convergence among my personal intellectual development, changes in the discipline of anthropology, and my switch to tourism as a new field of study. My aim was to write tourism as others were writing culture and to apply a radically reflexive ethnography to tourism research. This was a good fit. Contemporary tourism involves travel, however temporary and fleeting, by Western peoples on a massive scale to the margins of empire and to the peripheries of modernity; it is one of the greatest population movements of all time. In response, Third World people, with tour agents and local producers, actively strive to understand tourists' desires. Throughout the world they rework their indigenous cultures to construct new emergent cultures specifically for tourist audiences. Tourist performances represent new culture in that they have been modified to fit the touristic master narrative, have been shortened to fit the tour schedule, have been edited so as to be comprehensible to a visiting audience, and are performed regularly at set times and usually on stage. I was ready to study tourism because it so perfectly incorporates my interests in travel, movement, encounters, reflexivity, agency, contested narratives, and emergent culture—precisely the themes reflected in this book.

Stories Foreign and Domestic

John Urry (1990, 1), in his important work on the tourist gaze, says that tourists travel to consume "experiences which are different from those typically encountered in everyday life." We go away to see something different. His statement is more accurate for foreign tourists than for domestic ones. On their journeys to Kenya to see the primitive Maasai or to Bali to experience that South Sea island paradise, American and European travelers may indeed be foreigners seeking difference. But urban Toba Batak who visit Taman Mini (chapter 8), an ethnic theme park in Jakarta, may go to a reproduction of a Toba Batak house located within the park to reexperience their own village culture and identity, seeking not difference but similarity. Urban dwellers from Nairobi going to the ethnic displays at Bomas (chapter 2) to witness the tribal dances of Kenya are domestic tourists who are consuming themselves. American tourists to New Salem (chapter 5), a reconstructed Abraham Lincoln heritage site, reinforce their own sense of American history to strengthen a patrimony that is already theirs.

The contrast between foreign and domestic tourism has long been recognized in the scholarly literature (Smith and Wanhill, eds., 1986), but the importance of the distinction has not yet been fully appreciated; nor have the nuances and complications received sufficient theoretical attention. All too often anthropologists speak of tourism only when they mean foreign or international tourism. These issues are discussed further in chapters 2, and 8. There are cases when the difference between what is domestic and what is foreign depends on one's standpoint, and other instances when there is a transition between the two.

For example, the former slave fort of Elmina Castle in Ghana (chapter 3) has been developed into a tourist site that attracts a large number of African American tourists. Most come to Ghana to seek their roots, to return to Mother Africa, to search for similarity based on origin and skin color, but the Ghanaians perceive the African Americans as foreigners, as Americans, as different from themselves. So difference and similarity depend upon position and perspective. African Americans may see themselves as domestic tourists returning home, but Ghanaians do not share this view.

Some tourists to New Salem, the Lincoln site, are immigrants who come by chartered bus from Chicago in preparation for their examination to become U.S. citizens, to learn about Abraham Lincoln, and to experience first-hand an aspect of American history. They are foreign tourists in transition to becoming domestic ones. What is initially difference will become similarity if they pass their examinations and become American citizens.

Contested Sites

Tourists come to New Salem for many reasons, and some are not particularly interested in either American history or Abraham Lincoln. They visit because of the many craft making displays at the site, including presentations of blacksmithing, weaving, shoe making, and the production of candles and quilts. For these visitors New Salem evokes earlier times before industrial production, when life was simpler, when craftspeople produced by hand what was consumed. These tourists see themselves as returning to a cherished past as pioneers, making a journey not in space but in time. They are time tourists to the past. New Salem is a contested site in what might be called a soft contestation between a narrative about Abraham Lincoln's place in American political history and a narrative about folk culture in nineteenth-century America (chapter 4). Or to put it another way, the Abraham Lincoln story is the one told at New Salem by the state, which is the official producer, and by academic historians, while the folk culture story derives from American popular culture. The two narratives struggle for dominance as the tourists resist or undermine the official interpretation of the production. Professional historians, too, write against popular interpretations.

Masada, in Israel, is a historic site in Jewish history visited by domestic and foreign tourists alike, and it too is strongly contested, but this is a case of hard contestation. People fought and died in the past over control of the physical Masada, and they are fighting and dying today for what Masada means (chapter 6). The struggle is between those for whom Masada is a symbol of Jewish resistance against imperial Rome in the years A.D. 70–73 and those for whom Masada is a living symbol of the suicidal isolation of Israel from its Arab neighbors. The past merges with the present and time frames become blurred as the question is posed, then and now: Should the Jews fight or accommodate? Historic sites like Masada are invariably contested as tourist tales merge with national narratives of origin. For two thousand years Masada has moved in and out of history, sometimes silent, at other times pregnant with meaning, a site of fierce struggle, subject to reinterpretation as circumstances change so the struggle is always contemporary, always in the present.

Contested sites such as New Salem, Masada, and Elmina Castle in Ghana raise the key narrative question of who has the right to tell the story. The sites themselves are not passive for they are given meaning and are constituted by the narratives that envelope them, which initiates a dialogue. Without a story, New Salem would be an empty place on the prairie, Masada a massive rock in the desert, and Elmina an abandoned fortress. These sites remind us to be cautious about monolithic interpretations that are static and ahistorical, that homogenize meaning, and to be careful about assuming that the official version of the site is accepted by all parties, as if reception were identical with production. The traveler's and the local's understanding does not always correspond with the producer's intentions.

MacCannell (2001) has written a helpful paper titled "Tourist Agency," but my reaction is that of course tourists have agency, as do the local people, the producers, the tour companies, and even the anthropologists—all actors in the coproduction of the touristic drama (Jules-Rosette and Bruner 1994). There are no persons without agency, without active selves, except possibly as described in the pages of some 1930s academic journals. To conceive of tourists without agency, or of natives[11] as objects, would be to write about them as if they were automatons. Tourist and native are not fixed, irreversible slots, as local people who are the object of the tourist gaze in their own country may themselves subsequently travel to Europe or America as tourists and direct their gaze at those very same Euro-Americans. I argue against a fixed, static model that sees producers as in control, natives as exploited, and tourists as dupes. The research studies in this book analyze tourist sites and performances as evolving and historical—or to put it more simply, as alive.

On the other hand, to view tourism solely within the frame of interaction among the various actors is too narrow. A site is not fully described from the actors' perspective, but must be seen in its larger political and economic context as mediating between the global and the local. A key advantage of studying a specific attraction in a single place is that the researcher can examine local and world politics ethnographically as they manifest themselves in the site, as opposed to resorting to facile overgeneralizations about tourism. Not all the chapters in this book achieve these objectives equally well, but taken together they do analyze tourist productions in their multilayered, living complexity from multiple perspectives.

Home, Away, and the Touristic Borderzone

In his early articles on the anthropology of tourism, Nelson Graburn (1977, 1983) describes tourism as a sacred journey from home to away, followed by a return to home. He continues in the classic tradition of H. Hubert and M. Mauss (1898/1964), Arnold Van Gennep (1909/1960), and Victor Turner (1969), applying their analyses of ritual and pilgrimage to tourism, considering it as a rite of passage characterized by three stages: travel from the familiar everyday world to another location; temporary residence in the nonordinary place while in a liberated, liminal state; then a return to home, transformed by the ritual experience. With variations this threefold scheme has appeared frequently in tourism literature, although scholars have problematized the concepts of home and away (Urry 2000). There is some validity to the model, and I use a modified form in a later discussion of tourist narratives. My critique, however, stems from ethnographic observations about what happens on tour and from what I have learned by interviewing tourists. I extend my understandings beyond an examination of home and away and reconceptualize tourism space altogether.

There is a diurnal rhythm to touring. Typically, the tourists are housed in a hotel or similar accommodation in the evening, and it is during the day that they go sightseeing to the places on the tour itinerary. Thus within the larger frame of the entire journey, there is an internal daily fluctuation of being in the hotel, their temporary home, during the evening, and out sightseeing each day. Tourist brochures and advertising emphasize this division. They contrast the luxury of the accommodations they provide—the spacious rooms, gourmet food, swimming pools, excellent service, comfort, and safety like that of home—with the uniqueness of the sights to be seen in such foreign places as Indonesia or Kenya during the day. Thus the tour is not all "away"; it is also home because it oscillates between the two within the larger frame of the vacation (Price and Price 1992, 48).

For example, in 1999 I participated in an Intrav tour to Africa by private jet that started in Cape Town, then proceeded to game parks in South Africa, Zimbabwe, Botswana, Tanzania, and Kenya, and ended in Egypt (chapter 2). It was a three-week tour that cost $36,800 per person because the crew of fourteen and the private jet remained with the group throughout the entire trip from one end of Africa to the other.[12] It was the ultimate tour, so certain features that other trips possessed were exaggerated and enhanced. The tour provided superb information on luxury tourism.

In Cape Town the group stayed at the Mount Nelson Hotel, described in the brochure as "Surrounded by seven acres of peaceful, lush parkland at the foot of Table Mountain. Boasting dignity and elegance, the Mount Nelson reigns as one of the world's greatest hotels—a true international destination in the grand tradition. The hotel features heated swimming pools, all-weather tennis courts and a squash court for recreation [and] several golf courses." The booklet for the Victoria Falls Hotel in Zimbabwe describes the history of the hotel; here I summarize portions.

When the hotel was opened in 1904, the manager was the Italian Pierre Gavuzzi, who had formerly been with the Carlton and Savoy hotels in London. "His chef was a Frenchman, the barman came from Chicago, and the waiters were Arabs." The first royal visitor was Princess Christian of Schleswig Holstein, and in 1961 the visit of His Majesty King George VI of England, Queen Elizabeth, and the two princesses, Elizabeth and Margaret, was the "highlight" of the season. There is a Stanley bar and a Livingston suite, and the booklet recalls the time in 1869 when Stanley, a reporter from the *New York Herald*, uttered the famous words, "Dr. Livingston, I presume!"

What is being sold here? First, the hotels are not just places to sleep, they are tourist attractions in themselves. Second, the tour is not just about Africa, it is about social class in America and Europe. Third, the tourists are placed in a colonial subject position as they survey the landscape, the primitive tribes, and the wild animals of the African bush. They are tourists, but given their wealth, they are American royalty, and they expect to be treated as such. Fourth, there is no compromise on luxury, which at least replicates what these wealthy tourists are accustomed to in everyday life. When the Intrav private jet returned to the United States, at least two tourist families I knew had their own private jets waiting at the airport to take them to their home destinations, although commercial flights were readily available.

My colleague Alma Gottlieb (1982), in a frequently cited paper, argues that a class inversion happens in tourism: working-class people on tour desire to emulate the wealthy, while the upper classes favor a more modest and folk-like experience, although the inversion can take the form of either dissolution or accentuation. The American tourists on the Intrav tour and on other, less extravagant tours for which I have served as a guide may have wanted the destination to be wild, exotic, and different from everyday life, but they were adamant that their hotels, food, lodging, and service be first-class.[13] Nevertheless, I would resist viewing luxury tourism simply as a form of conspicuous consumption, although such consumption may be an important aspect of it.

Rather, many of these older wealthy tourists revealed in their conservations with me that they saw travel as a project of self-development, as a way of learning about the world. Tourism for them was not just a reaffirmation of their current status, but a statement about the future—that life can go on, that their world can expand, that they can acquire yet more knowledge and experience.

The modes of transportation were spectacular on the African Intrav tour. The private jet, an L1011, which regularly has 362 seats, had been reconditioned to accommodate only eighty-three persons, all in first-class sleeper seats. A grand buffet with a bar was always available in a lounge at the back of the plane, and the food was served with "elegant china, crystal and linens." The tour featured helicopter rides around the Cape of Good Hope; an overnight in a private compartment on the legendary Blue Train of South Africa, "one of the greatest in the world . . . where everything is refined," according to the Intrav brochure; another helicopter ride over Victoria Falls; a hot-air balloon excursion over the Masai Mara game reserve in Kenya; flights on chartered small aircraft to places where the wide-bodied L1011 jet could not land; and cruises down the Nile "aboard the exclusively reserved M.S. Nile Maxime."

The tour did not just present a view of Africa from a colonial position, but with the private jet, chartered aircraft, helicopters, and hot-air balloons, the gaze was from above, a lofty perspective from which to look down at Africa and the Africans. There was a vast discrepancy between the tour and the realities of African life, of people working and raising their families, sometimes in the context of famine, poverty, the AIDS epidemic, and military conflict. Most important, there was little exposure to the everyday life of African people.

While the Intrav tour may have expanded the envelope, tourism is always as much about the accommodations and forms of transportation as it is about the destination. This is true not only of luxury tourism. Backpackers delight in finding out from the Lonely Planet guidebooks or from travelers like themselves distinctive youth hostels or other inexpensive places to sleep, they talk of eating local foods in picturesque restaurants, and they tell stories about their ride in a crowded public bus with chickens flying about. Backpackers, too, have their own vision of appropriate accommodations, modes of travel, and narrative structures, and a segment of the tourism industry caters to their desires. Backpackers are adamant in distinguishing themselves from tourists, but they are, after all, the children of the middle-class mass tourists they despise, and their travel represents just a stage in the life cycle within the touristic enterprise. Though they are more adventurous in seeking new destinations and there are other differences, they generally journey to the same places and see the same attractions group tourists do.[14]

What do the tourists talk about among themselves while on the tour? When I was traveling in Indonesia and Africa, I listened carefully to the tourists' conversations and was surprised to learn that they talk less about Indonesia or Africa than about tourism and themselves. After all, they do not know much about the peoples or the cultures of the countries they are visiting, as they lack knowledge at the outset and they are never entirely sure about what is presented to them on tour. There is an existential ambiguity about the constructed tourist performances they witness and about the explanations offered by their guides because they have no independent or positive ways of knowing the validity of what they are seeing and hearing, unless they are willing to do serious research before the tour. Some accept what is presented, but many others develop what I call the "questioning gaze" (chapter 2). While they may be uncertain about the destination culture, however, most travel regularly on different tours, so they are experts on tourism.

Much of the dialogue among tourists as they are traveling, sightseeing, and eating together is about the hotels, the food, the transportation, and the other specificities of the tour at hand and about other tours as well. During one lunch around a large table in central Java, the entire conversation was about China, in part about what the tourists had seen there, but also about who had been the first to visit after China was opened to tourism, and about other tourists they had encountered while on their China trips. It was a conversation about status and about the tourists' own authenticity as experienced travelers.

The tourists also told family stories and personal narratives and discussed problems they were having with their businesses or with their children or grandchildren. These were tales about home and about themselves. They were the kinds of conversations that might be held among casual friends at a dinner party in their home community. Although I tried not to ask direct personal questions, by the end of each tour I knew almost everyone's occupation, lifestyle, and approximate level of income.[15] My wife and I were not exempt: I found myself talking about my life as a professor, my wife talked about her work as a reading specialist and counselor, and we told stories about our children. The anthropology of tourism tends to neglect tourist talk, possibly because that talk does not focus on the distinctive anthropological characteristics of the destination culture.

The stories tourists tell depend in part on the social context of reception; on whether one is traveling alone, with family or friends, on a school trip, or with a tour group; and on whether stories about the trip will be told after the tourists have returned home. All tellings are situated and no story is told in a vacuum, for at the very minimum the teller is also an audience of one.

Because New Salem is located in Illinois and is readily accessible by car, many visitors come in family groups, and many parents see themselves as teaching their children about American history. In other cases the context of reception of tourist talk may override or modify the intentions of the production the tourists have come to witness. Group tours to Africa usually recruit strangers from similar socioeconomic backgrounds, and this structure of reception is highly significant in determining what the tourists talk about. Thus, there are two ethnographies of travel, one of performances in the destination culture, and a second of the traveling unit, which may be conceptualized as its own site of cultural production, a performance in itself. The total tourist experience encompasses both the destination country and the journey to that destination.

Tourists, then, experience home while away, a home created by the tourism industry in the accommodations and modes of travel, and a home constructed by the tourists themselves in their conversations.[16] Home consists of the familiar, of expected comforts, and of interactions with persons like oneself. Where then, for these foreign tourists, is the away part—the Maasai and the Balinese, Africa and Indonesia, the exotic Other, the content of alien cultures and places, what the tour is supposedly about?

In the main it is located in what I call the touristic borderzone, a point of conjuncture, a behavioral field that I think of in spatial terms usually as a distinct meeting place between the tourists who come forth from their hotels and the local performers, the "natives," who leave their homes to engage the tourists in structured ways in predetermined localities for defined periods of time (chapter 7). The concept of the borderzone focuses on a localized event, limited in space and time, as an encounter between foreign visitors and locals. The two groups approach it from very different perspectives. Tourists are mobile; they travel through the sites and usually never return. Locals remain in the area and witness a stream of different tour groups flowing through. Tourists seek peak experiences; locals and producers organize these experiences for the tourists but live mostly in the everyday. Although the borderzone is about the local, what is performed there takes account of global and international flows as tourism development in the Third World requires the involvement of the nation-state and transnational networks. The focus on borderzones in these studies makes possible the ethnographic exploration of local practice in specific sites within a larger frame. The symbolic interactionist position I studied at Chicago as a graduate student applies here: although pretour tourist tales structure the engagement, the final meaning for the tourists, locals, and producers is not given a priori but emerges in dialogic interplay during their interactions in the borderzone.

Although the borderzone is located in an actual place in the world, what is created there is a cultural imaginary, a fantasy, in itself not a real-life culture but a constructed theatrical one (cf. Ness 2003). In the borderzone each group knows its part in the touristic drama. It is like a hospital setting in which, hopefully, the patients are compliant, the nurses caring, the doctors knowledgeable, and the administrators efficient so the hospital works well as a system. In tourism, hopefully, the natives act primitive, the tourists suspend disbelief, the producers put on a superior show, and the government provides adequate infrastructure. Of course, it doesn't always work well, and there are conflicts of interest—natives can become hostile, performances can be uninteresting, the narrative structure can become muddled, the tourists can reject the performances, and the politicians can become too greedy. In these cases tourism declines. Therefore, all parties will gain to the extent that each plays its proper collaborative role. Still, the roles are not fixed or a priori, for in my conceptualization locals are not passive recipients of a touristic invader from the outside. Rather, both locals and tourists engage in a coproduction: they each take account of the other in an ever-shifting, contested, evolving borderzone of engagement.

My use of the term *borderzone* differs from the that of other writers. Gloria Anzaldúa (1987) and Guillermo Gómez-Peña (1993) theorize about the U.S.-Mexican border, but the situation is different for tourism to the underdeveloped world, as the touristic borderzone is not like a fixed national boundary separating two different cultures and nations. Tourists are not migrants. The performances by Gómez-Peña work so well precisely because of their penetrating insights and ironic criticisms of borderzone practices. But if peoples like the Maasai or the Balinese were to step out of their assigned roles in exotica, or if they were to portray their culture with too much irony or political commentary, it would be bad for business.

MacCannell's (1992, 2) empty meeting ground is somewhat similar to the touristic borderzone, especially when he writes that it is "vibrant with people and potential," a site of new subjectivities and consciousness where new culture and relationships emerge. Mary Louise Pratt (1992, 6) defines a contact zone as "the space of colonial encounters," but for her the relations that develop in the zone usually involve "coercion, racial inequality, and intractable conflict," a quite critical view that I would hesitate to impose on all touristic borderzones. I very much agree with Homi Bhabha's (1994, 2) statement that what he calls the Third Space cannot be read as a "reflection of *pre-given* ethnic or cultural traits set in the fixed tablet of tradition."

My conceptualization, based more on performance theory (see Edensor 2001), sees tourism as improvisational theater with the stage located in the borderzone, where both tourists and locals are actors. Borderzones may be located anywhere, even within the tourist hotels where organized dance or musical performances are held in the early evenings. I have witnessed Maasai wildly dancing with spears in the cocktail lounge of an elegant hotel in Tanzania, certainly an incongruous setting, but a touristic borderzone nevertheless. After the dance, the Maasai do not sit at the bar and order a beer, which they may do elsewhere, but they leave the hotel entirely after the curtain closes on their act. Maasai dancing in this context is a tourist performance for an audience with a defined beginning and ending, where the Maasai arrive as actors and rework their culture while the tourists watch, and after which they leave the stage and the tourists move on. Occasionally tourists and natives do move into each others' space as boundaries are not absolutely rigid and there are transgressions and resistance. In upscale group tourism, however, the kind described here, the entire itinerary is arranged in advance, and the encounters most frequently take place in the borderzone. On the 1999 Intrav Africa tour there were visits to native villages, but the villagers were prepared in advance, they were paid, they expected to be photographed, and they displayed souvenirs for sale.

Narrative and Experience

Thus far I have used the term *tourist tales* rather loosely, and some conceptual clarification is called for.[17] So much has been written about narrative in the past few decades that Jerome Bruner (2003, 111) refers to the "narrative turn," but various scholars use the same terms differently. Thus it will be helpful to define my terms and explain my usage, as narratives appear so frequently in the studies that follow.

I make a distinction between the trip as lived: as it actually happened, the reality; the trip as experienced: consisting of the images, feelings, desires, thoughts, and meanings that emerge in individual consciousness; and the trip as told: usually a story, but possibly a series of photographs or other forms of expression (E. Bruner 1984b, 7). Some scholars do not make a threefold distinction. For example, Cheryl Mattingly (1998) merges life as lived with life as experienced and places them in opposition to life as told. I believe the threefold distinction is helpful. The trip as lived, as experienced, and as told are never exact replicas of one another, and there is no precise mimetic correspondence, but this does not mean that there is no influence or mutual interdependence of one on the other. Indeed, the problem in ethnographic narrative analysis is to sort out the interdependencies between life as lived, as experienced, and as told. In literary analysis, on the other hand, there is no life as lived, but only text.

Among scholars of narrativity, there is wide agreement that no story could possibly encompass the entire trip as lived or experienced as there are always omissions, distortions, and condensations, and in any case, to tell the entire story would take as long as the trip. No representation is ever an exact replica of an event; there is always an existential residue, a part of the experience that remains untold. Furthermore, stories have conventions of telling that are dependent on the narrator, the audience, and the context. Each subsequent telling, although based on the previous one, is in itself emergent because the situation of the telling has changed. Jerome Bruner (1986) and Cheryl Mattingly (1998) suggest that stories are told primarily about the breaches in everyday life, about the extraordinary. Such incidents do provide material for good stories, but my data suggest that tourist tales are about the routine as well as the unexpected.

Almost all theorists agree that narratives make meaning, and some suggest that narratives are required for meaning to be made (J. Bruner 2003). Experience may be the ultimate tourist commodity (chapter 1), but in itself experience is inchoate without an ordering narrative, for it is the story, the telling, that makes sense of it all, and the story is how people interpret their journey and their lives. As a guide in Thailand I took a small group of tourists on a small open boat on the Mae Kok River from the town of Chiang Rai to the town of Chiang Mai. It was a bleak, unfamiliar scene. There was no sun, rain was coming down in buckets, and a soldier from the Thai army was seated in the back of the boat, armed with a rifle, to serve as a guard. The tourists were nervous and somewhat disoriented until one said, "This is like the movies about the Vietnam War along the Mekong." The statement became the frame for the rest of the journey, for with that guiding narrative the tourists were transformed into American soldiers scanning the river bank for Vietcong.

In 1984 I lived in Benares, India, for six weeks with a student group and concluded that it made a poor tourist site, as there was no clear narrative structure about the place. There were no markers, boundaries, or framing, and the site was interpretatively intimidating. For foreign tourists it was not readily accessible, although the scene was fantastic, with Hindu holy men bathing in the River Ganges, cremations held along the banks of the river, cows in the roads, colorful costumes, and ancient buildings. There were very few foreign tourists, but a large inflow of domestic Hindu pilgrims. Our student group read about India, Hinduism, and Benares, spoke to local scholars, lived with families, attended ceremonies, did ethnography, and went to yoga classes, but they never got a handle on it. In the end, I just surrendered to the sights, sounds, and smells of Benares, to the memorable experience of being there, but I never did write or tell about it. Possibly the dominant narrative of indigenous Hindu pilgrims was so overwhelming that a presentation of Benares for foreigners had not yet been developed. In any case, for me it was unstoryable, possibly because of my own failure to devise a coherent travel narrative.

I make a distinction between metanarratives and the tourist tales told before, during, and after the trip. Metanarratives are the largest conceptual frame within which tourism operates. They are not attached to any locality or to any particular tour, and they are usually taken for granted, not brought to consciousness. For example, Lisa's story, which sees tourist performances as representations of an authentic culture, and my view of tourist performances as constructed and historically situated are what I call metanarratives. Lisa was probably not aware of her metanarrative, and I am aware of mine only because my story arose in opposition to hers, as there was at the time a lively debate on the subject within anthropology. On one occasion when I was serving as a guide, when we were about to witness a performance one of the women in the group said to me, with a smile, "Here comes the tourist dance." Her statement constructed a touristic frame around the event so that, irrespective of cultural content, tourism itself became the context that conferred meaning. Just traveling as a tourist, applying the label to oneself, constitutes the locality visited as a tourist destination.

Another metanarrative, which guided the organization of the Intrav African tour as it does many others, is one of privileged Westerners viewing the wildlife and peoples of Africa. Tourists see themselves as elite members of the civilized world who have the resources, leisure time, adventurous spirit, and discriminating taste to travel to see less developed, more primitive populations (E. Bruner 1991). It is primarily a narrative of older, wealthier whites viewing younger, poorer darker-skinned people. As I have written previously, "narratives are not only structures of meaning but structures of power" (E. Bruner 1986b, 144). To participate in such a tour in the Third World is to buy into and reinforce a story of unequal power relations, neocolonialism, and elitism.[18] A subtext is that of the disappearing savage, the idea that authentic primitive cultures are being eroded by the forces of modernization. The iconic white colonialists in Africa presented themselves as controlling the wildlife and the people. In replicating the colonial experience, tourism is conservative and even reactionary, frequently retelling outmoded stories, reproducing stereotypes, replicating fantasy, or simulating a discarded historical vision (E. Bruner 2002).[19] Susan Sontag (2003, 110) makes an observation that may be applied to tourism performances: "To speak of reality becoming a spectacle is a breathtaking provincialism. It universalizes the viewing habits of a small, educated population living in the rich part of the world."

Less encompassing in scope and more attached to particular regions are tourist tales. Because there are no naive travelers, tourists begin each trip with some preconceptions about the destination—a pretour narrative. The tourists then reshape and personalize the pretour narrative in terms of their lived experience on tour. Upon returning home, tourists further alter their stories about the journey into what is usually a more coherent narrative.

Before the tour group comes together, tourists gather information about the destination that is based on many sources, including Western popular culture themes—for example, the African primitive, the Balinese island paradise, Egypt as the land of the pharaohs, or the strong and honest but humble Abraham Lincoln, and each of these is expanded into a story.[20] The tourism industry organizes the tour with these master stories in mind. They are the basis for tourist brochures and serve as a script for the tourist production, although no tour can be so well scripted that there are no gaps or surprises.

When a new area is being developed for tourism, the local government and tourism consultants strive to devise an appropriate story line for the site, for without it a destination may be difficult to sell. Encompassing narratives require less detailed explanation by guides or markers at particular sites on the itinerary, as the interpretation flows from the master story and is more self-evident. Tour brochures, government tourism bureaus, travel agents, travel writers, media, airlines, and hotels work within the frame of the pretour master narrative in their writing, advertising, photography, decor, and depiction of the destination. It is marketing, branding, presenting a product, selling an experience. Here is Out of Africa, Wild Kingdom, The African Queen, National Geographic, all skilled presentations of popular culture images. Tourism is not that innovative in inventing new narratives but rather seeks new locations in which to tell old stories, possibly because those stories are the ones that the tourist consumer is willing to buy. The disadvantage of such scripted stories, of course, is that so much cultural content is left out or masked; it is what I call the "touristic untold," and it is part of the politics of selection (Trouillot 1995).

One finding from my studies is that especially in areas with well-established tourism, as new culture is developed for tourists, the way local peoples tell stories about their traditions to foreigners influences how they talk about and express their own culture to themselves. Cultural performances constructed for tourists in Bali begin to be performed in Balinese ritual and may indeed be described by subsequent ethnographers as parts of traditional Balinese culture (chapter 7). Further, American narratives about Africa that are performed in Africa by Africans for American tourists are presented and viewed as African culture (chapter 2). It has been suggested that the attention given by professional historians to the early years of Abraham Lincoln in the community of New Salem is a direct consequence of the reconstruction of New Salem as a heritage site for tourism (chapter 4). The development of Elmina Castle in Ghana as a tourist attraction has given rise to multiple conflicts between foreigners and Ghanaians about who owns the castle and who has the right to tell which story (chapter 3). Tourism changed life as lived. Tourist tales are not fixed, self-contained entities. Our stories merge with theirs, genres become blurred, the border between tourism and ethnography becomes porous, and the line between subject and object becomes obscure.

Given the authority of pretour narratives as constructed by the tourism industry and embedded in Western discourse, what can tourists learn on a tour that is new, and what are their responses to the master narratives? The tour guides retell the pretour narrative, but also provide random information about the site or the country and describe amusing incidents to keep the tourists entertained. Tourists' reactions are varied. I have known some tourists who accept the pretour narrative and rarely question it, while others are less passive and challenge the narrative as well as most of what they are told by the guides. The tour group is not monolithic. However, aside from these individual differences, which are important in themselves, the question remains: How does one go beyond the closed circle of simply replicating an a priori narrative? Are tourists just revisiting their own former stories?

To paraphrase Ricoeur (1984, 74, as quoted in Mattingly 1998, 46), tourists travel in quest of a narrative, for tales to tell as well as for sights to see, like Rosaldo's (1986) Illongot, who hunt for stories as well as for meat. The tourists' objective is to hunt for experiences that will make prime stories in which the tourist is a main character, so as to dramatize and personalize the tour and to claim the journey as their own. Although many tourist stories are about the everyday, the ones most cherished are those about experiences outside the regular itinerary that lead to improvisation as they introduce spontaneity and unexpected elements of adventure. Tourists may seek these experiences on their own or they may just happen.

Once when I was in Java, our tour bus was delayed by an accident on the road that blocked traffic for hours. I took advantage of the moment by bringing a group of tourists into a Javanese home, with permission. There we were welcomed and served tea as hoards of children looked at us through the window. Another time, at a Balinese ceremony in Batuan, we unexpectedly met Hildred Geertz, who was there as part of her long-term study of Balinese ethnography. She took the tour group to meet a Balinese artist, and along the way we passed the home occupied in the 1930s by Margaret Mead and Gregory Bateson. That merging of tourism and ethnography was, for the tourists, a highlight of their Indonesian trip. They were enamored by the metaethnography of people and places connected to famous past ethnographers, like Mead and Bateson, who had the aura and romantic distance required to become tourist attractions; still, the tourists had no patience for ethnography as actually practiced.[21]

The photographs and souvenirs that tourists gather (S. Stewart 1984) may have intrinsic value in themselves, but they also perform the key function of providing tourists an opportunity to tell and personalize the story of the journey. A souvenir becomes the focus of a story, less frequently about how the object is used within the indigenous culture, and more often about the details of the purchase—the bargaining and the acquisition. Photographs taken of tourists proudly smiling in front of historical sites or familiar icons are not just shown, but serve as mnemonic devices for storytelling. And the tales do not merely repeat a pretour story, they embellish, privatize, and transform the master narrative. Any item may serve as a mnemonic—even a postcard, an airline ticket stub, or a restaurant menu. Thus, the tour is not just a replay of an old story; it is in itself a site of cultural production that generates new experiences and new stories. The tour is a story in the making. The vision of the posttour telling, which will be delivered in a living room full of family and friends once the traveler returns home, is present in the tourist's mind during the tour, and it structures the actual tour as lived. The quest for stories changes the experience of the tour, for the tourists are not just living in the moment, but are directing their actions toward encounters that will form the basis of future stories.

Another way tourists move beyond the pretour narrative during the tour stems from the sheer materiality of being there, engaging in the practice of the tour, enacting the itinerary, and moving through the site, be it a Maasai compound, a Balinese dance performance, a five-hundred-year-old castle in Ghana, or an 1830s Abraham Lincoln heritage site. To perform the site is to inscribe the pretour narrative within the body of the tourist. Conversely, so much of what tourists see, especially in places like Kenya and Bali, where what is being sold are local peoples rather than landscape or heritage, is the dancing native. From the producers' point of view, organizing dances for the tourists is a way to make the experience more intrinsically interesting than it would be if they saw locals just standing around, but it also features the body in movement, with its aesthetic, erotic, and exotic overtones, which is part of the tourist narrative. The work of the tour is to transform a preexisting tourist tale from an abstract text into an embodied narrative, a somatic experience (Farnell 1999; Macnaghten and Urry 2001; Franklin 2003). On the Intrav African trip the tourists in the helicopter or the hot-air balloon not only experience a view from above, but also move beyond the gaze to the corporeal sensation of soaring above the landscape. These physical feelings are still powerfully inscribed in my memory of the trip and in my body, however resistant they may be to being put into words. I can feel them now, even as I write.

Different sensory codes are brought into play. In Kenya my wife purchased a carved Maasai doll with beadwork and clothing, which she now keeps on a shelf in her study. Every time she picks it up she reports that she smells the Maasai, as there is a distinctive odor about a Maasai village, possibly from the presence of cattle or something in the environment, and the doll has the same smell. Thus that doll becomes evocative of her Maasai experience, not just by its physical resemblance to a Maasai child, but by its olfactory association. One Abraham Lincoln buff, a judge, loved to come by himself to New Salem very early on snowy winter mornings because, as he explained to me, by walking alone on the same hallowed ground as Lincoln he was better able to feel his presence and to identify with the values he represented. His identification with Lincoln was enhanced by his movement through a special physical setting. With the ground and houses covered by snow and few other visitors present, the silence of the site spoke loudly to the solitary judge.

In the castle of Elmina in Ghana, tourists enter the dungeon where slaves were herded together to wait to be transported in the mid-Atlantic slave trade. It is a dark, dank cavity beneath the ground, and for the African American tourists, it is a tremendously emotional experience, not only because of the story of the slave trade but because they are physically positioned in the very dungeon where their ancestors had been located. The tourists assume the position of the slaves, moving beyond text to embodied experience, and within the dungeon they are better able to feel the predicament of the slaves, torn from family and community, robbed of human dignity. The slaves may not have known the fate awaiting them, but the tourists know what was ahead, as they have in their minds mental pictures and stories of the horror of the Atlantic passage and of the conditions on the other side of the ocean once the slaves were sold to their new owners. In the tactile encounter in the dungeon, the tourists relive the slave experience.

Thus a site may be generative and may construct meaning not as a silent text, but in action, in social practice, by the responses of the visitors to its physicality. The site itself has agency. This is most apparent in such places as Elmina Castle, New Salem, and the fortress of Masada, in part because of their massive presence, but also because they tell grand historical stories of the formation of peoples and nations. Monumental stories are attached to monumental places, as each gives meaning to the other. Such structures are consistently contested, giving rise to conflicting stories as one story arises in response to another in what I call dialogic narration. Any tourist attraction is subject to multiple interpretations even if the producers attempt to impose a monolithic meaning. Master narratives provide a preexisting structure, but they are not determinative, nor can they possibly encompass the many possible tourist responses. The tourist story is emergent in the enactment.

Posttour stories may be the most interesting of all because it is there that slide shows are organized, videos presented, photo albums constructed, and digital images arranged on the computer. An audience is waiting to hear about the trip.[22] Posttour settings provide new sites of cultural production, new opportunities for situated tellings, so that the semantic ordering takes place after the conclusion of the tour. The plot of the story is usually ordered chronologically, following the itinerary. I made it part of my ethnographic methodology to visit with individual tourist families in their homes after the tour was over to see their slides, turn the pages of their trip albums, and listen to their posttour retellings. I was welcomed on these occasions because after the initial meetings with close family and friends following their return from a trip, the tourists usually lacked an audience for their tales of travel and adventure.

The epitome of posttour tellings occurred at one tourist reunion. Some months after a trip to Thailand-Burma, the Sullivans (a pseudonym), a popular couple on the tour, invited us to come on a Sunday to the reunion at their home in the suburbs of Chicago. The husband was a retired military officer who had a second career as a bank executive, and his wife owned a clothing boutique. In the morning eight of us who had gone on the tour together showed our slides. If anyone had a striking picture, others would ask for a copy, but there was considerable similarity in the images, possibly because everyone had taken photos at the same time when the bus stopped and because the collections of photos were guided by a shared narrative. There were many romantic images of buffalo in the rice fields, of saffron-robed monks, of smiling Third World children, and of Buddhist temples. Another reason for the similarity was the presence on the tour of *National Geographic* magazine, which the Sullivans had brought with them and circulated among the tourists as we traveled together. The photographs in the magazine served as a template for the images taken by the tourists. The Sullivans informed me that they had a huge stack of old copies of *National Geographic* in their basement that they consulted before every trip.

At about noon, other guests arrived to join us for a buffet lunch. All had traveled with the Sullivans on other tours, but many were strangers to each other. What they had in common was tourism. Guests were asked to fill out name tags, and after listing their name, to list the tours they had taken with the Sullivans. My tag, for example, read "Ed Bruner, Thailand-Burma." Other tags listed the East African safari tour, the walking tour in Germany, the English countryside tour, or some other tour. The walls of the home were covered with photographs grouped together not by theme but by prior tour.

The centerpiece of the buffet table was quite remarkable as it contained a number of the souvenirs the Sullivans had purchased on their many trips. There was a cloth from India, a mask from Africa, Chinese pottery, a Bavarian-type Swiss clock, a Maasai spear, a German beer mug, Thai temple bells, an Australian boomerang, and a Mekonde statue. The display reminded me of Steven Mullaney's (1983, 43) description of a sixteenth-century European wonder-cabinet: "what comes to reside in a wonder-cabinet are, in the most reified sense of the phrase, strange things: tokens of alien cultures, reduced to the status of sheer objects." The objects survive the period and the context that produce them. A wonder-cabinet has absolutely no classificatory principle at work except that the items contained within it are all strange. The items in the Sullivans' centerpiece had nothing in common except that they were collected on tours, and the Sullivans had a story about each object.

The reunion provided an extraordinary opportunity to tell tourist stories, using name tags, photographs, and souvenirs as points of entry. From the tourists' point of view, it was a posttour gathering made in heaven: an improvised construction of tourist identity that established a social community of travelers who could share tourist tales and experiences.

Posttour narratives have no ending. They are never finished, for with each retelling the circumstances, the audience, and the situation of the narrator changes, providing the opportunity for novel understandings and new narratives to arise. Travel tales, told and retold throughout the life course, have a synchronic dimension as they construct and reconstruct the self as well as the memory of the original travel experience. It has been fascinating for me to observe how in sequential retellings tourists recapture aspects of a travel experience that had been omitted the first time the story was told. Experience as consciousness is often fleeting, unmarked, and inchoate, requiring a period of "working through," to use Freud's psychoanalytic phrase, or just reflection or the passage of time before being articulated in story form (Arendt 1958, Jackson 2002). When articulation happens, it changes the recollection of the trip as lived and reorders the experience so that the tour comes to be both told and remembered differently. The past is reconstructed and memory refashioned. It is not the first telling but the subsequent retellings that are truly constitutive.

A Tour of the Book

This introduction tells the story of how I entered tourism studies, placing it against the backdrop of how the discipline of anthropology has changed; the chapters that follow present my research studies; and the last chapter ends on the same note as the introduction, with a partly autobiographical account of the theoretical shifts within ethnography since I began my anthropological career. Thus my personal biography intertwines with paradigm transformations in ethnological inquiry, providing a beginning and an ending that frames the tourism studies that constitute the middle of the book.

The volume is divided into three sections, "Storytelling Rights," with three chapters on Africa; "Competing Stories," with three chapters on the United States and the Middle East; and a concluding section called "Tales from the Field," with three chapters on Indonesia. The unity of the book stems from a consistent theoretical perspective based on constructivism, which views performance as constitutive of emergent culture; narration, stories, and retellings as active expressions that structure and express the tourism experience; mobility, travel, and encounters as inherent not just in tourism but in social life; human agency and reflexivity as characteristic of anthropologists, the tourists and the toured; culture as always contested and in process; dissident voices and challenging readings as embedded in interpretations of heritage sites; ambiguity, irony, and paradox as tropes characterizing the human predicament; skepticism of master binaries as reducing and simplifying cultural complexity; and historical specificity as necessary in any account of cultural productions. These theoretical themes are woven in and out of the pages that follow.

Each chapter is an ethnographic research study. No chapters deal exclusively with theory, but theory pervades every account in the book.[23] Every chapter is marked by ethnographic and historical specificity. In each case I did field work and gathered data by talking to people, by observing them in action, and by participating in their activities. None of the studies is based solely on the reading of texts, images, postcards, advertising, travel writing, and other documentary sources, although I utilize these sources when they are available. Practice and ethnography are central to these studies, which distinguishes them from more literary or cultural studies approaches. Excellent work has been produced within other frameworks, but I work as a more traditional ethnographer, privileging performance, experience, process, and practice, with the aim of constructing an embodied tourism and studying it ethnographically. Tourist productions are viewed as systems in themselves, with many different players, to be studied for what they are in the present, not for what they are assumed to represent when seen through the lens of simulation, hyperreality, authenticity, or orientalism. I have tried not to belittle tourists or to make them the butt of jokes, and this has been hard to do as the denigration of tourists is so pervasive in tourism discourse. Most important, I have listened to tourists and to the producers of tourist attractions carefully and have made every effort to understand them on their own terms.

I have had fun doing these studies and putting them together in this book, as I enjoy traveling and observing other cultures, so it is fortunate that I can turn these joys into a professional product. I have done hard ethnography—living in villages without electricity, running water, or sanitary facilities; speaking a foreign language; confronting political turmoil; suffering tropical diseases—but as I get older, I become more appreciative of upscale travel and of making ethnographic observations from a more comfortable setting. I value the ambiguity of being betwixt and between tourism and ethnography, observing concurrently the tourists, the indigenous people, and myself. It is a reflexive delight. My hope is that these studies delight the reader too.

PART ONE Storytelling Rights

1

Maasai on the Lawn
Tourist Realism in East Africa

Edward M. Bruner and Barbara Kirshenblatt-Gimblett

MAYERS RANCH IS a tourist attraction near Nairobi that is privately owned by the Mayers, a British ex-colonial family who are now Kenyan citizens.* The site features Maasai "tribal" dancing followed by tea and scones on the Mayers' lawn.[1] The site enacts a colonial drama of the savage pastoral Maasai and the genteel British, playing upon the explicit contrast between the wild and the civilized so prevalent in colonial discourse and sustained in East African tourism. The master narrative of tribal resistance and colonial containment is performed daily at Mayers Ranch for an international audience of tourists and visitors, reproducing in the postcolonial era a story that emerged at the turn of the century, early in the colonial period (Knowles and Collett 1989). The Maasai at Mayers Ranch make their living by performing the noble savage in a carefully and collaboratively constructed ethnographic present. A key to the success of Mayers Ranch is its ability to produce what we are calling tourist realism, an effect closely linked to the ultimate tourist commodities—experiences and the tourist tales they generate.

Tourism gives tribalism and colonialism a new space by bringing them back as representations of themselves and circulating them within an economy of performance. Mass tourism routinely recycles dying industries, dead sites, past colonial relations, and abandoned ethnographic tropes to produce industrial parks, living historical villages, and enactments like Mayers Ranch.

* To reflect the more euphonious local usage, we refer to the members of the Mayers family collectively as *the Mayers* rather than *the Mayerses,* and for the possessive form we use *Mayers'* rather than *Mayers's.*

Catering to the "imagination of others" (Waller 1993, 301), mass tourism stages fantasy not only within hermetic theme parks located anywhere, but also within geographically specific historical sites and life worlds—and blurs the distinctions among them. What Renato Rosaldo calls "imperialist nostalgia" (1989) is not just a sentiment. It is also a scenario for tourist productions—itineraries, environments, and performances—and the marketing of them.

Anthropology has responded to the growing importance of tourism by exploring everything from the uneasy historical relationship between travel writing and ethnographic discourse to studies of the industry itself and its local impacts.[2] Dean MacCannell's *The Tourist: A New Theory of the Leisure Class* (1976) continues to inform the analysis of tourist sites some decades after it was written. Both "a sociology of leisure" and "an ethnography of modernity," a project MacCannell sees himself as sharing with tourists themselves, *The Tourist* frames the crisis of modernity, as seen through tourism, in terms of authenticity. While we do not share this concern, we do admire MacCannell's analysis of the "semiotic of attraction" and hope to extend its possibilities in our analysis of one site, Mayers Ranch as a tourist production.

We ask of Mayers Ranch: What is being produced here and how? How did the site arise historically? How is it staged, who has artistic control, and how does the performance develop in space and time? How is the production organized in social and economic terms, and who gets what from the event? Because the Maasai and Samburu, the tourists, and the Mayers do not experience the site in the same way, we ask: What does the event say and what does it mean to its varied producers and audiences? We argue that close attention to the tourist production itself—to the performance—holds clues to the nature of Mayers Ranch as a tourist commodity and to its success within Kenya's tourism industry.

International tourism draws travelers from affluent capitalist democracies to virtually all parts of the world. In the recreational geography of tourism, hard currency from people with the money and leisure to undertake such trips flows through international corporations to local sites, and many countries are now dependent on income from tourism as a major part of their gross national product (Sinclair, Alizadeh, and Onunga 1992). As the number of tourists to Third World countries increases, the income from foreign visitors becomes a mainstay of some local economies. In Kenya, for example, there were 5,000 tourists in 1958; 110,200 in 1963; 352,200 in 1981; 676,900 in 1988, and over one million by the mid-1990s, so that tourism has become second only to coffee and tea as a producer of Kenya's foreign exchange. In Kenya in 1996 tourism receipts were 448 million dollars; three-fourths of the tourists come from Europe and North America (D. Harrison 1992).

Pastoralism and the Moran

Tourism at Mayers Ranch performs a paradox. It sells Maasai pastoralism as pristine and independent but depends for the production of this idealization on Maasai adaptability and interdependence. East African pastoralism never has existed in isolation. Its very survival depends upon the maintenance of relationships among farmers, hunters, and others in a regional ecosystem. Since the Eastern Nilotic ancestors of the Maa-speaking peoples from the Sudan border migrated through the Rift Valley into what is now Kenya and Tanzania, the Maasai have survived by adaptation (Spear and Waller 1993).

At the end of the nineteenth century, the Rift world was in disarray. Herds were being decimated by rinderpest and pleuropneumonia, human populations were falling to smallpox, and droughts were devastating the economy when British and German troops arrived. The pastoral Maasai had survived by taking up agriculture and by moving in with other tribes, but during the colonial period, many Maasai returned to pastoralism, which had a revival under the British. The colonial government established reserves for the Maasai as a solution to a long-standing conflict over the control of land. The British needed land for the colonial settlers, and this pressure on the land has continued since independence in 1963 to the present day as the Kenyan government has taken land for farms, ranches, and game preserves. Some Maasai have become farmers and ranchers, some have received an education and have moved to the cities, and some have become part of the modern capitalist economy of Kenya, but many others have remained pastoralists, a Maasai ideal.[3]

In Kenyan cultural politics, the Maasai are the quintessential pastoralists, and the *moran* (junior warriors) are the quintessential Maasai.[4] State efforts to weaken Maasai autonomy focus on diminishing the age-grade system and the institution of moranism, which brings Maasai youths into full Maasai adulthood and keeps them out of Kenyan schools. In recent years, the state has insisted that Maasai attend school. Many Maasai parents protest that the integrity of their way of life is being threatened. And school is not the only threat; pastoralism itself is increasingly difficult to sustain in the face of drought, disease, overgrazing, and other pressures on the land as the population expands, as does a tourist industry built upon game parks. Ironically, it is the contested institution of the moran—specifically the activities of moran in the *manyatta,* their village—that is performed at Mayers Ranch.

Mayers Ranch is built on the close fit between the requirements of a tourist production and the performance culture of Maasai youth. Living together in a manyatta, the morans at Mayers perform an idealized colonial construction of themselves. Featured at Mayers is the bravery of the Maasai warrior, the glorification of youth and maleness, the Maasai as the "Lords of East Africa," cattle raids, lion hunting, male circumcision, the diet of raw foods (milk and blood), the primitive Maasai, the "natural man," and the affinity between tribesmen and wildlife.

The Landscape and the Lawn

Framed by the big-game hunt or by the biblical Garden, situated before the Fall or after the Apocalypse, created by God in six days or through billions of years of evolution, untamed wilderness or transplanted lawn, nature is the star in East African tourism—raw, wild, untouched, given. But nature is a cultural construction, as the formulaic descriptions of generic scenes, animals, and peoples in East African travel brochures make clear. As Theodor Adorno states, "Natural beauty is an ideological notion because it offers mediatedness in the guise of immediacy" (1984, 101). The East African landscape has long been coded in ways that remove it from human agency. Hence we have the recurrent trope of the Kenyan landscape being untouched and its contrast with the power of the Mayers' garden to make the African desert bloom—with British flowers.

Four nature thematics structure East African tourism and inform our analysis of Mayers Ranch. The safari, as the big-game hunter's encounter with the Dark Continent, is the model for tours and the iconographic source for tourist amenities and gear. *Safari* is coded in terms of the hunt, a wilderness inhabited by quarry, the violence of manly sport, and taxidermic trophies of its success. Tourists wearing khaki are delivered to Mayers by companies named for one kind of safari or another. The Garden of Eden is the destination of a voyage to the dawn of creation itself, where "our primitive ancestors," who have not yet eaten of the tree of knowledge that is "modern civilization," can be found. Characterizations of the Maasai as shepherds whose flocks live in harmony with their predators also evoke the peaceable kingdom of Isaiah 11. The gorilla safari models the tourist as the naturalist and appeals directly to the notion of the evolution of man from ape. Female primatologists assist tourists armed with weapons of vision—binoculars and cameras. Tours of European gardens, usually on the grounds of grand homes, are testaments to cultivation—which is to say, civilization. The lawn at Mayers Ranch, lush and green in an arid landscape, is to be read in this context.

Gorilla Safari

The ultimate destination, the one beyond which it is not possible to go, is the gorilla safari—the new frontier in the Darwinian universe of evolving forms. In these tours, safari coalesces with the Garden of Eden and Adam is a gorilla. Recalling the moment of first encounter, novelist Janice McIlvaine McClary describes in the travel section of the Sunday *New York Times* how she tramped through the jungle in Zaire to stalk a mountain gorilla: "It was an unforgettable moment. Somehow the gorilla symbolized what is left of the wilderness, of a world belonging to the animals, free and unbridled by men and materialism. To see the greatest of the great apes at close range was to see a glimpse of Eden, of the world as it once was, without computers or condominiums, schedules and the draining sense of time" (1985, 37).

What McClary actually saw through the leaves was an ape, and what she read into the experience was all the Western intellectual baggage about a return to origins, to primitiveness, to what we once were—unspoiled, unpolluted, uncomplicated. The imagery suggests that we have exhausted the metaphoric potentiality of primitive man and must recede even further to the irreducible ape. The glimpse of Eden, of course, was not in the Zairean forest, but in McClary's head. Her account tells us more about the subject, McClary, than about the object, the gorillas.

Her note in the article that there are fewer than four hundred mountain gorillas left in the world and none in captivity adds a sense of loss and urgency to her quest for the unspoiled, vanishing primitive. She describes her local guide, John, as "mission-taught and mountain-knowledgeable." She writes that just before seeing the gorillas, John, "as if sniffing the wind, like the leader of a herd scenting water . . . said we would soon come upon a group" (37). In McClary's Western reading the local guide, animal-like, mediates mission and mountain, culture and nature.

McClary did not just come upon the gorillas by accident. She had joined a very expensive "gorilla safari," one of several organized adventure tours recently promoted by the tourist industry as the ultimate travel experience for those who can afford to go off the beaten track. The mountain gorillas, like the game parks of Africa, are a tourist event—framed, labeled, and sold. A subsequent note in the *New York Times* travel section explains:

> At a height of more than 9000 feet, on heavily forested African mountainside . . . live two families of the last of the world's mountain gorillas. They are typical of their species—with one exception. Over the years these animals have been habituated to visits by humans. . . . Each day the gorilla families move from feeding area to feeding area, and a group of tourists . . . is taken to see them. . . . Guides accompanying the visitors use a gorilla sound, similar to a clearing of the throat, to let the animals know that friends are approaching. That established, the group may move to within a few feet of the animals [and] take pictures. (*New York Times*, October 27, 1985)

Rather than McClary's glimpse of Eden, of unspoiled origins, what we actually have are tourist gorillas. Some of the young gorillas may never have known any environment other than one in which friendly tourists have come, every day, to peer at them through the leaves. The tour group has become, as it were, part of the ecosystem of the forest. The article concludes by noting that from New York the cost of the gorilla safari is $4230 per person, double occupancy.

In both Zaire and Rwanda, gorilla tourism has become such a successful multimillion dollar enterprise that efforts to expand it include domesticating additional gorilla groups. Jean Kahekwa, a guide in Kahuzi-Biega National Park, was reported in the *New York Times* as saying, "We're trying to get two other gorilla families accustomed to people" so as to handle more tourists (Greenhouse 1988, 15). If this trend continues, one wonders if eventually the entire species of the mountain gorilla, human beings' nearest primate relative, may become incorporated into our Western capitalist system of international tourism, domesticated and co-opted to appear appropriately "wild" and "natural" (cf. Haraway 1989).

Mayers Ranch

In contrast with the gorilla safari and animal watching venues more generally, Mayers Ranch is a side trip rather than a main event within East African tourism. The ranch is located only thirty miles from Nairobi, and most groups opt for the excursion, returning to Nairobi in the late afternoon. Independent travelers may rent a car or arrange transportation with a tour company. UTC, the local Hertz agency, dispatches a minibus to Mayers Ranch that leaves each day at 2:00 in the afternoon and arrives in time for the 3:30 performance. There is only one performance a day.

The tropes of East African tourism discourse pervade promotional descriptions of Mayers Ranch, which foreground the completeness of the excursion. In a matter of a few hours, tourists will experience a panoramic view of the Great Rift Valley, a "Maasai Tour," and tea on the lawn of a British colonial homestead, as advertised in this brochure for the tour company, H.A.T.S:

> This afternoon we visit Mayers Ranch. Leaving Nairobi, past hundreds of colorful farmholdings, the road emerges from a belt of forest to reveal the most magnificent valley in the world. The Great Rift Valley. . . . We wind our way to the base of the Valley . . . before proceeding to Mayer's [*sic*] Ranch where we are treated to an awesome display of traditional Masai dancing. You will be able to watch, from close-up, the legendary Masai enact warlike scenes from their past. These warriors are noted for being able to leap high into the air from a standing

position. The experience is truly a photographer's delight. After English Tea on the lawn of the Ranch house we return to Nairobi.

In such tourist discourse, landscape is staged from a distance. This is the idiom of the commanding view. Animals and people, however, are best watched *close-up*, a term that evokes not only the camera, but also the range finder on a gun that is pointed at a target. Indeed, because it bills the excursion —and especially the proximity to the Maasai—as "a photographer's delight," the brochure reads like a plan for a camera shoot, complete with pans and zooms, long shots and close shots, providing one more indication of how profoundly the camera structures the tourist experience. The thrill of being so close to wildness is located here in animals and in people more than in landscape: the "legendary" Maasai "enact warlike scenes," perform "awesome" dances, and "leap high into the air from a standing position." Concluding with English tea on the lawn of the ranch house, the description then supplies the missing term in the wild-civilized polarity and makes explicit the principle of contrast that structures East African tourism more generally—the assurance that the wild will be experienced under the most civilized of circumstances and that their surreal juxtaposition will be enjoyed in its own right.

Tour companies historicize the experience of visiting Mayers Ranch in various ways. Maupintour evokes the period before Kenyan independence: "The colonial days are remembered and local tribal villages are visited." Travacoa casts Kenya's history in terms of its tourist amenities: "Only sixty years ago, Nairobi was a camping station for settlers and traders trekking westward to new lands and adventure." In contrast, Njambi Tours, owned by an African Kenyan (Belle Njambi), makes no mention whatever of the Mayers, and its literature has no word of what other accounts call the family's "privately owned country estate"—no hint of tea and lawn and colonial days or for that matter the Great Rift Valley prospect. Rather, Njambi Tours, which bills the excursion to Mayers Ranch strictly as a "Masai Tour," refers to the "proud past" reenacted in the warriors' dances: "Visit a Masai Manyatta (homestead) where you can see young warriors (Moran), performing their tribal dances which re-inact [*sic*] their proud past. Extremely good looking, classically athletic, they dye their tall bodies with ochre clay and fat, wearing only a red cloak tied to one shoulder."

The Mayers

Early in the twentieth century, Cyril and Hazel Mayers, a British family in Kenya, were pioneers in establishing sugar and coffee plantations. They later established a cattle ranch that grew to almost one hundred thousand acres. Their latest land acquisition, in 1947, was of six thousand choice acres in the Kedong Valley. Fed by a natural spring, an eternal source of fresh water in the semiarid environment, this paradise-in-the-desert became their homestead. The Mayers explain that the government encouraged British and European farmers and ranchers to settle the Kedong Valley during colonial times. Their presence was a way of driving a wedge between the upland Kikuyu and the Maasai in the Rift Valley, who, the Mayers reported, were at war with each other.

In the early 1960s, when they realized that Kenya would achieve independence and sever the colonial relationship, the Mayers decided to sell off most of their land. The problem was not simply the postindependence squatters, with whom the settlers who remained usually developed a working relationship. More threatening were the "walk-ons," Kenyan families who simply appropriated the settlers' land on the not-unreasonable basis that the land had formerly been appropriated from them, the Africans, by the British. Since independence, all the other European settlers have left the Kedong Valley; the Mayers are the only Europeans remaining. Reluctant to sell their homestead, the Mayers kept 250 of the six thousand acres in the Kedong Valley, including the house and the natural spring. This exceptional property, close to Nairobi, is tucked away in its own ecological niche in the Rift Valley. Invisible from the main highway, its lush green vegetation comes as a surprise at the end of the dirt road leading to their home.

The problem became how to make a living on 250 acres in independent Kenya. Cyril Mayers was not in good health, the ranch had been drastically reduced in size, and the hilly land that remained was only partially arable. Around 1968, Hazel Mayers, with English garden tours in mind, thought of opening their homestead to visitors in order to generate additional income. There in the classic setting of the escarpment, where giraffe and zebra could be seen from the road leading to the property, guests could have tea on the rolling lawn and stroll along the banks of a reflecting pond fed by a spring and shaded by a giant fig tree. Luxuriant beds of asters, zinnias, daisies, chrysanthemums, hibiscus, and other flowers were set off by majestic views of the vast escarpment that extended as far as the eye could see. A staff of eight gardeners who watered morning and evening kept the garden green and blooming the year round.

The tour operators were unenthusiastic. Why would European tourists come to Kenya to visit an English garden, however beautiful? They could do that at home. Not to be daunted, Hazel Mayers turned to another major resource, the Maasai who had for decades served as herders on their cattle ranch, which was adjacent to the Maasai reserve, and were now unemployed. Hazel approached a group of Maasai elders from Ewaso Kedong and explained her idea. She would have them construct on the Mayers homestead a Maasai manyatta, a settlement for Maasai junior warriors, one of the Maasai age-sets, as well as traditional dwellings for their female relatives on an adjacent piece of ground. For one hour a day during the tourist season the warriors would sing and dance for the tourists. Before leaving, the visitors would be served tea on the lush lawn and chat with the Mayers.

The project was executed with discretion and panache, and it became a great success. Combining the wild and the civilized, the site sets itself apart from many other stops on the itinerary by its tasteful and personal style, its small scale, and its fastidious attention to detail. Visitors feel like exclusive guests in the private homes of both the Maasai and the Mayers. Hazel's daughter-in-law Jane Mayers, who now manages the operation, says the entire project was Hazel's inspiration and that "it's what kept us going."

The Maasai and the Mayers, tribalism and colonialism. What an unlikely pairing in a postindependence Kenya that saw the end of colonial rule and the creation of a new nation. Of tribalism and colonialism, Jane Mayers says, "They are anachronisms, but one is privileged to be part of it." The tourists come to Kenya for a very short time, she points out, and where else could they see, close up, authentic Maasai and a gorgeous colonial garden? She asks, "How long can it last?"[5]

John Mayers, Hazel's son and Jane's husband, now runs a flower export business on the ranch[6] with irrigation from the natural spring, and he may expand into vegetables. The family maintains a small vegetable garden for their own consumption. Their two children, ages thirteen and eleven, attend St. Andrews boarding school. John notes that his family has been in Kenya for four generations. His grandfather emigrated there from England; his father, Cyril, built up the land and the businesses. It is "remarkable," says John, that his two children are going to St. Andrews, the same school from which he graduated. After all, he notes, in his grandfather's day people said the British could not last, and here the Mayers have lasted for four generations.

Economics

When they were younger, John and Jane Mayers emigrated from Kenya to South Africa, but in 1979, after Cyril suffered a massive stroke, they were called back to the homestead to take over the operation. At that time they found the farm run down. There were no locks on the doors, and things had to be put in order. John devoted himself to building up the farm and developing the irrigation system. Jane took charge of the tourist business, which Hazel had already been operating for about ten years. Jane tried to increase business by making the rounds, "chatting it up" with tour agencies in Nairobi. The Mayers do not advertise for tourists because that would place them in direct competition with the tour operators on whom they depend. The tour business and the farm now produce an approximately equal amount of income.

John speaks of having two labor camps on the ranch and two sets of employees on the payroll: about fifty Maasai and Samburu who perform for tourists and about fifty farm laborers (Kikuyu, Luhya, Kipsigis, Tariki, Turkana, and Tugen, among others). The exact number of farm employees fluctuates with the seasonal nature of the flower export business. The tourist attraction operates for ten months a year, which the Mayers speak of as a season, and then closes down for the two rainy months. The tourist high season starts at the end of December and peaks in January and February.

The Mayers have a sliding scale for the cost of admission. The tour company pays the Mayers fifty Kenyan shillings per adult, but the tourists never know this, as the money is paid by the bus driver directly to a member of the Mayers staff. Those on a packaged tour pay for everything in advance in the currency of the country of origin. Individual tourists who make their own arrangements with UTC or with one of the other Nairobi agents pay 240 shillings for round-trip transportation with a driver; that includes the price of admission. Those visitors who come in their own cars pay fifty-five shillings per person, but the cost is only fifty shillings for a resident of Kenya. On the basis of 1984 exchange rates, fifty Kenyan shillings is approximately U.S. $3.60.[7] The Mayers do not offer discounts to large tour groups, but they do give the tour operators complimentary tickets.

The distinction in the cost of admission, however slight, between visitors (tourists) and residents (Kenyans) is indicative of the role of Mayers for expatriate Europeans, mainly members of the British community in Kenya. They come to Mayers Ranch on weekends, usually Sundays, especially if they have overseas guests. But they also visit on their own. They typically remark, according to Jane, that "the Maasai are interesting, but the garden is lovely." Some are friends of the Mayers. Jane says some do not even bother to go down to watch the Maasai performance, preferring to stay on the lawn and visit with the Mayers.

Expatriate visits to Mayers Ranch are one reason for higher weekend attendance, which reaches as many as 150 admissions per day during the high season. International airline schedules—the arrival of Air France or British Airways flights—can also swell attendance figures, which vary by day of the week and time of the year. On average fifty to sixty tourists come each weekday during the high season. On February 7, 1984, there were seventy guests, a good day, but on February 8 there were only 40.

The Maasai and Samburu on the payroll receive a daily rate, paid weekly. If a performance is scheduled on any given day, the performers are paid, even if only two tourists come. We were not told what the wage rate is, but Jane did explain that the performers receive less than the farm laborers because they work fewer hours, and in any case rural wages are not comparable to wages in Nairobi. Although the farm workers receive a higher daily rate, the performers do better than them financially because they receive food from the Mayers, sell handicrafts, and are given tips by the tourists. Let us consider each source of income in turn.

The Maasai and the Samburu performers receive one measure of ground maize and one pint of milk per day. They may purchase additional milk from the Mayers for one shilling a pint. The Mayers have eight Holstein cows, which produce enough milk for the family's consumption, for sale to their employees, and for the tourists, who mix it with their tea or coffee. The Mayers report that they make no profit on the sale of milk.

The traditional diet of the pastoral Maasai consists of milk, meat, and blood, although they also consume grains.[8] The warriors in the manyatta slaughter about ten sheep or goats a week to provide meat for the twenty-three Maasai warriors and sixteen Samburu warriors. The meat is grilled or mixed with herbs in a stew. Because initiated women are not allowed to observe the junior warriors eating meat, the warriors slaughter and eat the meat in their all-male age group. Jane tells of the time a foreign professional photographer came to Mayers Ranch to photograph Maasai drinking blood from their cattle. After the bloodletting the Maasai refused to drink the blood on the grounds that women were present. After the women left the scene, they repeated the procedure. Jane reports, however, that the Maasai will eat meat and drink blood in front of her.

After the performance the women sell beadwork and handicrafts to the tourists, and the men sell spears that they have made—for seventy shillings each. The sale of crafts is a Maasai-Samburu concession, and the Mayers take no cut. The Maasai and Samburu do not sell the spears they ordinarily carry, but make special tourist spears that can be taken apart so travelers can pack them in a suitcase and take them home on the airplane. The Maasai do not do the metalwork; instead they purchase the metal tips from Kikuyu dealers who come to Mayers Ranch. The Maasai and Samburu women who sell to the tourists are female relatives of the warriors, mothers and sisters who live apart from the manyatta in one of three Maasai villages. The women keep the entire proceeds from their own sales. The beads are imported from Czechoslovakia to make jewelry and other handicrafts, but this is not a new pattern. Maasai beadwork has been sought by travelers and tourists at least since the late nineteenth century (Klumpp 1987).

Photography, a central part of the Mayers scene, provides another source of income for the Maasai. The tourists usually do not pay for candid photographs, the kind that they take most often, but if they ask the Maasai to pose for a group picture that includes members of the tour group or the tourist's family, then the Maasai may receive a tip, usually paid in Kenyan shillings.

The Maasai and the Samburu put much of the income they derive from the tourist operation into the purchase of more livestock, usually cattle, sheep, and goats. The cattle are slaughtered on ceremonial occasions; the sheep and goats are everyday fare. The Mayers have set aside land on their homestead where Maasai may keep some livestock, and they also allow Maasai herds access to the homestead's relatively abundant water supply. Most of the livestock, however, is located in the Maasai's home area, on the reserve. Although the Samburu keep no livestock on the Mayers property—the Samburu district is too far away—they still use their income to increase their herds.

The Age-Set System

Mayers Ranch is based on the performance culture of Maasai moran, junior warriors. The moran are traditionally segregated in their own manyatta, where they spend their time grooming, dancing, tending their herds, and learning what they need to know to function as adult male Maasai. As the Mayers discovered, the performance culture of the junior warriors is easily adapted to tourism—with important consequences for the Maasai.

Hazel began the tourist business with twelve Maasai junior warriors. The warriors later brought their mothers and uninitiated sisters to do their washing and the cooking of food other than meat. The junior warriors also brought their young uninitiated brothers, who were primarily responsible for herding. In accordance with traditional Maasai practice, the women and the young boys did not live in the manyatta itself, which was the exclusive domain of the warriors, but in an adjacent village.

According to Hazel, the Maasai were very uncomfortable at first, and the women, who were shy, accepted Mayers Ranch only very gradually. The Mayers needed to gain their trust. Hazel reports that the Maasai had to learn, for example, that photographs would not kill them. Once, a film company proposed to shoot the Maasai, an undertaking that would provide an additional source of income for all parties. They set up a sound system with portable speakers in the women's village about a mile from the ranch. Hazel recalls that when "loud American voices" suddenly emanated from speakers, the women "scattered like birds."

One day, Hazel reported, a band of about fifteen Samburu came to the ranch, moving in formation and singing away. The lead Samburu, she said, was a sight. He had on starched khaki shorts, bright blue socks, and army boots, but he was a fantastic leader. Some of the Maasai had intermarried with the Samburu, and that particular group of Samburu were coming to visit their relatives. When they asked if they could dance with the group at Mayers Ranch, Hazel told them they were welcome to join the performance and they would be put on the payroll on the condition that the Maasai accepted them and they could get along together. Hazel felt that their dancing was very good and that they enhanced the total performance by creating an interesting counterpoint to the Maasai dancing.

The Samburu warriors joined the Maasai. The men moved into the manyatta and the women into the villages, which were eventually built closer to the manyatta and incorporated into the performance. In the performances that we witnessed, the Maasai danced first, then the Samburu, and the two groups could be distinguished not only by their clothing, hairstyles, body painting, and ornaments, but also by their dance forms. The Samburu and Maasai did not merge into one troupe; they maintained separate group identities.

Each season the Mayers hire several new Maasai performers from the reserve to supplement those who come back every year, the "holdovers." The performers in January 1984 ranged in age from about thirteen to twenty-six. The longest any of them had stayed at Mayers was twelve years. In the case of Maasai performers who are children of herders who used to work on the Mayers' cattle ranch, the relationship to the Mayers extends across two generations. On the other hand, some dancers were in their first season in 1984. Thus, although performers circulate through the troupe, at its core is a group of dancers who have been with Mayers for a long time.

Of the twenty-three Maasai performers, thirteen are junior warriors and ten are senior warriors. There are also Maasai elders on the payroll, although the elders neither dance nor stay in the manyatta. Some direct the flow of tourist traffic before the performance, and others cluster in front of Maasai houses when tourists stroll through the village before the performance. Of the sixteen Samburu warriors, three are married. The married men sleep in the village with their wives at night, and during the day they go down to the manyatta with the warriors. Some of the Maasai senior warriors are also married. Except for the half-dozen preadolescent girls who dance, all the performers are male.

Because the age-grade system and the manyatta are so central to Mayers Ranch, we quote from the handout the Mayers distribute to the tourists:

> Among the Masai soldiering is not just a chosen profession. It is an inevitable—and proud—stage in the life of every male. A young boy spends

> his early years herding his father's flocks, in solitude and with unquestioning obedience. His great day arrives when the chief priest (*laibon*) of the Kekonyeke tribe, one of the sixteen Masai tribes and the one to which these moran belong, decides that there are a sufficient number of adolescent boys clamoring to become young men. The laibon declares the circumcision period to be open and all boys over the age of fourteen, perhaps slightly younger, leave their families, gather into groups and march off to establish their manyattas. There they live by themselves for approximately eight years, learning their tribal traditions, songs and dances and oral history: practicing, of necessity, the basic rules of self-government; organizing lion hunts; and defending the tribal lands, livestock and people. In the old days they raided the herds of others also.
>
> As a new circumcision period is declared, the entire age-grade system moves up a notch; the young boys become junior warriors, the junior warriors become senior warriors, the senior warriors become junior elders, the junior elders become senior elders, and the senior elders retire. The circumcision period remains open for several years.

Not mentioned in the Mayers' handout is that Maasai boys have the option of going to Kenyan government schools and that some Maasai do not enter the age-grade system and never become junior warriors. Instead, the handout stresses the warrior role: the junior warriors hunt lions; they are soldiers; the manyatta is an "army barracks." The handout does not mention the expectation that the moran will roam about, serving as a communication system on the reserve. Or that they were expected to perform difficult tasks for the elders, escort women over long distances between kraal camps, report on pasture conditions, search for lost cattle, and during the dry season bring cattle to water when it would be too difficult for the herdsboys to do it themselves. The handout is correct, however, about the centrality of the age-set system to Maasai social structure.[9] An age-set is a corporate group with its own local leader and an area of pasture land usually reserved for its exclusive use.

The junior warriors follow special rules. They cannot drink milk alone but only in the company of their age peers. They cannot eat meat that has been seen by an initiated woman; nor are they allowed to marry or engage in sexual activity with initiated women. Their mothers are not permitted to have sex with members of their sons' age-set, although some do (Galaty 1983). Moran may have sex with uninitiated girls—that is, girls who have not yet had the subincision ceremony. Moran do not cut their hair but wear it in a braid and treat it with fat and red ocher. Once a man becomes a senior warrior, he cuts and shaves his hair, has rights to initiated women, and can marry.

Both the handout and our account use the language of ethnography to describe the Maasai age-set system. This almost clinical approach to recording symbols of masculinity—warfare and hunting, fierceness and bravery, hair decorations and sexual behavior—is cast in the third person and refers to the normative practices of "the" Maasai. There are warriors and elders, initiated and uninitiated, a village and a manyatta, and a strict separation of men and women in many spheres of life. But this manner of speaking is deceptive. In the conduct of daily life and in the actual operation of Mayers, there have emerged forms of organization and practice that are unique to Mayers Ranch and unlike anything recorded in ethnographies of Maasai culture. It might be said that a new Maasai-and-Samburu-dancing-for-tourists-at-Mayers culture has evolved from the interaction of the Maasai with the Mayers and with the tourists, tour agents, film crews, travel writers, and anthropologists. The attempt in the handout to compare Mayers Ranch with a hypothetical original—and the suggestion that what tourists see at Mayers is the original—misses the mark, but not because of any question of authenticity.

The structure and ideology of the moran are ideal for the Mayers' purposes. The Mayers have utilized a culturally appropriate complex that both fits the Maasai life cycle and meets the expectations of the tourists. The junior warrior stage is a life phase in which unmarried Maasai leave their home villages and go off by themselves for exploring and learning. Why not go to Mayers Ranch? The Mayers provide a plot of ground for the Maasai livestock and good access to water, and they even hire crews to construct and repair the manyatta. The dances the moran perform for tourists are the same dances they perform for themselves in the manyatta. Of course there are crucial differences. At Mayers the moran dance for tourists in the afternoon when the light is good; for themselves they perform their dances in the evening. At Mayers the moran perform seven days a week for the entire season; for themselves they dance on ceremonial occasions and whenever they feel like it. At Mayers the dances are commercial and are theater; on the reserve some dances are performed at sacred rituals and some just for the fun of it.

There are many other differences, of course, primarily that the manyatta at Mayers was constructed for a tourist performance, but two paradoxes stand out. First, the Maasai have become resident nomads. In contrast with the pastoral Maasai, who are seminomadic, Maasai who work at Mayers return to a fixed place every year and stay there for ten months. Second, the discrete period of seclusion during which junior warriors prepare for adulthood has become the time when they display themselves to tourists. Segregated within Maasai society, they are exposed to tourists. Even in Maasai society, however, the moran are on display and are very concerned with their appearance: their hair and body decorations, their good looks, and their skill in dancing. Galaty writes that the moran enjoy the "favor and attention of society" (1983, 368), but the Maasai performers at Mayers have placed themselves in the position of receiving the favor and attention of two societies simultaneously. They have become warrior performers. They are liminal but on stage. While learning to be themselves they are asked to participate in a representation of themselves for others.

A major predicament is that many of the traditional activities of the Maasai are now against the law, and some of those illegal activities are precisely what appeals to tourists and are featured at Mayers. The British banned, unsuccessfully, the practices of the moran in 1921, and the Kenyan government has laws against lion hunting, cattle raiding, and the conducting of clitoridectomies. Even the length of time one can be a moran is regulated by the Kenyan government, as the age-grade system is thought to hinder development. Yet what the government condemns is celebrated in tourism. Indeed, tourism is a safe place for practices that are contested in other spheres, for in tourism they function in a privileged representational economy.

We asked eight Maasai if they had ever killed a lion. Four replied that they had, two that they had not, one that he had gone on a lion hunt but they never found a lion, and the last that he did find a lion but it ran away. But among these eight moran were some who had been to the Kenyan government school. One man had gone to school at the age of five, had remained in school for seven years, and then, in his words, "went to work at Mayers." He did not say that he became a junior warrior. He said that he went to work. Mayers is where he is employed.

Experience Theater

We now turn to an examination of how tourists move through Mayers Ranch and experience the site. There are, of course, many kinds of tourists (Cohen 1974), but those we observed at Mayers were mostly on packaged tours. They were middle class or professional, they were older, and many were retired. Tourist discourse denigrates tourism and tourists. Not only cultural critics, but also tourists themselves are quick to condemn the ersatz and exploitative aspects of the industry and the naiveté of "other" tourists. Those we met at Mayers, however, were intelligent and adventuresome. They wanted to learn about the world, and although they realized the limitations of the mass tour, they lacked the knowledge, expertise, time, money, or inclination to make the necessary travel arrangements themselves. Further, many preferred the security of the group and the companionship of others to traveling on their own.

Many of the tourists had been on group tours before to other areas of the world, and they considered themselves experienced travelers. Nevertheless, they spent less than two hours at Mayers Ranch, which was simply one site on a long itinerary. Their sources of information were also limited. To our knowledge, no complete description of Mayers Ranch exists. The tourists had a brief description from the tour agency brochures; they received the one-sheet handout at Mayers, which some did not have the time to read on-site; and they received explanations from their own tour leaders and from the Mayers guides. The general theme of Mayers—the wild and the civilized—was, however, a well-established metanarrative for their East African experience and was coded into even the briefest of descriptions of Mayers Ranch. Most tourists knew in advance that they were about to see Maasai dancing and a colonial garden.

Mayers Ranch operates in the mode of tourist pastoral (Clifford 1986; Empson 1950; Williams 1973). The traveler starts from home or royal court or a familiar place and goes on a journey to the wilderness, to a dream world, to an island, to the desert, to the Garden of Eden, to a place that is rural, simpler, primeval, and then the traveler returns, transformed. The Maasai, themselves pastoralists, and Mayers Ranch with its bucolic gardens offer the tourist pastoral in a distinctively East African idiom: the colonial order staged as a peaceable kingdom in the safe representational space of a tourist production within a touristic borderzone.

Immersed in a total environment, tourists move through the site in order to experience it. This is *experience theater,* an imaginary space into which tourists enter and through which they negotiate a physical and conceptual path. Mayers Ranch and tourism more generally are built on environmental and improvisational principles; they are in large measure unscripted ensemble performances. There is at work here a performance epistemology that places a premium on physical experience—visceral, kinesthetic, haptic, intimate—and a performance pedagogy more akin to the nascent medium of virtual reality than to older models of learning. Immersed in an experiential situation, tourists actively engage the site and those in it. The virtual world they are experiencing pushes back. Mayers Ranch constructs an effect we call *tourist realism,* which we distinguish from *authenticity,* the concept that has dominated much critical writing about tourism. There are several ways in which the site produces this effect.

Movement through the Borderzone

The tour minibuses leave the main highway from Nairobi and turn off on a dirt road at a crude sign that says simply "Mayers" in a black, hand-painted scrawl on a small, white beat-up panel. After a short descent into the Rift Valley, past land that appears to be uninhabited, they soon arrive at the Mayers parking lot, which is adjacent to the main house. There they discover other tour buses and are met by a representative of what Jane refers to as the "European staff." In early 1984 there were three members of this staff; two were British, Dan and Fiona, and one was American, Gail. All three were young, in their midtwenties; they were attractive, personable, and informally dressed.

One of these staff members greets the tour bus, collects the price of admission, distributes the modest handout describing the Maasai and giving a history of the ranch, and suggests that the tourists wander on the lawn until the performance begins. At 3:30 everyone is recalled from the lawn and told to return to their vehicles. In a journey that takes only a few minutes, they drive, caravan-style, down to the first Maasai village, where they are greeted by a tall Maasai elder, who directs traffic. The elder wears an enormous feathered headdress and carries a spear and a club, which he uses to point the drivers of the automobiles to the parking area. At the same time he poses for pictures (fig. 1).[10]

As the tourists pour out of their vehicles, cameras ready, they confront a Maasai woman seated at the thornbush entrance to the village, surrounded by eight to ten Maasai children all under the age of five and dressed in red robes. It is an exceedingly photogenic scene. The background is uncluttered, the light is perfect, and it is as if the tourists were traveling in the bush and just happened to come upon a charming domestic scene. Of course, it is not entirely clear why a Maasai woman would surround herself with such a group of children at the entrance to a village precisely at 3:30 in the afternoon—every day. It is also remarkable that the children just sit there, posing, and do not run around. But it makes an interesting photograph, and it is exemplary of how Mayers is set up: as a series of tableaux vivants designed for a live photographic encounter.

As the tourists enter the village, they see a semicircle of a half-dozen Maasai dwellings—each a twig armature covered with dung and mud to form a low, rounded dome with one small entrance. Some of the houses are open for tourist inspection; others are locked. Maasai women are seated or standing by the side of the houses, posing for pictures. Some women have children on their backs, but there are no crawling babies, no livestock, and very few of the flies so common in other Maasai villages. In the center of the clearing, the tourists gravitate to three charming Maasai girls, approximately eight to ten years old, bare to the waist, with red ocher markings decorating their backs, and wearing an abundance of beaded bracelets, necklaces, earrings, and head ornaments. The girls pose willingly for the army of cameras (fig. 2).

1. Maasai elder. Photo by Barbara Kirshenblatt-Gimblett.

The tourists enter a second, adjacent village, where the scene is repeated, then move down to the manyatta in a procession led by the European staff, the Maasai elders, the Maasai women, and occasionally Hazel or Jane. There are no signs, microphones, uniforms, or badges—none of the markers familiar at other tourist sites, such as Bomas of Kenya, the national ethnographic park. The staff, who serve now as tour guides, mingle with the guests, make comments, answer questions, and provide brief explanations, but it is all very informal. As there are three staff members, each can chat with a small group or even one person. There are no formal remarks addressed to the group as a whole.

The tourists enter the manyatta through a narrow thornbush opening. On the right are seven Maasai dwellings in a row against a backdrop of lush green trees; on the left, rows of logs arranged as seating for the tourists, forming a rudimentary amphitheater (fig. 3). Between the seating area and the Maasai dwellings is a large open area, the performance space. There, Maasai warriors—torsos wrapped in red cotton, hair braided, and bodies decorated with red ocher—dance to their own singing and jump straight up into the air in their signature movement. The Samburu, torsos wrapped with red and white cotton cloth, wait in the wings for their turn to perform.

Three girls are joined by three others, and together they form a line facing the warriors, with whom they dance. The guides explain that the warriors are allowed to have sex only with uninitiated girls, which gives this performance a provocative and erotic turn. At one point the dancing stops and groups of Maasai youths pair up for a stylized athletic display in which they throw sisal stalks at each other and deflect them with decorated shields. The three guides, mingling with the tourists, explain that stalks are an effective weapon for disabling the herdsboys during cattle raids. The dancing resumes and the guests are encouraged to leave their seats and mingle with the dancing warriors. The tourists wander into the performance space, moving close to the Maasai and Samburu performers, examining them in detail and photographing them from various angles or close-up.

As the performance concludes, the women begin setting up shop. They place their handicrafts in front of the manyatta (fig. 4) while the warriors display rows of Maasai and Samburu spears nearby. While some tourists continue to watch or photograph the performers, others purchase souvenirs. The

2. Prepubescent girls. Photo by Barbara Kirshenblatt-Gimblett.

3. Dancing for tourists

sellers wait until the tourists approach them, and there is no hard sell or hawking, no price tags or signs, no booths or stalls—just goods arranged in an orderly fashion on a blanket on the ground by each woman who presumably made the items and is selling them. At about 4:30 the dancing stops, the women bundle up their wares, and everyone leaves together.

But the performance is not over. The tourists return to their vehicles and are driven to the Mayers' place, where they find garden furniture awaiting them on the lawn. Standing behind a long table piled with pikelets, cookies, and scones are two Kenyans. They are not Maasai or Samburu or fierce warriors; they are more likely Kikuyu. Their uniform is not red cloth and ocher body paint, but the white chef's hat and apron of the domestic servant whose job it is to pour the tea and coffee in an idyllic, even romantic tableau devoid of any hint of aggression or sexuality. The European staff have set up a table to sell postcards and picture books about the Maasai and the Samburu, who are absent from this white social space except as reproduced in those quintessential genres of tourist representation. Jane and Hazel circulate among their guests, welcoming them, volunteering information about the Maasai or Kenya or Africa or themselves with utter charm. There are even two Scottish terriers, the family pets, on the lawn.

Tribal Resistance

Mayers Ranch, like East African tourism more generally, is built on a series of binaries. The two terms alternate for a varied itinerary, or one term is suppressed in the interest of total immersion in the tourist real, or the two are juxtaposed to produce the tourist surreal:

culture	nature
Mayers	Maasai
civilized	wild
European	African
white	black
green lawn	brown earth
cultivated garden	wild vegetation
fertile	arid
agricultural	pastoral

Although Mayers Ranch is open to different readings, the converging interpretations of the guides, the brochures, and the tour literature become

4. Handicrafts for sale

authoritative. Their collective interpretation is built on the theme of tribal resistance and the Maasai as the exemplar of fierce independence. The Mayers brochure emphasizes Maasai conservatism: the Maasai "cling tenaciously to their traditional way of life" and are "very reluctant to adapt to modern ways." In their review of colonialist writings, Knowles and Collett mention "constant references in the literature to the Maasai as 'unchanged,' 'museum pieces,' 'obstinately conservative' and 'anachronistic in modern society' " (1989, 449).

The guides stress Maasai resistance: the British tried to change them and the Kenyan government has tried to change them, but the Maasai have fought back. They have resisted both the colonial government and the modern state. They are cultural minimalists who refuse to be trapped by our modern consumerism and materialism, and they will not capitulate. They are the few fighting against the many, a Kenyan David against a Western Goliath. They are willing to pay the price of doing without our modern technological apparatus, opting instead for a purer, simpler, more natural existence. They are the indestructible Maasai. They are self-reliant and they value their own traditions above the seductions of corrupting civilization. The Maasai are true to themselves and refuse to buckle under. This is how the guides at Mayers Ranch present the Maasai to the tourists. Anyone who doubts this interpretation, say the guides, only has to look at the Maasai. They are obviously proud, and there are no modern objects to be seen anywhere: no plastics, no metal cooking pots, no radios, not even a Japanese digital watch.

While the staff celebrates tribal resistance in the most explicit of terms, they also hint at a theme that works at the unconscious level: wildness and bestiality, with aggressive and sexual undertones. As represented at Mayers Ranch, the Maasai are warriors; they carry spears and clubs; they enact warlike scenes; they hunt lions and raid for cattle. They embody the potential for violence, at least in fantasy, and the potential for an unleashing of powerful primitive forces, including the erotic—as coded in the virility of Maasai youth coming of age in the manyatta and in the clitoridectomies, which are represented in authoritative tourist accounts as a containment of the sexual desire of Maasai women.

Mayers Ranch is an adventure. Its excitement is similar to that of the safari game runs held in the parks, where one never knows when an elephant could upset the minibus or a rhino could charge or a lion could turn. It is dangerous to get out of the bus in the game parks, but a temptation for tourists who see animals so used to their presence that they lie passively, as if bored with yet another caravan of tourists. In Nairobi tourists are advised never to take a picture of the Maasai without asking permission, the implication being that the Maasai, too, could revert to savagery—that it is not safe to come too close.

Tourist Realism

From the safety of a van or a seat in a performance space, or protected by the tour group, tourists mediate their immediate experience with technologies of seeing: still cameras, video recorders, and movie cameras. Photographic visualization is a key sensory mode in East African tourism, as in tourism more generally, and Mayers Ranch itself is staged as if for a photographic shoot.

We have asked ourselves why photography is so prominent, and we have sought insights beyond the truism that tourists take photographs to make a record of their trip and to show that they were there. We have no firm answers, but we are intrigued by the thoughts of Laura Mulvey, who follows Freud in associating scopophilia, looking as a source of pleasure, with "taking other people as objects, subjecting them to a controlling and curious gaze" (1989, 16). The key word for us is *controlling*. The tourists control the wild through photography and derive a pleasurable, even libidinous, excitement from photographing the Maasai. One goes on a photo safari, substituting the camera for a gun, and shoots a picture, captures an image. To speculate further, photography is an aggressive act, at least in the context of international tourism, where it is a means of dominating the object (Barthes 1981; Sontag 1973). The tourists make the Maasai safe for their own purposes by enclosing them within the white borders of a photograph or within a video frame and by reducing them to two dimensions, all by means of sophisticated Western technology. We suggest that at one extreme is obsessive voyeurism, a perversion, but at the more normal end is tourism, an engagement with the exotic Other, utilizing photography as the medium for fixing the sexualized images. These processes are on the level of the unconscious, for if tourists became aware of this, they would probably feel embarrassed.

If this analysis is correct, Mayers Ranch plays with Western fantasies about the savage. To make the Other into an object is to distance oneself and to allow fantasy to operate. Mayers is like a silent film: without dialogue, without a complicated narrative structure, a story told through a succession of images in cinematic style. Moving through Mayers, the tourists return from their experience in the manyatta, from their confrontation with the primordial, to the Mayers' verdant lawn, to a sea of white faces, to a cultivated and familiar place, to tea and cookies, with a sense of relief. The blacks are servants again, in their proper place, and the Mayers, their British hosts, are in firm control. The Maasai may be wild, but the Mayers have contained them, at least temporarily, until the next performance, when tourists will again visit them in their "native habitat."

The master narrative of Mayers Ranch is the unresolved tension between tribal resistance and colonial containment. Mayers not only is a tourist performance but also recuperates a historical drama. The Mayers family, as representatives of the colonial British, are benign, paternalistic, gracious; they are able to make the desert bloom and to live in harmony with indigenous people. They are informed about native ways; indeed, they can be counted upon to preserve those ways more effectively than the natives themselves, let alone the state. They reproduce a discredited colonial order (M. Wallace 1981), an Africa well-off, even better off, under the British, a version of history in the Mayers' own interest.

When the British annexed the East African Protectorate, now Kenya, they saw themselves as introducing the "gifts of civilization" (Knowles and Collett 1989, 436), as domesticating the backward "natives" to bring them from untamed nature into the realm of culture. From the early 1900s, the British saw the Maasai as warlike, militaristic, primitive, as "natural man" who drank blood and ate raw foods, and rejected cultivated plants (Knowles and Collett 1989, 435). As pastoral nomads interested only in cattle and warfare, the Maasai had seized more land than they needed, the British believed. This colonial characterization was at best simplistic and inaccurate because the Maasai were not instinctively warlike, they did consume grains, and they had always established peaceful trading relations with farming and hunter-gatherer societies. What the British saw as excess land the Maasai saw as provision for times of drought. Regardless of the historical accuracy of the colonial image (see Spear and Waller 1993), however, the important point for us is that this old colonial narrative is precisely what is enacted at Mayers Ranch.

Our reading of Mayers Ranch aligns the Mayers with the Maasai in a quiet rebellion against the Kenyan government. When the Mayers reconstitute and celebrate colonialism, even if only in a tourist performance, they are resisting the efforts of modern Kenya to establish a new independent nation. Many Maasai, for their part, refuse, if they can help it, to abandon pastoralism, conform to a European dress code, submit to state-mandated educational institutions, or end a whole range of cultural practices that the state opposes. The Mayers and the Maasai join forces in an anachronistic performance that resists the new political tide and offers the tourists a nostalgic return to a bygone era. They coproduce this site for tourists—each for their own reasons and with their own understandings.

Where is the Africa that rebelled, the independence movements and the Mau Mau in East Africa? The British gave up their colonial empire and withdrew. Powerful forces erupted, new states were constituted, and Africans regained control. One can see the power of local loyalties in the stance and demeanor of the Maasai here and elsewhere in Kenyan society. The Maasai may not be the only site of such resistance, but it is the one most celebrated in Kenyan tourism. Tribal resistance and colonial containment is enacted in every performance, and if our analysis is on the mark, it is also enacted within every tourist. The British could not contain Kenya, the Mayers cannot contain the Maasai, and we all struggle to contain the dark forces within. The tension is never resolved, and this is what generates excitement—and, outside the tourist representations of a peaceable kingdom, bloody violence.

The success of the tourism industry depends on stable government and guarantees of personal safety. The industry responds instantaneously to political instability with massive cancellations of organized tours, and the tourists simply book their vacations elsewhere. Thus, there are strong financial incentives for protecting the image that tourism sells. The issue is not about making the image conform to the Kenyan world that tourists do not experience. Rather, conditions in Kenya must be stable and peaceful if the industry itself is to function. Mayers Ranch offers tourists an image of the stability of the colonial order in which Europeans like themselves are in charge, and everything about the site speaks to their entrepreneurship, managerial abilities, affluence, and good taste.

Mayers Ranch offers itself to tourists as a host to guests, a trope found in tourist discourse elsewhere, and takes great pains to present itself as simply a place where two households, that of the Mayers family and that of the Maasai, live. The effect depends on the achievement of an aura of realism, on the simulation of realism—total immersion of all the senses in a seamless environment—with a calculated suppression of performance markers. The tourists are made to feel that they are watching the Mayers and the Maasai in their natural state, not that they are watching artful theater. Even when tourists detect markers of the staging, and even if they ask, "Are the Mayers and the Maasai for real?" all is not lost. The uncertainty and ambiguity, never fully resolved, add to the intrigue of the site and the complicity of the tourists with the site's producers, for a willing suspension of disbelief is necessary precisely at such moments.

Jane Mayers wants the Maasai to "look smart," and she fears that without her efforts they would "quickly disintegrate into a shabby lot." She assumes a curatorial role, and in a sense she edits the Maasai, for she maintains rigorous control of the production. She does not permit the Maasai to wear their digital watches, T-shirts, or football socks, and all radios, Walkmen, metal containers, plastics, aluminum cans, and mass-produced kitchen equipment must be locked away and hidden from the tourists' view. Jane supplies the red ocher and insists that the Maasai decorate their bodies and their hair. Morans would do so in any case, but at Mayers she helps set the standard. The performers must wear their earrings and the correct shoes—leather sandals for the Maasai and rubber-tire sandals for the Samburu. For performances the Maasai cloth must be solid red, not red and white like the fabric they frequently wear when they are not on the job. Sellers are not permitted to display elephant-hair bracelets or Kikuyu carvings; all the objects sold must be Maasai or Samburu—a condition not enforced at other sites, Bomas of Kenya, for example.

No cows are allowed in the village or the manyatta, for as Hazel explains, tourists may want the real Maasai, but they do not want to step into cow patties. Furthermore, the cows would attract more flies. Some livestock are permitted outside the residential compounds, but they are strategically placed for visual impact. The Maasai are not to touch the tourists, which they might otherwise be inclined to do, or to hassle them in any way or crowd them or intrude upon their personal space. There must be enough savagery for credibility but not so much as to frighten the tourists. In the performance and in tourist discourse the Maasai are wild savages, but in their personal relations with the tourists, they are professionals. They are cooperative and composed, and they pose for pictures, which is part of the contract between the Mayers, the Maasai, and the tourists.

Mayers Ranch is a skillful production designed to achieve tourist realism. Nothing about the performance is slick or high-tech, in contrast with the official government site, Bomas of Kenya, which features choreographed performances by a professional ensemble in a state-of-the-art amphitheater. At Mayers there are no trash cans, uniformed guides, formal lectures, or announcements over a public-address system. No signs are located on the property except the one on the worn signpost on the main road, and there is no printed program, only the modest handout.

The language of the handout is especially interesting because it is so different from the exaggerated language of the tourist brochure. Again we quote:

> Since they move with the grazing and water, the Masai are semi-nomadic. Matters affecting the camp as a unit are settled by the elders in that camp; matters affecting a locality (perhaps several dozen camps) are settled by spokesmen of each camp meeting together. Only rarely does the whole tribe act as a unit and then primarily to regulate the graduation of the age-grades. The sixteen Masai tribes have no mechanism of interaction as such, but the fact that the age-grades cut across all of them . . . provides a modicum of functional unity.

What we have here is ethnographers' talk, and those of us in the discipline will recognize the language as derived from British social anthropology. It is not just that tourist discourse and ethnographic discourse merge, but that the Mayers have appropriated the language of the masters of the realist genre, the ethnographers (Clifford and Marcus 1986; C. Geertz 1988). A tourist event is presented as ethnography, and when it is performed in the round as a total immersion experience, it is an ultimate case of ethnographic realism. The authority of ethnography is used to authenticate a tourist production that shares its realist effects. Indeed, Hazel tells us that their handout was written for them by an anthropologist.

The aim is to build the interpretation of the performance into the tourist production so as to eliminate the metacommunication that is the stock in trade of such productions. It is as if they understood, as native producers of tourism, the process of site sacralization delineated by MacCannell (1976) and systematically eliminated markers and explanatory devices—for even as markers help to define and elevate a site, to authenticate it and make it authoritative, to structure the way it is viewed and experienced, they also work against the effect of tourist realism. At Mayers Ranch performance and interpretation are folded into one another, and every effort is made not to pry them apart any more than necessary. For this reason tourists are encouraged to wander in the total environment, to mingle, to chat, to interact with each other and their hosts, to socialize, and to proceed with candor and spontaneity through the seamless space of the tourist imaginary. The opportunities for close-up, candid photography are predicated on catching people unaware, when they are presumably acting naturally. The candid, a species of the spontaneous, enhances the effect of realism (Trinh 1985).

This approach to the site also requires the suppression of markers of the commercial nature of the transaction. On packaged tours, the entrance fee is paid by the bus drivers on behalf of the tourists so there is no money exchanged between the tourists and the Mayers. The first time that we visited Mayers, the European staff introduced themselves as friends of the family, but actually they are paid employees unrelated to the Mayers. It was a ploy: if you are a guest in someone's home, even, as in this case, a paying guest, it softens the commercialism and enhances the naturalism.

Of course, the construction of realism and the control of the production does not mean that the Maasai are not real or that the performance is a hoax. Actually, Mayers Ranch is an excellent tourist performance, one of the best we have seen. The tourists thoroughly enjoyed it, and we certainly looked forward to our repeated visits to Mayers. Our intention is to distinguish realism, as achieved in this tourist performance, from authenticity, which we see as a problem of authentication—who has the power to determine what will count as authentic? The preoccupation with authenticity is a symptom of doubt, a preoccupation with the relationship of what is given to something that is posited as prior. Authenticity speaks in the language of copies and originals, of the spurious and the genuine.

Tourist realism is better understood in relation to virtuality and its effects. At Mayers these effects are achieved through theatrical conventions understood by the visitors. The performance must be short, preferably no more than one hour, fast moving, readily comprehensible, and hopefully framed for photography (which operates as a surrogate proscenium). Frequently there are opportunities to purchase souvenirs. The site itself should be safe, accessible, and clean, and the performance must be regularly scheduled and reliably performed so groups can book space and plan itineraries well in advance. Given that tourists, like museum visitors, will not stand in one place very long to watch a performance, seating of some kind—here the arrangement of logs on a slope—is a concession to comfort requirements. Hazel and Jane are well aware of tourist expectations. They strive to achieve informality and relaxed naturalness.[11]

Who Is in Control

How much control does Jane actually have over the Maasai? Jane sees herself as preserving the Maasai: she says, "We encourage them to be Maasai." She tells the performers that if they do not appear Maasai enough, then the tour operators will not bring the tourists. If a Maasai has a "tatty" loin cloth, then Jane will tell him to buy a new one. If he says that he does not have the money, Jane will offer to withhold a week's paycheck so he will have the money. The performers are expected to keep the area clean and to help in picking up trash, including the tourists' empty film boxes. If a child's face is dirty, Jane will tell the mother to take the child to the river and wash his face. When we were conducting our interviews, Jane reported that within the previous six months one elder and one warrior had been dismissed and told to leave the property.

While the Mayers and the Maasai have a reciprocal working relationship, it is not always an easy one. One morning John Mayers woke up at three o'clock to find Maasai cattle grazing on his front lawn. He was so incensed that he drove the cattle up the road and into the forest, forcing the Maasai to spend hours rounding up their livestock. But the next morning, in defiance, the Maasai placed the cattle on the front lawn again. This matter was eventually settled, but others are not. Once a Maasai got drunk and came out during a performance wearing a Burberry raincoat. Despite Jane's efforts to fire him, that Maasai is still living on the ranch. Jane suspected one Maasai woman of dishonesty and later caught her "making eyes" at the European men; she was simply dismissed. There was also a Samburu warrior who could not jump but just stamped his foot. When Jane went to speak to him, she learned that he had a wound that prevented him from jumping, so she decided that there was nothing she could do. If she tried to dismiss him, Jane felt, all of the Samburu would be very offended. Instead, she has stated that he will not return to work next season. When Jane is not sure of her grounds, she goes to the elders and says, "We have a problem here," and she solicits their advice.

The Maasai manipulate the Mayers and use their traditions to their own advantage. Sometimes the Maasai come with a request for help, knowing in advance that John and Jane are not prepared to give it, but then the Maasai say, "You are my father and my mother now." On occasion the Maasai remind Jane that whites are privileged, so as to make her feel morally responsible for their welfare. As a general rule the Mayers do not give loans to the Maasai, but they had recently loaned one Maasai two hundred shillings and another three hundred shillings. The two went off and defaulted on the loans; so Jane went to the elders, and the Maasai agreed to be responsible for their debts. On another occasion, a Maasai raped a fellow tribesman's wife and was fined by the elders for the offense. The warrior went to the Mayers to ask for the money to buy sheep and goats to pay the fine, but the Mayers refused on the grounds that he had committed an offense against his own people and so he should take care of it himself. Another time, the Mayers found that their driver's daughter needed an operation, so they arranged it, made a loan to the driver, and even made a donation to the hospital without the driver's knowledge.

The Mayers' relationship with the Maasai is a complex one; we have suggested only some of the complexities. But some things are clear. Jane likes the Maasai, has a good relationship with them, tries to be fair but needs to be in control, and feels that at times she has to discipline the Maasai. Hazel and Jane told us that the Maasai are sometimes "like children" and are "not far removed from the bush," with all that this implies about a maternalistic attitude. However, Hazel explained that the Maasai always respected the British because the Maasai felt that the British were brave, that they were pioneers in a new country, and that they had a straightforward way of thinking. The Maasai, Hazel believes, have similar characteristics, so in her view the two peoples share basic character traits. The Maasai and the Samburu have functioning indigenous social organizations, and the Mayers respect and work through them. Still, Jane does control the performance, in part because she is the employer but also because the Maasai have come to identify their interests with the interests of the Mayers in order to keep the business going. At the end of one of our interviews, knowing that we were American anthropologists writing about tourism, the Maasai asked us to "send more tourists."

The Picture

At the end of the season, the Maasai say that it is time to "close the picture." Both the Mayers and the Maasai speak of the performance as "the picture." It is a remarkable phrase. Those who are in the picture include the Maasai and Samburu warriors; the elders; the women who have parts in the performance and who dress up and pose, including the six prepubescent girls; Jane, Hazel, the European staff; and the two servants who pour tea on the lawn. The farm laborers, the domestic servants, and the Maasai living in the third village are clearly not in the performance. There is, however, an interesting problematic about the role of others, including the foreman, the bus drivers, and the anthropologists.[12]

The Mayers have hired a foreman to serve as a middleman between themselves and the Maasai, with whom the foreman deals on a daily basis. He records the names of those who are present at each performance so their paychecks will be calculated accurately, and he informs the Mayers if there are any problems. The foreman himself is neither a Maasai nor a Samburu; he is a Marigoli from Lake Victoria. He is more knowledgeable about the performers than the Mayers, who are the producers and artistic directors. The foreman plays the role of stage manager, operating somewhat behind the scenes.

One time we asked Hazel for the tribal affiliations of the six young girls, and she did not know, so she asked the foreman. He replied that three were Maasai and three were Samburu. Another time we saw a group of people on the top of a hill overlooking the manyatta, and we asked who they were. Hazel went to the foreman, who replied that they were visitors, friends of the Maasai—Africans, but not in the picture. They were a silent audience, and we were never clear whether they were watching the Maasai dancers or the tourists. If the latter, then they were an audience to an audience, watching the watchers. In any case, the foreman is physically present during the performance, but he is not part of the performance. From the tourist perspective, he is structurally invisible. He is not in the picture.

The bus drivers are known to the tourists because they provide the transportation to and from Nairobi. They have no role in the performance. Although like ushers in a theater, in many ways they are structural anomalies. The European staff say that the bus drivers are surly and provocative. Staff member Fiona reports that they will say, "Hey, white woman," and also that they try to cheat on the number of tourists in their bus. For example, she explained, they may claim that there are only five tourists and offer to pay 250 shillings, when actually there are six tourists so that they can pocket the extra fifty shillings. This conflict occurs among persons occupying two structurally marginal positions, the European staff and the bus drivers.

One day when returning from the manyatta to the lawn after a performance, we took the back way, past the servants' quarters, and came across five or six drivers having tea. We took one photograph, our cameras being ready after the performance, and then moved around to get a better view.

One of the drivers said, "Don't you ask before you take pictures?" "Sorry," we replied, "but may we take your picture?" "No," he said. So we put our cameras away and left. The interaction may be indicative of our own presumption, but it also comments on the difficult role of the drivers. They are black Kenyans from Nairobi, well-dressed in European clothes, that is, shirt, dress pants, and shoes, and we were behaving toward them as if they were "natives," appropriate objects for our camera—as if they were in the picture and part of the deal. We had confused them for Maasai, in effect, and we had also touched the boundaries of the picture, the line between actuality and virtuality. It is significant that although the drivers have tea, they are not invited to the Mayers' lawn, and they are not served cookies. The serving woman who brings them tea explained to us that only "English people" get tea on the lawn.

Anthropologists are clearly not in the picture, and their role is quite problematic. They present special problems for the Mayers. In many respects anthropologists are like tourists, but they keep coming back and asking questions. We did explain our mission honestly, and it did seem that the Mayers had accepted us, but Jane never gave us permission to visit the manyatta or the villages except during performance time or in her presence, even though Maasai and Samburu had invited us there. This severely restricted our ability to gather information directly from the Maasai and the Samburu and thus limited our study. The European staff invited us for supper, but Jane, who knew when we had been invited, said that it was a bad day for us to come and thus prevented us from having supper with the staff. And at one point in our research, near the time we were preparing to leave, Jane suggested that it would be best if we finished our study. Since Jane informed us by letter, we do not feel that it would be a violation of confidence to reproduce the letter here, especially as it gives some understanding of our relationship.

P.O. Box 43298
Nairobi
10th February, 1984

Dear Ed:

Many thanks for your note and the book for Hazel. She was not here to receive it this afternoon but I'm sure she'll be delighted with it.

Thank you so much for inviting us to dinner but we, unfortunately, have a prior engagement for tomorrow evening. For the same reason I will not be able to spend time with you tomorrow chatting to the Maasai after hours.

I suggest Tuesday, 14th would be a good day for you to come. If you came for the normal performance we could stay down in the manyatta for an hour or so afterwards. I think you should be prepared to finalize your researches next Tuesday.

I do feel I cannot continually impose on the privacy of the Maasai, which is one of the things that I have guaranteed them I would protect. Although they are agreeable, it is to please me and I do not like to take advantage of them. The next two weeks also will be fairly busy for me as I will have guests staying and children home from school for half-term.

I look forward to seeing you on Tuesday. Perhaps we can finalize the dinner date at that time.

I'm sorry tomorrow is not convenient.

Sincerely,

Jane

It is a lovely letter. We realize that they are running a business, that their time is limited, and that we never did offer to pay for the information received. In fact, after our first visit to the ranch, Jane refused to accept the fifty shillings per person admission fee for subsequent visits even though we volunteered it. And we certainly ate our share of cookies. The times we were there the Mayers invariably were gracious and patiently answered our questions. On that Tuesday, the last day we were at Mayers, we had a very productive session with the Maasai with Jane present, after which Jane and John invited us for gin and tonic at their house. Again we had approached the limits of the picture. Being allowed in the manyatta in the morning to photograph the Maasai with their Western clothes and modern objects would have been the equivalent of receiving permission to photograph Joan Collins without her makeup. Even worse, it would have confused performance time with real life and would have dissolved the frames so essential to maintaining Mayers Ranch as a life space.

The problem is that the Mayers and the Maasai are not only in the performance, on stage, for a few hours a day at Mayers Ranch, but they also live there. It is their home. When they are in the picture, their homes become a stage, but when the tourists leave, the stage becomes their homes again. They must be able to distinguish between tourist time and life time. If they cannot delineate the frame that puts them in or out of the picture, then they confront the Batesonian paradox of not being able to distinguish between a nip and a bite, or between a play fight and a real one. If Gregory Bateson (1972) is correct, the effect of such confusion is schizophrenic.

Imagine a troupe of Broadway actors who live in a theater—not just for fun but really live there, sleep there, and cook there. At 8:00 each evening an audience comes and pays admission, and the actors put on *Death of a Salesman.* After the show, the audience leaves but the performers remain. From the audience's perspective, it makes no difference whether the actors live at home and come to the theater every evening or whether the actors live on stage. All the audience knows is that from 8:00 to 10:00 p.m. they watch the show. But from the actors' point of view the distinction is critical, for at the very least they must know when to put on their costumes, start speaking their lines, and stop treating each other as housemates.

Of course, it would not matter if one of the actors really was Willy Loman or only acted as though he were because the role is scripted into the play and does not require either condition. Here is where the analogy with Mayers Ranch breaks down because the Mayers are the Mayers and the Maasai are the Maasai and tourists come expecting to meet those who really live at the site. But then again the Maasai of Mayers Ranch and the stage Mayers are in the picture for only part of the day and part of the year. Who are they and where are they the rest of the time?

Dancing in a Burberry raincoat during a performance, having anthropologists as unaccompanied guests in the manyatta, and taking photographs of the bus drivers are acts that violate frames and blur boundaries. Being in the picture defines the limits of the borderzone. If farm laborers were to dance in the performance, if bus drivers were to be on the lawn, or if the Maasai were to have tea with the tourists and talk to them in English or to graze their cows on the lawn, then the picture would be operating on different principles, in more of a surrealist mode than a realist one—that is, in a mode predicated on jarring juxtapositions that follow the logic of dreams. Mayers Ranch might even be a more interesting place. It would certainly be a very different place from what it is now. As for the ranch's commercial success, the tourist surreal generally preserves the comfort of the tourists in their encounter with the wild. It is about minibuses on the savannah. Not Maasai on the lawn.

Mayers Ranch as it now exists is not only framed, like the proscenium stage or the cinema screen, as a picture; it is also reproduced as a picture (Benjamin 1969). Not just amateurs, but professional photographers, film crews, sound technicians, and writers come to Mayers to photograph and record the Maasai because it is such a convenient setting. It is easy to make arrangements with the Mayers, the Maasai are cooperative, and the scenic locale is already organized as a picture. All of the postcards and photo books sold by the staff at Mayers, which also appear in many bookstores in Kenya and around the world, include photographs taken at Mayers Ranch. We find this quite startling. This live event of the Maasai for tourist consumption is mechanically reproduced as a representation of all Maasai. The Maasai of Mayers Ranch have become canonized as *the* Maasai. They are an icon of East Africa reproduced infinitely on such postcards and in such books and in the illustrations of travel brochures. The Maasai at Mayers come to stand not only for all Maasai but also for African tribespeople generally, for the primitive.

Exploitation?

An American university student at the performance commented that it was disgusting how the Mayers were exploiting the Maasai. In her view, whites were exploiting blacks by producing black culture for a predominantly white audience. Although the Mayers are now Kenyan citizens, they are British and they are ex-colonials. This American liberal reaction selects color and colonialism for emphasis. The term *exploitation* has different meanings, ranging from the general sense of one group taking advantage of another group, to the more specific Marxist sense involving surplus value.

The power relations between the Maasai and the Mayers are clearly unequal: the Mayers can fire the Maasai, who are wage laborers. The question of exploitation in the precise economic sense directs us instead to the issue of the distribution of profits within the Mayers Ranch community. Is there an equitable allocation of the proceeds? We simply do not have enough information to answer this question. There are, however, some economic and political issues about which we do have data.

We began by posing the question of exploitation to Jane. Her response was that the Maasai are free to leave at any time, that no one is holding them, that more Maasai want to work at Mayers than they could possibly employ, that the Maasai are quite well off and have large herds of livestock, that when there is a drought on the reserve the relatives of the Maasai at Mayers come to join them, and that the Mayers themselves are not getting rich off the operation. That is Jane's position.

The Maasai explained their own view to us: they say they are in it for the money. With the income generated by their work at Mayers they are able to increase their herds and maintain their culture. As far as we have been able to determine, the attainment of these two goals is absolutely essential to the Maasai. When we interviewed them, they made it clear that maintaining their herds and their culture was the most important thing to them. In Kenya one frequently hears that the Maasai have too many cattle and that they overgraze, but according to Alan Jacobs,[13] the Maasai are extremely efficient pastoralists. Having surplus cattle is like having money in the bank for the Maasai; it is how they save for the future, and it is highly functional because the large number of cattle enables them to survive recurrent droughts.

The Maasai are sophisticated in their negotiation of the complex world of Mayers Ranch. We have already seen how they use their traditions to manipulate the Mayers. With regard to the tourists, the Maasai see themselves as having a direct exchange relationship, one that is not mediated or controlled by the Mayers. The Maasai told us that they do dance for the tourists and that the tourists do take their pictures, but that the tourists also buy their spears and necklaces, so it is a reciprocal relationship. Out on the reserve, they say, while the tourists may take pictures, the Maasai have nothing to sell, and so there is no exchange. Thus, the Maasai at Mayers presented themselves to us as entrepreneurs with an independent business that they conduct directly with the tourists. Within the framework of Mayers Ranch, they have carved out their own economic niche. The Mayers' role is to bring the tourists and thus enable the Maasai to sell their handicrafts.

During those brief times when the Mayers permitted us to speak with the performers, we found that the Maasai themselves were skilled interviewers and did not hesitate to put us on the spot. After a long session in which they answered our many questions (fig. 5), we asked them if they wanted to know anything about our culture. One part of the conversation went as follows:

> *Maasai:* In America, do you have female circumcision?
> *Anthropologist:* No.
> *Maasai:* Did you recently stop circumcising girls, or did you never circumcise girls?
> *Anthropologist:* We never did.
> *Maasai:* Then how can you tell the difference between a girl and a woman?

The Maasai also asked if we can have two wives, and when we replied that we can have only one, they asked why. Circumcision and polygamy are political issues in Kenya. Westerners are usually fascinated by them, and tour guides are ready to answer tourists who ask these questions about the Maasai. Here the Maasai turned the tables on us.

When we asked about their hiding material objects from tourists' view before the performance and about their masking their modernity, the Maasai replied that it is what the tourists expect, and that anyway tourists come to Kenya to see Maasai things, not European things. Further, they replied, if they were to wear socks and carry radios, the tourists would not know if they were Maasai or Kikuyu. They added that the Kikuyu had become educated and had lost their traditions. When we asked how that came about, the Maasai explained that when the Europeans came during colonial times, the Kikuyu were poor and the Maasai were rich. The Maasai had their own food and their own cattle, while the poor Kikuyu had to work for the Europeans, which is why the Kikuyu got educated and why they lost their traditions. The Maasai have kept their traditions, they said. The Maasai are proud of their culture and

5. Interviewing the Maasai. Photo by Barbara Kirshenblatt-Gimblett.

willing to defend it. Knowles and Collett write that the Maasai never accepted the superiority of British culture and never used the honorific *bwana* when addressing Europeans (1989, 444–45). The Maasai do have a very positive image of themselves, and they chose not to give up their culture to become like the Mayers or the Kikuyu.

The situation of the Maasai at Mayers Ranch is not a unique one in Maasai history. Pastoralists have always placed themselves within trading networks to obtain metalwork, honey, cloth, and other necessary items (Berntsen 1979; Spear 1981). In the past those relationships have served the Maasai well during times of disease or severe drought when pastoralism was not feasible; they provided the Maasai not only trade items but also the connections that enabled them to change their economy when that proved necessary. In a sense, the Maasai's collaboration with the Mayers and the tourists is simply the most recent in a long line of trading partnerships.

What do the Mayers get from the tourist operation? We suggested to Jane that the lawn is to the Mayers what the cows are to the Maasai. Jane admitted that English people do admire lawns and that the lawn is costly to maintain, but she insisted that most of their profits go toward building up the farm.

Tourism supports their farm and enables them to maintain their homestead. Thus, both the Maasai and the Mayers get essentially the same thing from tourism—the ability to maintain a contested, some might say anachronistic and even reactionary, lifestyle in contemporary Kenya, a lifestyle at once signified and subsidized by the tourist production. The Maasai and the Mayers are in business together.

Conclusion

In the largest sense, the Maasai and the Mayers are merely players in a show written by international tourist discourse. Both are positioned by that discourse and are allocated space within it (Foucault 1973; Lyotard 1979). The Maasai and the Mayers are on display and their culture is for sale, but the lines they speak are written for them by the real producer of Mayers Ranch, the tourist industry. As mere actors in a much larger tourist tale, the Maasai and the Mayers have to articulate themselves in terms acceptable to international tourism. The story line of the show, the guiding narrative of the colonial drama of the primitive Maasai and the genteel British, of resistance and containment, of the wild and the civilized, was in place long before the Maasai or the Mayers mounted their production. They did not invent the story they tell at Mayers Ranch. Rather, tourism is unyielding in its demands. It insists on recidivism, atavism, and anachronism. It insists on true tribespeople and archetypal colonialists. But the Maasai and the Mayers are not powerless pawns. They do not have to perform for tourists. If they choose to do so, however, they must follow the script.

2

The Maasai and the Lion King
Authenticity, Nationalism, and Globalization in African Tourism

EARLY WORK on the anthropology of tourism documented the variety of tourist experience in terms of a typology of tourism that included ethnic, cultural, historical, environmental, and recreational tourism (Smith 1977/1989, 4–6) and a typology of tourists that included explorer, elite, mass, individual, backpacker, and charter tourists (Cohen 1979; Pearce 1982; Smith 1977/1989, 11–14). Though all tourism and all tourists were not the same, scholars in the field tended to reduce the variety by seeking the essence of the tourist experience—as a quest for authenticity (MacCannell 1976), a personal transition from home to elsewhere (Graburn 1977), a form of neocolonialism (Nash 1977), or a particular type of "gaze" (Urry 1990). The typologies of tourism and tourists ordered the data but yielded few insights. The generalizations had so many exceptions that their usefulness was rendered questionable; one was never sure when or where these general propositions were applicable.

More recent field studies of tourism among particular peoples have tended to avoid typologies and monolithic generalizations, but still there is a predilection for the homogenization of local tourist displays. The Maasai are represented as male warriors (chapter 1), the Pueblo as female potters (Babcock 1990b), the Balinese as people who live in a magical world of dance and drama (chapter 7; Picard 1996; Vickers 1989), and the Tahitians as representatives of South Seas sensuality (Kahn 2000). In such cases, a single form of tourism becomes associated with one ethnic group in a given locality. The effect is similar to that which Arjun Appadurai (1988) observes for ethnography, where the connection between topic and place becomes the defining characteristic of a people to the exclusion of other perspectives—for example, caste with India, lineage with Africa, or exchange with Melanesia. Tourism scholarship thus aligns itself with tourism marketing in that scholars tend to work within the frame of the commercial versions of their sites. Grand statements about the nature of tourism in Bali or in Africa or, even more broadly, in the "Third World" are sometimes the result, to the neglect of more ethnographically based and nuanced analyses of the variety of tourist displays within each culture area.

To open up the theoretical dialogue in tourism scholarship, here I apply a method of controlled comparison (based on Eggan 1954), to consider how one ethnic group, the Maasai, are exhibited for tourists at three different sites in Kenya.[1] Although all three sites present a gendered image of the Maasai warrior, the personification of masculinity, a controlled comparison enables us to examine three ways of producing this image—postcolonial, postindependence, and postmodern. Each site tells a different story, its own version of history with its own perspective on the role of ethnicity and heritage within the nation-state and in the world community. A critical comparison of these performances provides an opportunity to depart from the monolithic discourse that has characterized so much of tourism scholarship and to highlight the breadth of meanings, ironies, and ambiguities that emerge.

The comparative approach shows that familiar concepts in the literature, such as authenticity, tradition, and heritage, are relevant only in certain touristic contexts. The wide-ranging impact of globalization on the staging of local tourism becomes apparent, as does the important distinction between domestic and foreign tourism, one not yet fully appreciated in the literature.[2] On the basis of these comparative data, I show that forms of tourism are historically parallel to forms of ethnographic writing and develop the concept of the "questioning gaze," tourists' expressed doubts about the veracity of what they are seeing. The tourists' questions and skepticism penetrate the commercial presentation of the site, undermining the producer's dominant narrative.[3]

• • •

Kenya achieved independence from Britain in 1963. Its population of approximately thirty million is made up of members of about forty-two ethnic groups. The tensions among these ethnic groups have at times been severe. The Maasai are a seminomadic pastoral group with a total population of about four hundred thousand in Kenya; Maasai also live in Tanzania (Spear and Waller 1993).

The three Kenyan field sites are Mayers Ranch (chapter 1), a privately produced performance organized by local entrepreneurs; Bomas of Kenya, a public production developed by the national government; and an "Out of Africa Sundowner" party, arranged by a tour agency, held at the Kichwa Tembo tented safari camp near the Masai Mara National Reserve. Other chapters in this volume offer humanistically oriented descriptions of tourist performances privileging political complexities and local voices. My emphasis here is on the production and the tourists, not on indigenous perceptions. The juxtapositions between one site and another become grist for the theoretical mill. I use material from Mayers as a comparative baseline as the site is a superb example of postcolonial tourism that eventually gave way to newer modes of production, but I devote more analytic attention to the other two Maasai sites.

A thumbnail sketch of each site follows. The production at Mayers, designed for foreign tourists, staged proud and aloof Maasai dancing in their warrior compound, chanting and carrying spears (fig. 6, fig. 7). The production hid all outside influences and manufactured objects, presenting Maasai as timeless and ahistorical. Mayers reproduced a nineteenth-century colonial narrative (Knowles and Collett 1989) of Maasai men as exemplars of an African primitive, as natural man. It depicted Maasai men as brave warriors, tall and athletic, who, at least in the past, would raid for cattle, kill lions with but a spear, consume raw foods such as blood and milk, and (as "Lords of East Africa") instill respect and fear in others. The producers strived for tourist realism, the aura of authenticity, and the site was designed as a series of tableaux that were set up for tourist photography. The tourists viewed the Maasai from a colonial subject position, as did early explorers and ethnographers.

Mayers began in 1968 and flourished until the late 1980s but was eventually closed by the government because the colonial aspects were offensive to many Kenyans. The critique of colonialism within anthropology (Asad 1975; Hymes 1972; Marcus and Fischer 1986) was part of the same worldwide anticolonial movement that led to the closing of Mayers Ranch in Kenya.

Bomas has a national folklore troupe that presents the dances of Kenyan ethnic groups, including the Maasai, primarily for an audience of modern urban Kenyans. The mechanisms of production are prominently displayed. The dances are staged in an auditorium with rows of seats and a bar in the back for the sale of refreshments. The theme of the production is Kenyan nationalism, to show that all the ethnic groups of Kenya are equally valued. Representatives of Bomas say that their aim is the preservation of Kenyan heritage; it is as if each ethnic culture is in the past and has to be recuperated in a museum-like setting. Bomas is an ethnic theme park for domestic tourists, a genre of tourist production that is now found in many areas of the developing world and is the basis of chapter 8.[4]

6. Maasai warriors with spears at Mayers Ranch

7. Maasai at Mayers dancing and chanting

The Sundowner presents Maasai men dancing in the context of an "Out of Africa" cocktail party near an upscale tented safari camp on the Mara reserve. The Maasai performers mix with the tourists, who are served drinks and hors d'oeuvres by uniformed waiters. Globalizing influences are apparent, as Hollywood pop culture images of Africa and blackness are enacted for these foreign tourists as they sip champagne, alternately chatting among themselves and dancing with Maasai, all the while on safari in the African bush. These are posttourists (Feifer 1985; Urry 1990, 100–102), beyond traditional tourism, who want a gracious African experience, all the comforts and luxury of home, and a good show rather than staged authenticity.

At all three tourist sites, Maasai men perform for an audience, but there are important differences. These differences are evident in the modes of transportation the tourists take to each site; the journey to a tourist destination is an inherent part of the tourist experience. Mayers is located in the Rift Valley about fifty minutes by car from Nairobi. Most tourists reached Mayers over dirt roads as passengers in a minivan provided by a local tour company. Bomas is located on the outskirts of Nairobi along the public bus route, and convenient ways of going are driving or taking a city bus. Kichwa Tembo safari lodge is located by the Masai Mara reserve. In 1999 I visited the lodge with a group of tourists on the Intrav agency "Out of Africa" tour. The group first visited Ngorogoro Crater in Tanzania, then went by small charter aircraft directly from Kilimanjaro Airport in Tanzania to the Kichwa Tembo private airstrip in Kenya. The planes did not stop in Nairobi or go through Kenyan immigration or customs.[5] The tourists flew directly from Tanzania to Kenya, over nation-states in a seamless journey from one game park to another—indeed a transnational experience. From the perspective of the tourists, there was no border crossing, and the nations of Tanzania and Kenya were not really experienced. The tour was above borders, traveling not just in airspace but in global space. The travel by van, public bus, and charter aircraft characterizes the differences among the three tourist attractions.

Mayers Ranch

The day after I returned to Kenya in 1995, I learned that the performance at Mayers Ranch had come to the attention of the Kenyan parliament and that the government had closed the site down in the late 1980s. I drove to the ranch, and over lunch Jane and John Mayers explained to me why they had been put out of business. They did so, of course, from their own perspective as descendants of a white British colonial family.

The closure resulted from a combination of factors, they said, including local politics, but the primary reason was that the government thought they were exploiting the Maasai. Jane and John reported that an African American tour group visiting the ranch to watch the Maasai performance had objected strongly, complaining about its colonial aspects—specifically, that the Mayers lived in a big house whereas the Maasai lived in mud huts, and that the Mayers gave food to the Maasai as part of their compensation, which the tourists felt was paternalistic. The Mayers brochure said that the Maasai were a linguistic subgroup of the Nilotic, but other black American tourists objected strongly to the term *subgroup,* which they regarded as insulting. The key factor, however, according to the Mayers and others in the tourism industry with whom I spoke, was that many Kenyans felt the performance of Maasai warriors dancing at a European homestead was simply too anachronistic in modern Kenya.

After closing the tourist performance, the Mayers remained on their ranch and engaged in other income-producing activities. They missed the income from tourism, but Jane expressed a feeling of relief, saying they had felt "totally invaded" having as many as 150 tourists come to their home on any given day. John felt their mistake had been that their admission price was too low, suggesting that they had underestimated the value of their attraction and had failed to appreciate the vast sums of money involved in international tourism. Jane acknowledged, as she had ten years earlier on my first visit, that a performance about tribalism and colonialism was indeed an anachronism. She felt it would be best if the Maasai were producing their own performances. Some of the Maasai who had worked at Mayers went on to the hotels in Mombasa and elsewhere on the coast, where they found employment as performers in Maasai tourist productions, and a few became involved in the sex industry, catering mainly to European women seeking a sexual experience with a Maasai man.

Cultural tourism recreates in performance idealized colonial images and other representations of the past, the pastoral, the original, and the unpolluted. Tourism performances throughout the world frequently enact imperialist nostalgia (Rosaldo 1989) and regularly reproduce stereotypic images, discredited histories, and romantic fantasies. The performances manipulate the past to serve the expectations of the tourists and to perform their master narratives about their destinations, stories already in place before they begin their sojourns.

Mayers Ranch was a brilliant postcolonial enactment of the dominant East African tourist tale, produced for foreigners. After the young warriors performed their dances for tourists at the manyatta, the tour group would move to the Mayers' lawn for tea and crumpets. The physical movement from the mud huts and brown dust of the Maasai compound to the lush green garden adjacent to the Mayers' main house crystallized the contrast between the primitive Maasai and the genteel British and evoked the broader contrast between the wild and the civilized. The tourists vicariously experienced the wildness of the Maasai only to return to civilization on the cultivated lawn and in the veritable sanctuary of the British garden. On the elegant lawn the Mayers graciously told stories about colonial times while black servants, dressed in white aprons and white chef's hats, served tea and cookies. As white settlers the Mayers themselves were part of the tourist attraction, nostalgic relics of the colonial era.

Tourists told me they found the production fascinating, in part because it was so carefully edited and produced. The Mayers (directors of the drama) did not allow the Maasai performers (or actors) to wear or display modern clothing, watches, or any industrially manufactured objects. The only souvenirs sold at Mayers were those handcrafted by Maasai. The entire performance was produced to achieve tourist realism, an ambience of authenticity, the appearance of the real. The Mayers directed the Maasai to act as if they were what the foreign tourists regarded as nineteenth-century tribespeople, the African primitives. The rituals performed at the Maasai village were made to seem natural, as if the Maasai were dancing for themselves and the tourists had just appeared there by chance. The constructedness of the site was masked. Some of the Maasai dancers had been to school and spoke English, but during performance time they remained aloof and mute.

The performance may have been brilliant, but it was nevertheless an instance of whites producing blacks, where the whites spoke graciously in a British accent and the blacks were silenced. The show featured the tribal, unchanging Maasai in a nation trying to develop its peoples into national citizens. Mayers Ranch catered to the darkest desires of the tourist imaginary, fixing Maasai people in a frozen past, representing them as primitive, denying their humanity, and glorifying the British colonialism that had enslaved them.

Bomas of Kenya

Bomas of Kenya constructs a different picture for a different audience. Opened to the public in 1973, Bomas is a government museum of the performing arts, an encyclopedic presentation of the cultural heritage of the nation performed by a professional dance troupe whose members are government employees.[6]

Its Web site says that Bomas "offers Kenya in Miniature" (Bomas of Kenya 2000). Like Mayers, Bomas has regularly scheduled daily shows. The patrons pay admission, move into a 3,500-seat auditorium for the performance (see fig. 8), then exit from the building to walk to the eleven traditional minivillages.[7]

Each village features the architecture of a particular ethnic group—Kikuyu, Kalenjin, Luhya, Taita, Embu, Maasai, Kamba, Kissii, Kuria, Mijikenda, or Luo—and consists of a few houses typical of that group or, as the Bomas Web site says, "the original traditional Architecture . . . as built by the ancestors" (Bomas of Kenya 2000). Significantly, there is no claim that the houses are those of contemporary peoples. Handicrafts are available for purchase in each village. The crafts shown, however, are not restricted to those produced by the members of any one ethnic group but are representative of all Kenyan groups and are comparable to the crafts that can be found in any souvenir shop in Nairobi. Nor are the sellers necessarily members of the ethnic group represented by the village in which each array is located. A Kikuyu seller, for example, might be found in the Maasai village. Further, no one actually lives in the villages; they are for display only.

National dance troupes have been established in Uganda, Senegal, Mali, and most other African nations as part of government policy, just as performance troupes, ethnic-village complexes, nations-in-miniature, and national museums have been established in many countries of the world. These sites differ from one another, of course, but their general aim is to collect, preserve, and exhibit the art, culture, and history of a nation. A mimeographed information program distributed by Bomas of Kenya announces, "We specialize in

8. Dancers at Bomas. Photo by Richard Freeman.

traditional dancing and preservation of Kenya Cultural Heritage." The word *preservation* is key. Whereas at Mayers the claim is that the Maasai are still living as they have for "a thousand years" and that they are essentially unchanged, Bomas talks of preserving culture, which implies that traditional ways are in danger of disappearing or no longer exist and that they belonged to the ancestors. Bomas makes a claim very different from that of the discourse directed toward foreign tourists. At Mayers the Maasai occupy space in the ethnographic present; at Bomas they and the other Kenyan groups are in the traditional past.

At the top of the Bomas program one sees: "REF: NO.BK/15/11." This is the sort of reference number that typically appears on government documents everywhere. Other evidence of a nationalistic emphasis is easy to find. For example, the performance troupe calls itself the "harambee dancers." Coined by Jomo Kenyatta, the first president of Kenya, *harambee* is a powerful national slogan that means, roughly, "all pull together" (Leys 1975, 75). In Kenya there are many harambee groups, sometimes called self-help or cooperative groups, and there is a national harambee movement. The program distributed at Bomas when I was there consisted of six pages, including advertising, and described each act or scene of the performance in sequence; there were twenty-two in all. The last act, called the finale, was described as follows: "This is a salute in praise of His Excellency Hon. Daniel Arap Moi the President of the Republic of Kenya." Such statements render the performance of traditional dances explicitly nationalistic.

The Bomas harambee dancers are of many different ethnic groups, and any member of the troupe may perform the dances of any of the other groups. At Mayers, Maasai performed Maasai dancing, but at Bomas a Kikuyu dancer, for example, can do the dances of the Maasai, the Samburu, the Kikuyu, or any group. Bomas creates an ensemble of performers from different groups who live together at Bomas as a residential community in a harambee arrangement, almost an occupational subculture, apart from their extended families and home communities. The harambee dancers from Bomas are available for hire all over the world and have made overseas tours to the United States, the United Kingdom, Sweden, Japan, and other countries.

The troupe acts as a single functioning unit, detaching ritual dancing from its home community and putting it in a museum, in a professional theater, or on the national or international stage. The troupe becomes an explicit model of the nation, melding diversity into a modern organization, disconnecting heritage from tribe. The implicit message of Bomas is that tribal dances belong to the nation. By separating cultural forms from tribal ownership, Bomas asserts that the multiethnic heritage of Kenya is now the property of all Kenyans. As an expression of nationalist ideology, Bomas speaks about tribalism as memory, and it does so in performance, where it is less threatening.

Bomas tells a story for Kenyans about themselves, and it appeals most to urban Kenyans. Its Web site states that visitors can see "rural Kenyan life" (Bomas of Kenya 2000). On Sunday afternoons, Bomas is crowded with local families who come with their children. Whereas the Mayers were hosts to foreign tourists and, on Sundays, to a resident expatriate British community, Bomas is host mostly to urban Kenyan families and only a few foreign tourists.[8] Businesspeople meet there for conversation over beer or coffee. It is a place for Kenyans to honor their ethnicity in an urban setting and to see dances they might not otherwise have an opportunity to witness. Bomas also arranges special shows for schools and educational institutions two mornings a week.

For purposes of this chapter, it is important to understand how Kenyan tourist discourse uses such terms as *tribalism, traditional, modern, primitive,* and *civilized.* The six-page program of Bomas does not once contain the terms *tribal* or *tribesmen,* and it uses the word *tribe* only twice, and then merely as the equivalent of *people* or *group.* In contrast, *tribal* and *tribesmen* are crucial terms in tourist discourse for foreigners. The tourist brochures issued by private tour companies advertising trips to Kenya for American and European audiences use *tribal* with the implicit idea that the people so characterized are primitive and are representative of an earlier state of existence. Significantly, the term used in the Bomas program is *traditional* (see fig. 9), which contrasts with *modern.* The Kenyan audience at Bomas consists of modern urbanites, and what they witness on stage are their own traditional dances that are part of a previous historical era and reflect on their own present modernity in complex, multilayered ways. The terms *tribal* and especially *tribalism* are sometimes used in the Kenyan media. They have a negative connotation in contemporary Kenya, as they have in many of the multiethnic nations of the world. The Kenyan government has long acknowledged deep-rooted ethnic identifications as a serious national problem (Chilungu 1985, 15; Okumu 1975).

In brief, *tribal* is a term for foreign tourists used at Mayers, *traditional* is a term for domestic tourists used at Bomas, and *ethnic* is a more neutral term used by some Kenyans and anthropologists to avoid the derogatory or misleading connotations of *tribal* or *traditional.* The terms elicit different associations in touristic, ethnographic, and political discourse. In a sense, Bomas has taken the concept of the tribe and put it in the archives or in a museum where hopefully it will be safe and out of the way.

The language of the Bomas program is revealing. Here are excerpts describing two of the Bomas acts:

9. Bomas sign using the term *traditional* two times

> The background to this item is the assassination of Nakhabuka, a young and beautiful girl of Abamahia clan in Bunyala, (Western Kenya). Her jealous boyfriend shoots her with an arrow at the river, because she has married someone else. Her great spirit enters the body of one of the villagers and demands that a wrestling dance be performed occasionally in her memory. . . .
>
> This item features a Giriama couple who are getting married. Unfortunately, the bride, having been bewitched just before the ceremony, threatens to refuse her man. It takes the skill of a famous medicineman to bring her back to agreement before the wedding can continue. The events of the wedding are heralded by the Gonda dance (performed mainly around Malindi on the Northern Coast of Kenya).

This is the genre of the folktale, indigenous stories. Embedded in the Bomas program are minifolktales, dramatic narratives about everyday life. The stories are culturally and geographically specific. They refer to the Abamahia clan or to a Giriama couple and to such actual places as western Kenya or the north coast. These are real places. There is none of the generalized language of much of the tourist discourse produced for a foreign audience, with its references to the untouched African primitive.[9] The function of such generalized references to tribesmen or primitives is to distance and depersonalize the object, to separate the tourist from the African. The Bomas stories, on the other hand, tell about the heritage of specific groups, ones with which the Kenyan audience can identify. That the stories tell about being bewitched, about a famous medicine man, and about spirits is part of the magical language of the folktale, but it also reflects a reality of Kenyan cultural life (Geschiere 1997).

Mayers was performed in a Maasai compound, and all Western objects were hidden from the audience. Bomas is performed in a modern auditorium that contains a restaurant and a huge bar. Before, during, and after the performance, members of the audience can order drinks. Mayers was characterized by the absence of signs; at Bomas there are signs everywhere, including ones that give the price of admission, directions to the auditorium, and directions to the traditional villages. Each village has its own sign, and there are even signs that advertise Coca-Cola.

Bomas is professionally produced, and with such technical virtuosity that it seems like a Kenyan Ziegfeld follies, with professional lighting and sound effects and with performers in matching costumes. At Bomas, the performers are clearly on stage, and they smile at the audience, whereas at Mayers the Maasai were preoccupied with their dancing. Toward the end of the dancing at Mayers the audience was invited to come on to the outdoor stage to view the performers close up and to photograph them, whereas at Bomas the audience does not mix with the actors on stage. Bomas gives one the feeling of being at a concert or at a theatrical production; indeed, Bomas employed an American producer for a time.

Mayers had a close fit between the performance and the setting, and that was part of the message. Bomas has a lack of fit between the performance and the setting, and that too is part of the message. The genre of Mayers was tourist realism. The genre of Bomas is nationalist theater. Although both were studiously produced, Mayers was made to seem underproduced, and Bomas overproduced. The aim at Mayers was to mask the artifice of production. The aim at Bomas is to expose the processes of production so as to create a discontinuity between the production and what it is designed to represent. Mayers denied change. Bomas highlights change. Bomas detaches culture from tribe and displays it before the nation for all to see and share, and in the process it aestheticizes, centralizes, and decontextualizes ritual. Ironically, Bomas represents what British colonialism was trying to achieve, the detribalization of Kenya. The British failed in their attempt to turn Kenyans into colonial subjects. Bomas succeeds, in performance, in turning Kenyans into national citizens. Disjunction at Bomas is a rhetorical strategy, whereas at Mayers the strategy was to stress continuity. Mayers was a Western fantasy.

Bomas is national wish fulfillment. Mayers and Bomas are equally political, each trying to present its own version of history. Mayers was not an accurate reflection of contemporary Maasai culture; neither is Bomas an accurate reflection of Kenyan traditionalism.

Out of Africa Sundowner

Kichwa Tembo Tented Camp is described in the brochure as "luxurious enough for even the most pampered traveler," with private sleeping tents that have electricity, insect-proof windows, verandas, and indoor bathrooms with hot showers.[10] So much for roughing it in the African bush. The camp is located near the Masai Mara National Reserve, which is an extension of the Serengeti. The main attraction at the camp is viewing game from safari vehicles, but the Maasai are also prominent. There are Maasai at the private airport welcoming the incoming tourists, Maasai dancing at the camp, a scheduled visit to a Maasai village, and a briefing on Maasai culture by a Maasai chief, who began his talk to the tour group I joined by saying in English, "I think all of you must have read about the Maasai." I choose, however, to discuss the Out of Africa Sundowner party held on the Oloololo escarpment on the bank of the Mara River.

This performance introduces a new note into ethnic tourism in Kenya. The Sundowner is basically a cocktail party with a buffet on a riverbank in the bush. The Kichwa Tembo staff set up a bar, which is attended by a bartender in red coat, black pants, white shirt, and bow tie. The name of the attraction, the Out of Africa Sundowner, comes from the 1985 Hollywood movie starring Robert Redford and Meryl Streep that is based on Isak Dinesen's 1938 book about colonial days in Kenya. The movie, *Out of Africa,* was shown to the tour group on the airplane en route to East Africa. The brochure from the tour agency describing the Sundowner says, "Standing at the precipice of the escarpment, the sun setting low amidst an orange and pink sky, it is easy to see why Africa so inspired Karen Blixen and Dennis Finch-Hatton." The brochure thus invites the tourists to experience the Sundowner not from the point of view of the movie or the actors, or from that of the book or the author, but rather from the point of view of the main characters in the story. It is all make-believe.

At the Sundowner waiters serve drinks and food to tourists standing in groups or seated together in clusters of folding chairs. Then the Kichwa Tembo employees form a line, singing and dancing for the tourists, and the Maasai men begin their chanting and dancing (see fig. 10). The performance is remarkable in a number of respects.[11]

During the dance individual Maasai dancers move among the tour group, take the hands of tourists, and bring them into the line to dance with them.

10. The Sundowner setting

11. Smiling Maasai dancing with tourists at the Sundowner

The other Maasai dancers smile in approval and visibly express their appreciation of the dance steps, now also performed by the tourists. The remaining tourists laugh and comment; most nod in sympathy and enjoyment. A few of the dancing tourists look uncomfortable but make the best of the situation, while others rise to the occasion, dancing away, swinging about wildly, improvising, introducing dance steps ordinarily seen in an American disco (see fig. 11). After the dance the Maasai again mix with the tourists, this time passing out free souvenirs—necklaces with carved wooden giraffes for the women and carved letter openers for the men. These curios are given as if they were personal gifts, but actually the tour agency at the camp buys these items for distribution at the Sundowner. It is all smiles and politeness.

At the Sundowner the Maasai warrior has become tourist-friendly. Gone is the wildness or the illusion of wildness or the performance of wildness; it is replaced by a benign and safe African tribesman. At Mayers Ranch the appeal was precisely the tension between the wild Maasai and the cultured English, but at the Sundowner that binary opposition is dissolved. At the Mayers performance the tourists moved between two distinct spaces, the Maasai manyatta and the Mayers' lawn, the African space and the English space, the wild and the civilized. The Maasai did not enter the Mayers' area, for to do so would have been a violation and would have destroyed the touristic illusion. At the Sundowner the two spaces have merged—there is no separation between the Maasai and the tourists, and there is only one performance space, where the two intermingle. By this breaking of the binary, ethnic tourism in Kenya is structurally changed (Sahlins 1981).

During the dancing at the Sundowner, the camp employees begin to sing a Kenyan song called "Jambo Bwana," written in the mid-1980s by a musical group called Them Mushrooms.[12]

The song was first performed in a tourist hotel in Mombasa. It became an instant hit and is still known throughout Kenya. Them Mushrooms moved from Mombasa to Nairobi and established their own recording studio, and they have performed abroad.

The message of "Jambo Bwana" is that tourists are welcome in Kenya, which is characterized as a beautiful country without problems. One tour agent in Nairobi said it is now the "tourist national anthem" of Kenya because it is so popular with foreign tour groups. Prominent in the song is the Swahili phrase *hakuna matata,* which in one version is repeated four times. It means "no worries, no problem." The phrase itself has a history. *Hakuna matata* had always been part of coastal Swahili language, but in the 1970s, when there was political turmoil in Uganda and the other states surrounding Kenya, it came to be widely used as a political phrase to say that Kenya is safe. The phrase was reassuring to refugees as well as to the citizens of Kenya. After Them Mushrooms wrote "Jambo Bwana" in the mid-1980s, *hakuna matata* came to be associated more with tourism.

"Hakuna Matata" is familiar to tourist audiences as the theme song of the 1994 animated Disney film *The Lion King*, with music by Elton John and lyrics by Tim Rice. The lyrics repeat the phrase *hakuna matata*, defining it as follows:

> Hakuna Matata!
> What a wonderful phrase
> Hakuna Matata!
> Ain't no passing craze
>
> It means no worries
> For the rest of your days
> It's our problem-free philosophy
> Hakuna Matata![13]

The hotel employees at the Sundowner then sang "Kum Ba Yah," an Angolan spiritual popular in the United States as a folk, protest, and gospel song. Although of African origins, "Kum Ba Yah" is now established in U.S. popular culture and has taken on new American meanings. The phrase *hakuna matata* has been similarly appropriated and is associated with *The Lion King*.

At the Sundowner, the performers present "Kum Ba Yah" with the rhythm of Jamaican reggae, a musical tradition that to many North Americans equates with good times, blackness, dancing, and Caribbean vacations.[14] In other words, Africans have taken a phrase and a song originating in Africa and have performed it for the tourists with a New World Caribbean reggae beat. This musical tradition and the songs themselves, "Hakuna Matata" and "Kum Ba Yah," have been widely interpreted in American popular culture as expressions of Africanness and blackness and then have been re-presented to American tourists by Africans in Africa. What is new is not that transnational influences are at work, that a song or an aspect of culture flows around the globe. Ethnographers are already familiar with these processes. Nor is it new that a global image of African tribesmen is enacted for foreign tourists, as this was also the case at Mayers. What is new is that the Americans at the Sundowner, who have presumably made the journey in order to experience African culture, instead encounter American cultural content that represents an American image of African culture. The Americans, of course, feel comfortable and safe, because they recognize this familiar re-presentation; they respond positively, for it is their own.

This is globalization gone wild: Paul Gilroy's "Black Atlantic" (1993), transnationalism as a Lacanian mirror image, and Appadurai's "scapes" (1991) as a Ping-Pong ball bouncing fantasy back and forth across the Atlantic. A reggae Lion King in the African bush. Points of origin become lost or are made irrelevant. Old binaries are fractured. The distance is narrowed between us and them, subject and object, tourist and native. Ethnography is transformed into performance, blurring the lines between genres in ways that go beyond Clifford Geertz (1983). What is left are dancing images and musical scapes flowing across borders, no longer either American or African but occupying new space in a constructed touristic borderzone (chapter 7; cf. Appadurai 1991) that plays with culture, reinvents itself, takes old forms and gives them new and often surprising meanings.

The colonial image of the Maasai has been transformed in the postmodern era so that the Maasai have become pleasant primitives, the human equivalent of the Lion King, the benign animal king who behaves in human ways. It is a Disney construction to make the world safe for Mickey Mouse. Presented in tourism are songs that have African roots but that in North America and probably globally are pop culture images of Africa and blackness. The Black Africa of the American imagination has been re-presented to Americans in tourism.

At the Sundowner, tourists receive drinks, food, a good show, an occasion to socialize, a chance to express their privileged status, an opportunity to experience vicariously the adventure of colonial Kenya, and a confirmation of their prior image of Africa. As posttourists in a postmodern era, they may also revel in the incongruity of the event, of dancing with the Maasai, of drinking champagne in the African wilderness. But what do the Maasai receive? The answer must be seen against the backdrop of what the Maasai received at Mayers and still receive at Bomas. The Maasai performers at Mayers received a small daily wage for each performance in which they participated, a measure of ground maize, and a pint of milk a day. They derived additional income from the sale of their handicrafts and from the tips they earned by posing for tourist photographs. They were wage laborers, as are the performers at Bomas.

The Maasai on the Mara, however, are part owners of the tourist industry and receive a share of the profits from safari tourism, but this is neither readily apparent nor ordinarily disclosed to the tourists.[15] Although tourists see only what is exhibited to them in performance, there is a vast behind-the-scenes picture. The Maasai receive 18 percent of the gross receipts of the "bed nights," the cost of accommodations at Kichwa Tembo per night per person. This can be a considerable amount as there are fifty-one units at the camp and the cost per night can be U.S. $300 to U.S. $400 in high season, for a total of over U.S. $100,000 per week with full occupancy (Kichwa Tembo 2000). There are a total of twenty-two camps and lodges on the Mara, some even more luxurious and expensive than Kichwa Tembo. Furthermore, the entrance fee to the Masai Mara Reserve is U.S. $27 per person per day, and the Maasai receive 19 percent of that fee. The odd figures of 18 and 19 percent resulted from a long process of negotiation. The funds are accumulated and given to two county councils, and one of these, the Transmara Council, which governs the area where Kichwa Tembo is located, divides the funds among the "group ranches," each based on one of the ten Maasai clans that own land on the reserve.

Maasai ownership of most of the land of the reserve, as well as the land on which the camps and lodges are built, is the basis of their right to a share of the gross receipts. Philip Leakey, a brother of celebrated paleoanthropologist Richard Leakey, reports that before the 1980s, the Kenyan elite and foreign investors derived almost all of the income to be had from international tourism (personal communication, February 19, 1999; see also Berger 1996). As a result most Kenyans, including the Maasai, were indifferent or even hostile to tourism, as they did not profit from it. Further, there was considerable poaching in the game parks. The depletion of the wildlife on the East African reserves not only threatened the tourism industry and with it a key source of foreign exchange, it also posed a danger to the national heritage of Kenya and to the natural heritage of the world.

Things changed in the 1980s when it came to be widely recognized that the way to gain the support of the Maasai for tourism development was to give them the stake in the industry that they had argued for. Since then there has been a drastic reduction in poaching on the reserve. The Maasai, who do not usually eat wild game, now have a financial interest in protecting the animals and in stopping the poaching. Further, a new law was passed stipulating that anyone caught poaching in Kenya may be killed on sight.

The Maasai profit from tourism on the Mara in other ways. There are 170 park rangers on the reserve, and all are Maasai. The Kichwa Tembo package includes a visit to a Maasai village, where the villagers receive the U.S. $10 per person admission fee as well as the profits from the sale of handicrafts. One day I counted eighty tourists, for a total income of U.S. $800. When the Maasai perform their dances for tourists, they receive compensation. One group consisting of about fifteen Maasai received U.S. $163 per performance. Again, tourists are not usually aware of these financial arrangements. Some Maasai on the Mara are wealthy by Kenyan standards, but that wealth is not visible to the tourists. Most Maasai have used their income to increase their herds of livestock—cows, sheep, and goats—which are kept away from the tourist routes.

Maasai are employed at Kichwa Tembo not only as waiters, chefs, and security guards, but in management positions as well. Yet the tourists do not see these employees as Maasai. In the hotel context, the Maasai waiters in their white uniforms are reserved and deferential, avoiding eye contact with tourists and speaking only when spoken to. If waiters were to overstep the bounds of appropriate service behavior they would be reprimanded, whereas if the same Maasai were performing for tourists as warriors and behaved deferentially in that context, they would be a disappointment to the spectators. All parties understand the behavior appropriate in each position, for the symbolic system is mutually understood and each party to the drama performs an assigned role.

Within the lodge the tourists are usually polite to the waiters but are disinterested, for the waiters are perceived as service employees. Kichwa Tembo camp is a space that provides the comfort, luxury, and safety on which upscale tourism depends. In contexts in which the Maasai are performing as Maasai and are on display for tourists, it is tourist time in another sense. The Maasai men—adorned with red ochre body paint; wearing beadwork, sandals, and red robes; and carrying sticks—change their demeanor and become warriors. In these performance contexts the tourists become voyeurs—amid the cornucopia of visual images there is the simultaneous clicking of many cameras. Ironically, on the same day a single individual might be a deferential waiter in the hotel during the serving of a meal and a Maasai warrior, one of the "Lords of East Africa," during performance time in the evening.

The Maasai, of course, are well aware of the discrepancy between their lifestyles and their tourist image, and they manipulate it, but there are many complexities in the situation. Some Maasai who have become performers in the tourism industry display themselves for tourists, to be observed and photographed, and if asked reply that they do it for the money. They play the primitive for profit, but have become what Dean MacCannell (1992) calls the ex-primitive. This is the case for performers at all three sites, at Mayers, Bomas, and the Sundowner. Tourism is their livelihood, a source of income. On the other hand, I knew one Maasai business executive who assumed "ethnic" Maasai traits only during his nonworking hours. He dressed in Western clothing with shirt and tie and spoke English during the workweek in Nairobi, but on most weekends, wearing jeans and a T-shirt and speaking Maasai, he would return to his native village to become a pastoralist and attend to his extensive herd of livestock. On ceremonial occasions, he would wear traditional Maasai clothing and dance and chant in Maasai rituals. What touristic or ethnographic discourse characterize as Maasai "ethnic" traits, may, in tourism or in life, be displayed situationally depending on the context, which is probably the case universally for all ethnicities. Identities are not given, they are performed by people with agency who have choices.

But boundaries are elusive. As Michel de Certeau (1984) suggests, spatial patterns are not composed of rigid, unbreakable regulations, flawlessly executed, but are spatial practices characterized by transgression, manipulation, and resistance as individuals appropriate space for themselves. I give two examples:

While watching the dancing at the Sundowner, I noticed one man, a waiter in black pants and white shirt, who picked up a club and began dancing along with the red-robed Maasai. He was out of place: apparently he was a Maasai waiter who had decided to join his fellow tribesmen, but it was a broken pattern.

At Kichwa Tembo one of the tourists, an African American woman, had taken an optional nature walk with Maasai guides. During the walk they came upon a pride of twelve lions. The woman reported that she had never been so scared in her life, but the Maasai guides urged calm and slowly moved the group away from the lions without incident. After that dramatic encounter, while the group was resting and chatting the woman showed the Maasai guides a picture of her grown daughter, a strikingly beautiful woman. One of the guides announced to the woman that he wanted to marry the daughter. The woman passed it off, and they continued on the nature walk. Later, back at the camp, the Maasai man came to the woman with his father, a marriage spokesman, and offered twenty-five head of cattle for the daughter, with the implication that a still larger offer would be made, a huge bride-price. The father urged the woman to consult with her own marriage brokers and then to meet again to negotiate—a Maasai practice.

When the woman told me about this incident, I playfully suggested that the least she could have done would have been to transmit the offer to her daughter and let her make her own decision. But the woman replied that her daughter was finishing her studies at a prestigious law school in California, that she was very driven and ambitious and would not want to be the second wife of a Maasai villager. Boundaries are not rigid—tourists and natives do move into each other's spaces.

Maasai, then, are incorporated into the safari tourism industry on the Mara in a dual capacity. First, they are part owners, possibly partners, and certainly beneficiaries. Second, they are performers in a touristic drama, a secondary attraction to the wild animals on the reserve, but clearly objects of the tourist gaze. As the Maasai receive a share of the profits and a stake in the industry, the question may be asked, To what extent do they control the images by which they are represented? My observations suggest that if the Maasai now have economic and political power, they do not exercise it to influence how they are presented in tourism. As the Maasai say, they are performing for the money, and they are willing to play into the stereotypic colonial image of themselves to please their clients, the foreign tourists. As one Maasai explained to me, the European and American tourists do not come to Kenya to see someone in Western dress, like a Kikuyu. The Maasai put on the red robes and red ochre and carry clubs so the tourists will be able to recognize them as Maasai.

Who is producing the Sundowner Maasai? Kichwa Tembo Tented Camp was built by the tour agency Abercrombie and Kent, but was recently sold to another company, Conservation Corporation Africa. Regardless of the particular company involved, the Out of Africa Sundowner is produced by tour agencies and, by extension, international tourism to meet a demand. Tourism is marketing, selling a product to an audience.

The production is skillful because the hand of the tour agency is masked in the presentation of the Maasai. It is the Maasai dancers who distribute gifts to the tourists at the Sundowner (though the gifts are provided by the tour agent), it is the Maasai chief who collects the ten-dollar fee to enter the village (though it is the tour agent who selects the village), and it is a Maasai (though hired by the tour agent) who provides explanations of Maasai culture. At Mayers the entrance fee was given to a member of the Mayers staff, and the staff or one of the Mayers provided the commentary on Maasai lifeways. It was apparent at Mayers that white Europeans were explaining and producing Africans, with all the colonial overtones such a process involves. At Kichwa Tembo, Maasai explain Maasai culture—but only briefly, as most tourists are not really interested in a deeper ethnographic understanding.

In Maasai tourism generally, as at Mayers, Bomas, and the Mara, there is a master narrative at work, but it is usually implicit, a background understanding. On-site textual content is less prominent than evocative visualizations, song, dance, and movement. In a sense, the producer is more important in Maasai tourist attractions than the writer. At the Mara, a casual observer might say that the Maasai are producing themselves, but I believe it is more accurate to say that the tour agents are the primary producers, with the Maasai at best relegated to a minor role. The role of the tour agent is concealed, and this concealment is part of the production.

If the Maasai at the Mara are behaving in accordance with a generalized Western representation of Maasai and of African pastoralists, then tourism in a foreign land has become an extension of American popular culture and of global media images. The startling implication, for me, is that to develop a new site for ethnic tourism, it is not necessary to study the ethnic group or to gather local data, but only to do market research on tourist perceptions. Is it too speculative to also contemplate the possibility that the Maasai will eventually become (rather than just appear as) the pop culture image of themselves? I do not believe the homogenization of world cultures is an inevitable result of globalization, for local cultures always actively assert themselves, and I would argue for the long-term integrity of the Maasai. But the issue remains: How well will the Maasai continue to compartmentalize themselves and separate performance from life? The line separating tourist performance from ethnic ritual has already become blurred in other areas of the world with large tourist flows, such as Bali. The Balinese can no longer distinguish between performances for tourists and performances for themselves, as performances originally created for tourism have subsequently entered Balinese rituals (chapter 7; Picard 1996). Where does Maasai culture begin and Hollywood image end?

Writing Tourism and Writing Ethnography

Mayers presented the tourist image of the African primitive, Bomas presents the preservation of a disappearing Kenyan tradition, and the Sundowner presents an American pop-culture image of Africa. At Mayers the tourists sat on logs facing the performance area in a reconstructed Maasai village, at Bomas they sit in tiered auditorium seats facing the stage, and at the Sundowner they sit on folding chairs on the escarpment as the performance evolves around them. The performance and the setting were concordant at Mayers and are detached at Bomas. At the Sundowner the most global message is delivered in the most natural setting, along a river bank in a game reserve. Mayers served English tea, Bomas serves drinks at the bar, and the waiters at the Sundowner pour champagne. The binary opposition at Mayers is between the African primitive and the civilized Englishman; at Bomas it is between traditional and modern Kenyans; and at the Sundowner, the binary is dissolved because the performance presents to the tourists their own transnational media image of Africa. The master trope at Mayers was tourist realism, at Bomas it is undisguised nationalism, and at the Sundowner it is a postmodern image.

Mayers, Bomas, and the Sundowner differ in many respects but all three sites combine tourism, theater, and entertainment. All take simultaneous account of prior colonial status, local politics, national forces, and global requirements. I have emphasized globalization at the Sundowner site, but there clearly are global dimensions to Mayers and Bomas as well. Mayers (as tourist realism) and Bomas (as national theater) are examples of transnationalism, and both arose in Kenya as an extension of the postcolonial condition, one for foreigners and the other for locals, for as Tim Oakes (1998, 11) says, both authenticity and tradition are themselves modern sensibilities. In the 1960s Mayers reworked a nineteenth-century colonial narrative for foreigners, and Bomas is a recent variant for domestic tourists of public displays of living peoples. Such displays have a history dating back to European folk museums (Horne 1992), World's Fairs (Benedict 1983), and even earlier (Kirshenblatt-Gimblett 1998, 34–51; Mullaney 1983). Bomas most resembles the ethnic theme parks of contemporary China (Anagnost 1993), Indonesia (chapter 8; S. Errington 1998; Pemberton 1994a), and other nations (Stanley 1998).

Viewed historically, the three tourist sites parallel three different forms of ethnographic writing. Mayers Ranch can be likened to ethnographic realism—it strove for an aura of authenticity based on a prior image of what was believed to be the authentic African pastoralist. When Mayers was opened in 1968, colonialism was gone in Kenya, a thing of the past, but there were still many British expatriates and a worldwide longing for a colonial experience—an enacted imperialist nostalgia that Mayers produced for the expatriate community and foreign tourists.

Authenticity has figured prominently in tourism scholarship since Boorstin 1961 and MacCannell 1976. Daniel Boorstin characterizes tourist attractions as pseudoevents that are contrived and artificial as opposed to the real thing. MacCannell sees modern tourists as being on a quest for authenticity but argues that what is frequently presented to them is "staged authenticity," a false front that masks the real back stage, to which they do not have access. For both Boorstin and MacCannell, there is a real authentic culture located somewhere beyond the tourist view.

Contemporary anthropologists would not agree with this early work of Boorstin and MacCannell, for we know that there are no originals, that a single real authentic culture does not exist. Of course, all cultures everywhere are real and authentic, if only because they are there, but this is quite different from the concept of authenticity that implies an inherent distinction between what is authentic and what is inauthentic, applies these labels to cultures, and values one more than the other. There is no single authentic Maasai culture in part because Maasai culture is continually changing and there are many variants. If one were to identify, say, a nineteenth-century version of Maasai culture as the real thing, one could then look further, to the eighteenth century or to a more distant region, for the locus of the really real Maasai. It is an impossible quest.

The same vision is apparent in ethnographic realism (Marcus and Fisher 1986; Rosaldo 1989; Tedlock 2000), the basic mode of ethnographic writing until the 1960s. The classic monographs on Africa (e.g., Evans-Pritchard 1940) did not describe what the ethnographers actually observed at the time of their fieldwork but were constructions based on the prevailing anthropological vision of a pure, unaltered native culture. As in anthropology, where the hypothetical ethnographic present was discredited and colonialism criticized, so too was Mayers Ranch disparaged and eventually closed. Mayers existed historically before either Bomas or the Sundowner, but even in its time it was an anachronism, doomed from the beginning.

Bomas, an effort to influence the political culture of Kenya, emerged in response to the same forces that led to political activism within anthropology during the 1970s, the era of the civil rights movement and the emergence of new nations. In the environment of intense nationalism that characterized many newly independent multiethnic Third World countries, the basic problem for each nation was how to express ethnicity while simultaneously containing it, a problem not yet resolved in many African states. The genre of Bomas is ethnographic activism. Bomas depicts traditional Maasai culture as fast disappearing and thus requiring preservation in museum archives or artistic performance. As one representation of the collective past, Maasai culture as displayed at Bomas becomes part of the national heritage of postindependence Kenya.

The Sundowner is an outgrowth of global media flows, electronic communication, and pervasive transnationalism. It is for foreign posttourists and produced in the style of postmodern ethnography. Unlike Mayers, it rejects the realist genre. Unlike Bomas, it rejects nationalist rhetoric. Postmodern ethnography describes juxtapositions, pastiche, and functional inconsistency; it recognizes, even celebrates, that cultural items originating from different places and historical eras may coexist (Babcock 1999). Contemporary ethnographers no longer try to mask outside influences, nor do they see them as polluting pure culture (E. Bruner 1984b, 1986a).

In performance, the Sundowner is more playful than the other two sites. It intermingles elements from the past and the present, is less concerned about points of historical origin, and does not strive for cultural purity. The comparison is not quite that neat, however, as the Sundowner tourists do occupy a colonial position and do want to view "primitive" Maasai. There has been a shift, nevertheless, in the stance of the audience: posttourists at the Sundowner are willing to dance with the Maasai and joke with them, and they are not that fastidious about authenticity. But postmodern tourists—and ethnographers—have not entirely overcome the contradictions of their modernist and colonial pasts. Many postmodern ethnographers still struggle with the inequitable colonial relationship and vast differentials in wealth and power between themselves and the people they study. Further, ethnographers, as those who write, control how culture is represented.

That the three sites correspond to different genres of ethnographic writing is not unexpected, as both tourism and ethnography are disciplinary practices and thus products of the same global forces. Ethnographers are not entirely free from the dominant paradigms of their times, and tourist tales have their counterpart in ethnographers' tales. When I study tourism as an ethnographer, ethnographic perspectives are reflected back to me by the very tourist performances I study. The predicament, of course, is not restricted to the anthropology of tourism; it is inherent in the ethnographic enterprise itself (E. Bruner 1986b).

The Questioning Gaze

I use the phrase the *questioning gaze* to describe tourists' doubt about the credibility, authenticity, and accuracy of what is presented to them in the tourist production. The key issue is that tourists have agency, active selves that do not merely accept but interpret, and frequently question, the producers' messages (chapter 5; Jules-Rosette and Bruner 1994). At Bomas, authenticity both is and is not an issue—it depends on which Kenyan is speaking, as there is no monolithic local voice. Some Maasai are illiterate, others have been educated at Oxford University; some live in the game parks, others in the city; some are pastoralists, others are doctors, lawyers, and businesspeople; some have a stake in the tourism industry, others do not. Urban Kenyans I know have told me they enjoy seeing their native dances at Bomas, as they do not travel frequently to their home areas, and even when they do they are not assured of witnessing a dance performance. They respect the ethnic diversity exhibited at Bomas, and they appreciate the performance and the entire Bomas experience. In addition to the dancing, Bomas features picnic sites, a children's playground, football, volleyball, badminton, table tennis, and a swimming pool. In other words, it is more than a display of Kenyan ethnic culture for intellectuals, ethnographers, and foreign tourists; it is a family recreational site.

Yet not all local observers share this positive view. Christine Southall, a scholar specializing in East Africa who is originally from Uganda, told me that many Kenyan intellectuals laugh at parts of the Bomas performance, criticizing the inaccuracies in its representation of tradition and calling its characterization of the various ethnic groups inauthentic. In 1999, Jean Kidula, a Kenyan musicologist who has worked with the Bomas performers, explained to me that Bomas is a failed project because the original objectives were not achieved. The aim in the early 1970s was to construct a national dance troupe that would accurately perform the ethnic arts of Kenya. She feels that the dances now performed are not authentic, so Bomas has become a tourist thing, folkloristic and commercial. The difficulty is that once the dance troupe was formed the performers began to innovate, and over the years the original tribal dance forms were changed. Kenyan people, she says, understand this but keep going to Bomas primarily because it is entertaining. To these two scholars, authenticity is important, and they criticize Bomas for not achieving it.

Commenting to me on Bomas, Jane Mayers said that "it's not true in any respect," meaning that the Maasai dance at Bomas is not necessarily performed by Maasai, that no one lives in the villages, and that their dance troupe is professional. The questions become: What do audiences see as true? From whom does a performance derive its authority? There are different meanings of *authentic,* but from my perspective, neither Mayers nor Bomas nor the Sundowner is authentic in the sense of being accurate, genuine, and true to a postulated original.

Anthropologists, at least in the past, have tended to regard tourism as commercial and shallow. From the perspective of realist ethnography, tourism is a disgraceful simplification, an embarrassment, and tourists are unwelcome intruders who keep appearing at cherished field sites (E. Bruner 1989; de Certeau 1984). Some American anthropologists, Kenyan intellectuals, and foreign tourists might experience Bomas as being superficial and inauthentic—but that would be to miss the point. At Bomas, traditional dances are placed in such a high-tech setting, and the production is so professional that the dances become detraditionalized. The modern auditorium, the bar, the signs, and the commercialism are not necessarily experienced by Kenyan visitors as an intrusion, for they serve to remind the Kenyans that they are not in a tribal village but in a national folklore museum. At the Sundowner, however, the juxtapositions and incongruities become surreal theater, what the tourists expect within the postmodern frame.

Although the issue for some Kenyan intellectuals is authenticity, my interviews suggest that the issue for many Kenyan tourists is doubt about the validity of the nationalistic message of Bomas. The message of the producers is not necessarily the one received by their tourist audience. Kenyan people from all segments of society are very well aware of the reality of ethnic conflict in Kenyan society, and hence those Kenyans who visit Bomas have their doubts about the ethnic harmony portrayed there. The understanding of Kenyans in this respect is similar to that of Americans who celebrate the Abraham Lincoln rags-to-riches narrative that anyone can be president, all the while knowing that no American of African, Native, Asian, or Hispanic descent, and no woman or Jew, has been elected president of the United States.

In this sense, Bomas is like Lévi-Strauss's definition of a myth (1967, 202–28) in that it tries to resolve the contradiction between a vision of Kenyan national integration and the reality of ethnic conflict and separatism, just as in the United States the Lincoln myth tries to resolve the contradiction between an ideology of equality and the actuality of discrimination. The function and the promise of national myths is to resolve contradictions, if not in life, then in narrative and performance. Yet these myths are not examples of a false consciousness, as the Marxists would have it, for most Kenyans and Americans are aware of these discrepancies.

At Mayers Ranch many tourists had doubts, which they expressed to me, for the performance was too picture perfect, too neat and well-scheduled, and the back stage of the performance and the actualities of Maasai life were too well hidden. Tourists vary, for being a tourist is not a fixed slot to be occupied but a role to be fashioned and performed (Jules-Rosette and Bruner 1994). Some tourists willingly surrendered themselves to the experience of the Mayers performance. One tourist told me that he was on vacation in Africa to relax, and he simply accepted whatever was offered to him. For him there was no questioning gaze, or if there was it was suppressed. Others behaved as if they were in a graduate anthropology seminar: They were obsessed with issues of authenticity and questioned the truth value of everything. They were never sure if the performances were bona fide.

One American student who was at Mayers Ranch during my visit kept muttering to herself and to anyone else who would listen that the Maasai were being exploited, which may have been the case. The African American tourists who complained about Mayers to the Kenyan government did not see the performance as the producers intended, as a story about the English and the Maasai, but focused on skin color, regarding Mayers as an example of whites producing blacks. This is interesting because it exports an American political sensibility to an African context (chapter 3). Tourists, however, like the rest of us, have the ability to simultaneously suspend disbelief and harbor inner doubts, and sometimes to oscillate between one stance and the other. Tourists may push the questioning gaze aside so they may delight in the excitement and danger of being with the Maasai and so they may play, in their imagination, even temporarily and tentatively, with the colonial slot into which they are being positioned. For them Mayers was good theater. Many made a conscious effort to engage the Mayers fantasy and to identify with the plot and the characters, at least during performance time, despite inner skepticism.

The Intrav tour agency that took the group to the Sundowner was skilled and sophisticated in catering to upscale tourists. It was an Out of Africa tour not just in the sense of the Isak Dinesen book or the Robert Redford and Meryl Streep movie, but in the sense of being literally out of Africa, above Africa, protected from hassles, waits, and crowds and shielded from the darker side of Africa, the poverty, brutality, disease, dirt, corruption, and civil wars.

Although the Sundowner itself went smoothly, there was an earlier instance, a memorable occasion in Tanzania, when Africa broke through the bubble. The tourists I spoke with were very disturbed about it. On a trip from Lake Manyara to Ngorogoro Crater, a ride of more than two hours, the cars carrying the tourists passed a number of painfully poor Tanzanian villages. As each village came into view, emaciated children dressed in rags ran after the cars with outstretched hands, hoping for a handout, and they continued running even after the cars had passed far beyond them. The drivers did not stop, but I saw many of the tourists continuing to look back along the dusty road at the desperate children. Afterward, with pained expression, one woman tourist commented on the shocking disparity of wealth between the members of the tour group and the Tanzanian villagers, stressing the contrast between our luxury and their poverty. Another said she felt ashamed to have spent so much money on a vacation while these villagers had nothing. It was a fleeting but important moment. The tourists talked about it for days and were obviously distraught. Its significance extended beyond that specific incident to the entire itinerary, raising the larger question in the tourists' consciousness: What else was being concealed on their tour of Africa? The incident materialized an inner doubt. By carefully orchestrating the tour, the agency had tried to suppress and silence parts of Africa, but they had not entirely succeeded.

The tourists' identification with Africans in this instance is reminiscent of the position of the character Dennis Finch-Hatton in Isak Dinesen's *Out of Africa* (1938). Finch-Hatton, a white colonialist, casts a critical eye on the institution of colonialism; identifies with the independent, pastoral Maasai; and is ultimately buried in a Maasai grave. In structural terms he is a bridge between the civilized and the wild, flying freely over the African landscape with the ability to move back and forth between the two domains of the binary. The tourists on the Out of Africa tour who participated in the Sundowner may want to be accepted, even blessed, by the primitive Maasai, if only temporarily, as a kind of absolution for holding the privileged position that haunts the edges of their dreams. They may relish the gifts, smiles, and dancing on the Sundowner as evidence that they are liked, or at least welcomed, by the Maasai. The African American woman who went on a walking tour with the Maasai and encountered the lions may retell that part of the story not only because it is a tale of unexpected adventure (always a source of good stories for tourists) but also because it is a way of identifying herself with the Maasai.[16]

At Mayers, Bomas, and the Sundowner, there are always doubts among the tourists about what they are seeing, doubts that differ from tourist to tourist but that move beyond what has been so artfully constructed for them. This is the case with all the studies presented in this book. As a tour group was seated in Bali to watch a Balinese dance drama at Singapadu, one man looked around and asked me, "Is this a temple or a theater?" Good question. The questioning gaze is a penetration of the constructedness devised by the producers, but it is also more in a number of respects.

First, there is always an unpredictability about the meaning of any performance, for individuals attribute their own understandings to each event, which may not be predicted in advance, and these understandings may change over time. Second, some tourists apply a frame to the activity of sightseeing and to everything else that occurs within the tour, like the woman who said to me as we were about to watch a performance, "Here comes the tourist dance." It made no difference to her what particular ethnic dance was on display; it mattered only that it was presented within a touristic frame. It was a tourist dance, period. For tourists who were more inclined to surrender, an immersion in the physicality of the dance activity itself was more important than any explanation or attribution of meaning. This verges on what Kirshenblatt-Gimblett (1998, 203–48) describes as an avant-garde sensibility, according to which the experience itself is more important than the hermeneutics. Further, in many cases, tourists simply do not understand what they are seeing, and they make no effort to interpret Maasai dance and culture.

Even to those tourists most willing to open up to the experience and to accept the producers' fantasy, there is, in MacCannell's terms, "an ineluctable absence of meaning to an incomplete subject" (2001, 34). It is what Kirshenblatt-Gimblett (1998, 72) has called the irreducibility of strangeness. Urry's tourist gaze (1990, 1992) is too empiricist, too monolithic, too lacking in agency, and too visual to encompass these varied tourist reactions. The tourist gaze does not have the power of Foucault's panopticon (1979), for it is not all-seeing and all-enveloping. It is variable, and there are seepages and doubts.

In Kenya the Maasai are displayed in these three tourist sites that originate in different historical eras and in disparate social milieus. Each performance has its own tourist tale, places its own frame around the travel experience, and has its own counterpart in historically constituted ethnographic modes of telling and retelling. Touristic displays of this single ethnic group are multiple and even contradictory. Ethnicity, culture, and authenticity gain and lose meanings in diverse touristic and world contexts. Constructionism, the main theoretical thrust with which I approach the study of tourist performances, is not an escape from history or ethnography. Rather, it is a theoretical foundation that enables the ethnographer to explore similarities and differences, to embrace complexity, and to open up to new possibilities.

3

Slavery and the Return of the Black Diaspora

Tourism in Ghana

RECENT LITERATURE on borderlands, hybridity, exile, and diaspora has taken us ever farther from the concept of culture as something stable and homogeneous and has opened up new theoretical and research vistas (Gupta and Ferguson 1992; Rosaldo 1989). The postmodern world is characterized by vast transnational flows of people, capital, goods, and ideas (Appadurai 1991), as the series of recent symposia devoted to the topic attests (e.g., Harding and Myers 1994; Lavie and Swedenburg 1996). As with many new intellectual currents, the first wave of enthusiasm was followed by more critical assessments and efforts at conceptual clarification. Paul Gilroy (1993, 205–12) and James Clifford (1994), for example, thoughtfully reexamine the term *diaspora* by comparing the experiences and trajectories of the Jewish and the black diasporas. As George Marcus (1994, 424) suggests, what we need in this field is theory that constructs our objects so they may be studied by fieldwork and the more traditional methods of ethnography.

The literature on diaspora and hybridity has, on the whole, neglected tourism, perhaps because tourist visits are thought to be temporary and superficial. But migrants, refugees, exiles, émigrés, expatriates, explorers, traders, missionaries, and even ethnographers may also travel for limited periods of time. To develop traveling theory, we need to know more about all patterns of travel (Clifford 1989), including tourism. This chapter contributes to an emerging discourse by describing the meeting in the borderzone between African American tourists who return to Mother Africa, specifically to Elmina Castle on the coast of Ghana, and the local Akan-speaking Fanti who receive them.[1]

In recent years Ghana has become an economically promising West African nation (Carrington 1994), and it now encourages a nascent tourist industry in its Central Region as a route to economic development.[2] Attractions include pristine beaches, the rain forest, and local cultures and rituals, but the star features are the historic castles of Elmina and Cape Coast, which were used as staging areas for the mid-Atlantic slave trade. Elmina Castle (fig. 12) was constructed in 1482 by the Portuguese (van Dantzig 1980). One of the great medieval castles, it was the first major European building in tropical Africa and has been designated a World Heritage Monument by UNESCO. In 1993 there were 17,091 visitors to Elmina Castle; 67 percent were residents of Ghana, 12.5 percent were Europeans, and 12.3 percent were North Americans. An important and growing segment of the visitor population consists of blacks from the diaspora, including many African Americans (Ebron 1998). Some of visitors from the black diaspora are upscale tourists in organized tour groups, while others are independent travelers. Some make the journey on a budget, and some prefer to stay in African homes and eat local food for a more intimate African experience. In general, however, they are a class-privileged and more educated segment of the larger diaspora population, those who have the money and the leisure time to make the long and expensive journey.

The Struggle over Meaning

As part of the tourism development project, much effort has gone toward the rehabilitation of the historic castles and the construction of a museum in Cape Coast Castle. The increased attention has precipitated discussion over the interpretation of the castles, particularly over which version of history shall be told (chapter 6).

What most Ghanaians want from tourism is economic development, including new jobs and other sources of income, better sanitation and waste disposal, improved roads, and a new harbor. The regional planning agency wants the tourist dollars to remain in the Central Region for the benefit of the community. Expectations are high.

Funds from tourism have already begun to flow into the local community, and there are numerous plans for small-scale business enterprises that will depend on the tourist trade. Many young people in Elmina want to tap into the market by offering their services as local guides. Some have plans for selling food and crafts; others want to provide home stays and even to organize performance groups for the tourists. Local people may benefit from such contacts with tourists in ways besides the financial remuneration. In addition to money, they may receive presents, and some have become pen pals or have gone abroad with tourists. The young Africans benefit most; those over forty-five years of age interact with foreign tourists much less frequently.

12. Elmina Castle

While Ghanaians see tourism primarily as a route to development, African American tourists have a different perspective. Understandably the slave trade is of primary interest to them, so they focus on the dungeons at the five-hundred-year-old Elmina Castle. Indeed, many African Americans come to Ghana in a quest for their roots, to experience one of the very sites from which their ancestors may have begun the torturous journey to the New World. It is for them a transition point between the civility of their family in Africa and the barbarism of slavery in the New World. One woman is reported to have fasted in the dungeon for three weeks and to have stated afterward that she had achieved a spiritual reunion with her ancestors.

For many African Americans the castles are sacred ground not to be desecrated. They do not want the castles to be made beautiful or to be whitewashed. They want the original stench to remain there. In Dr. Lee's eloquent words, a return to the slave forts is a "necessary act of self-realization" for diaspora blacks because "the spirits of the Diaspora are somehow tied to these historic structures" (Report of the Proceedings of the Conference on Preservation of Elmina and Cape Coast 1994, 3). Some diaspora blacks feel that even though they are not Ghanaians, the castles belong to them.

Richard Wright presents the meaning of the slave dungeons to African Americans in his book *Black Power,* where he constructs a master narrative and describes his own return to Ghana, including his visit to Elmina Castle. He refers to the "awe-inspiring battlements of the castle with [their] somber but resplendent majesty" and says that Elmina is "by far the most impressive castle or fort on the Atlantic shore of the Gold Coast" (1954, 340). Reflecting on the slave dungeons, he pictures

> a tiny, pear-shaped tear that formed on the cheek of some black woman torn away from her children, a tear that gleams here still, caught in the feeble rays of the dungeon's light—a shy tear that vanishes at the sound of approaching foot steps, but reappears when all is quiet, a tear that was hastily brushed off when her arm was grabbed and she was led toward those narrow, dank steps that guided her to the tunnel that directed her feet to the waiting ship that would bear her across the heaving, mist-shrouded Atlantic. (1954, 341–42)

Balancing this sadness is the sense of strength and pride many African Americans feel at the recognition that their ancestors must have been strong people to have survived these inhuman conditions (Jones 1995).

Most Ghanaians, on the other hand, are not particularly concerned with slavery. Although there was domestic slavery in Africa, that experience was different from the one undergone by those who were transported to the New World and suffered the indignities of the black diaspora. For Ghanaians, Elmina Castle represents a part of Ghanaian history; it passed from the Portuguese, who built Elmina in 1482 primarily to facilitate trade on the Gold Coast; to the Dutch, who captured the castle in 1637; to the British, who gained control of Elmina in 1872; and finally to the Ghanaians, who achieved independence in 1957. After independence the castle served various functions: it was the home of the Edinaman Day Secondary School, the office of the Ghana Education Service, the meeting place of the District Assembly, and a police training academy before it became a tourist attraction (see fig. 13). Having gone from trading post to slave dungeon to military fortification to colonial administrative center to prison, school, and office, Elmina Castle has had, over a period of five hundred years, a long and colorful history. First came the Portuguese, then the Dutch, followed by the British, and now the tourists.

Generally Ghanaians focus on the long history of Elmina Castle, while diaspora blacks focus on the mid-Atlantic slave trade, which reached its height between 1700 and 1850. Ghanaians want the castles restored, with good lighting and heating, so they will be attractive to tourists; African Americans want the castles to be as they see them—a cemetery for the slaves who died in the dungeons' inhuman conditions while waiting for the ships that would transport them to the Americas. Ghanaians see the castles as festive places; African Americans see them as somber places. Of course, some Ghanaians did express the hope that the restoration would not change the character of the castles and the dungeons.

In interviews and focus groups, many Ghanaians noted that African Americans become very emotional during visits to the castle and dungeons. From a Ghanaian perspective, they become almost too emotional, which suggests that the Ghanaians do not understand the feelings of diaspora blacks. Obviously Ghanaians have not shared the diaspora experience, and they may not have read works by such writers as Maya Angelou, Richard Wright, and Eddy L. Harris.

In black diaspora literature there is an almost mythic image of Africa as a Garden of Eden. For black American men in that popular literature, a return to Africa is a return to manhood, to a land where they feel they belong, where they can protect their women and reconnect with their ancestry. The kings and queens and paramount chiefs of West Africa represent royalty and dignity, resonating powerfully in the diaspora imagination. In Africa black people are in control, they are free and independent, in contrast to the disempowered minority in America. These themes pervade black diaspora literature: "Africa as motherland. Africa as a source of black pride, a place of black dignity" (Harris 1992, 13). Often the identification is intimately personal: "Somewhere deep in the hidden reaches of my being, Africa beats in my blood and shows itself in my hair, my skin, my eyes. Africa's rhythms are somehow my rhythms, and Africa speaks to me its languages of love and laughter" (Harris 1992, 27). Or as Maya Angelou writes, "I was soon swept into an adoration for Ghana as a young girl falls in love" (1986, 19).[3] In addition to Maya Angelou, other

13. Tourists in Elmina Castle, view from the women's dungeon. Photo © Frank Fournier.

African American intellectuals, such as W. E. B. DuBois and the anthropologist St. Clair Drake, have taken up residence in Ghana.

Kwame Anthony Appiah, a Ghanaian philosopher now teaching at Harvard University, describes some of the differences between the African and the black diaspora understandings of race in his book *In My Father's House.* He writes that many African Americans, raised in a segregated society and exposed to discrimination, have found that "social intercourse with white people was painful and uneasy" (1992, 6). But since Africans "came from cultures where black people were in the majority and where lives continued to be largely controlled by indigenous moral and cognitive conceptions, they had no reason to believe that they were inferior to white people and they had, correspondingly, less reason to resent them" (1992, 6–7). Although there has been resentment and resistance against colonialism, he continues, "the experience of a colonized people forced to accept the swaggering presence of the colonizer" must be seen in its African cultural context, for even educated African children "were fully enmeshed in a primary experience of their own traditions" (1992, 7).

Appiah is correct that the struggle against colonialism was conducted from within the base of a secure African family system and an active African religious tradition even though there were changes due to the colonial presence. Colonial penetration was not so deep that it led to alienation or a failure of self-confidence, a claim Appiah supports by reference to the works of such African writers as Chinua Achebe, Wole Soyinka, and Camara Laye. Interpreting the African and the diaspora experiences as similar, Appiah writes, would be to misread the psychology of postcolonial Africans.

Conflicting Interpretations

In addition to tourists and ordinary Ghanaian citizens, museum professionals have an interest in the castles. Members of the Ghana Museums and Monuments Board and their Smithsonian consultants strive for authenticity and historical verisimilitude (chapter 4). They want the castles to be represented and interpreted as accurately as possible. But the five-hundred-year history of Elmina Castle raises a difficult question: Which period will be presented for any given section in the restored castle? Particular rooms and locations changed in function over time. The site of the Portuguese church inside Elmina Castle—one of the oldest Catholic places of worship in Ghana—was converted by the Dutch into a slave auction market in 1637. The restoration could emphasize the early church, the place used for the selling of human beings, or the transition from place of worship to slave market. As a solution to the problem of restoring a castle that changed so much over five centuries, one museum professional suggested constructing a fifteenth-century Portuguese room, followed by a seventeenth-century Dutch room and then a nineteenth-century British room, but others felt this might compromise the integrity of the restoration.

Which story will be told? Vested interests and strong feelings are involved. Dutch tourists are interested in the two centuries of Dutch rule in Elmina Castle, the Dutch cemetery in the town, and the old Dutch colonial buildings. British tourists want to hear about colonial rule in the Gold Coast. Many Ashanti people have a special interest in the rooms where the Asantehene, their king Prempeh I, was imprisoned in Elmina Castle in 1896 after the defeat of the Ashanti forces by the British army. The king was later exiled to the Seychelles Islands and returned to Ghana only in 1924. He is important to all Ghanaians as a symbol of resistance to British colonialism.

The government guides at the castle are aware of and sensitive to their varied audiences. They know that all visitors are not alike and that different groups may bring their own constellations of interests. The guides cater to these varied interests by shifting the emphasis of the tour. If a group expresses a special concern with the architecture of the castle, for example, the guides will emphasize that aspect. The difficulty arises when different interests are expressed simultaneously. The problem at one point became so intense that the National Commission of Culture held a conference, on May 11–12, 1994, to decide on guidelines for the conservation program.

A restaurant-bar had been opened above the men's dungeons in Cape Coast Castle. The museum professionals saw the castle as a historic monument and museum, and as in similar institutions in other areas of the world, they wanted to have a restaurant where the tourists could go for rest and refreshments. Their view was that the restaurant would make the castle a more pleasant place so that the tourists might stay longer, have a more leisurely visit, and thereby learn more. But objections were raised that it was inappropriate to have a restaurant in a cemetery, that it was a desecration of a sacred site. The recommendation of the commission was that "facilities for restaurant, restrooms and shops could be located outside Elmina and Cape Coast Castles but appropriate musical performance and religious services should be permitted in the monuments" (Report of the Proceedings of the Conference on Preservation of Elmina and Cape Coast 1994, ii). The restaurant was closed.

An African American view has been expressed by Imahküs Vienna Robinson in a widely circulated newspaper article entitled "Is the Black Man's History Being 'White Washed?' "[4] Robinson is an American from New York who has moved permanently to Ghana with her husband, to a home on the coast with a view of Elmina Castle. The couple has established an organization called One Africa Productions, dedicated to the reuniting of Africans from the diaspora with Africans from the continent. For a fee they also conduct performances in the dungeons, primarily for African American tourists.[5] In addition, they have other development programs and contribute to the support of a local village. In her article Robinson describes the first time she visited the Cape Coast dungeons in 1987:

> As I stood transfixed in the Women's Dungeon, I could feel and smell the presence of our Ancestors. From the dark, damp corners of that hell-hole I heard the whimpering and crying of tormented Mothers and Sisters being held in inhumane bondage, never knowing what each new day . . . would bring. Strange white men that kept coming in to look at them, feeling them, examining their private parts as if they were some kind of animals; removing them for their own sick pleasures, while awaiting the Devil ships that would take them into a four hundred (400) year long hell.

After describing her own transformative experience in the dungeon, she comments on the restoration: "And here I am today witnessing the 'White Wash' of African History. But I cannot sit in idleness and watch this happen without sounding an alarm. . . . Restore, preserve, renovate, maintain? Exactly what is being done?" Robinson is objecting specifically to the installation of new glass windows, to the covering of the walls with fresh paint, and most important, to finding that the men's dungeon had been "painted a bright yellow."[6] She continues: "Gone was the musty, lingering smell of time and of Black male bodies, the lingering feel of the spirit of these ancestors who had been forcibly removed from their 'Mother' land."

The recommendation that emerged from the May 1994 conference was that the cultural heritage of all the different epochs and powers should be presented, but also that the area symbolizing the slave trade should be given reverential treatment. In keeping with this, there was a proposal to change the name from Elmina Castle to Elmina Castle and Dungeons, with an analogous name change for Cape Coast.

From the admittedly economic perspective of the Ghana Tourist Board and the tourism industry, the issue, at least in part, is one of marketing. In May 1994, when five hundred members of the African Travel Association, including many American representatives, held their convention in Ghana, for example, tours and visits to the castles were arranged as part of a conscious marketing and advertising effort. Marketing plans would be different if targeted primarily to an African American audience instead of a broader American and European one. Beyond marketing efforts, of course, there are larger issues of historical representation, and the key question becomes, What is best for Ghana?

The Representation of Slavery

Aside from the struggle over presentation and interpretation, there are other impacts of tourism. The attention of diaspora blacks to the dungeons and the slave experience has the potential consequence of introducing into Ghanaian society increased tension between African Americans and Ghanaians, and possibly a heightened awareness of black-white opposition, a sensitive and possibly controversial issue.

The Robinsons and other African Americans are not asking that the government guides discuss only the slave dungeons; they have no intention of suppressing history, and they want the guides to present the entire history of the castles. They understand that Africans themselves were active participants in the slave trade, that at first the Gold Coast was a slave importing area, and that the Europeans established positions on the coast and did not themselves conduct slave raids into the interior. It was African peoples who brought the slaves to sell to the Europeans on the coast. There was domestic African slavery and, in an earlier period (1400–1600), Arab slave trading across the Sahara to the Middle East and the Mediterranean.

Opposition between blacks and whites certainly exists in Ghanaian society, but it is not currently prominent. Emphasis on the dungeons and the slave trade calls attention to the European whites as oppressors and to the diaspora blacks as victims. All parties recognize that Africans and diaspora blacks have had a different historical experience, but some groups of African Americans, including the Robinsons' One Africa, see a need to educate Ghanaians about slavery and life in the diaspora. To help achieve this goal, on June 19, 1994, the Robinsons sponsored a ceremony in Cape Coast Castle called Juneteenth (see fig. 14) to commemorate the last day of slavery in America, which was June 19, 1865. In addition, American blacks have gone into schoolrooms to teach Ghanaians about these subjects. The youth of Elmina—and of other areas of Ghana—are very taken with the lifestyle of young, black Americans, which they regard as current and "cool," and are open to its influences. But what proponents of one point of view see as education, others might consider a rewriting of Ghanaian history.

The situation is full of ironies. When diaspora blacks return to Africa, the Ghanaians call them *obruni,* which means "whiteman," but the term is extended to Europeans, Americans, and Asians regardless of skin color, so it also has the meaning "foreigner." This second meaning is also ironic, since the diaspora blacks see themselves as returning home. So the term *obruni* labels the

African Americans as both white and foreign, whereas they see themselves as both black and at home. A white South African will be called an *obruni*, but black South Africans, as well as blacks from other countries of Africa south of the Sahara, such as Nigeria, Burkina Faso, and Kenya, will not be called *obruni* but will be referred to by another term, which means "stranger." Some African Americans who live or work in Ghana have confided to me that they find it galling that they are called *obruni* while a black person from Nigeria, who is also a foreigner, is simply called a stranger.

When I asked the people of Elmina who the tourists are, they mentioned, among others, Americans, Dutch, British, Germans, and Portuguese. (Though the Portuguese built Elmina Castle in 1482, there are not many tourists from Portugal these days.) The term *obruni* is applied to all. It suggests that in Elmina conceptualization, other than sub-Saharan Africans, all foreign visitors of the last five hundred years, including African Americans, are seen as similar. We in the West make many fine distinctions between traders, missionaries, colonialists, ethnographers, and tourists, and the Elminas do understand these differences. But the differentiations we make between types of travelers, between black brothers and sisters on the one hand and white oppressors on the other, between Europeans and Americans, are not made by the Ghanaians, who merge us all into a single inclusive category: we are all *obruni*.

14. Juneteenth celebration, 1994, Cape Coast Castle

Many Ghanaians have told me that they consider some African Americans to be racist.[7] They include the Robinsons in this group, though during my discussions with the Robinsons I did not hear one word of racism or hatred against any other person or group. One reason for the accusation is that the Robinsons' company, One Africa Productions, puts on a performance in the castle dungeon called "Through the Door of No Return—The Return," a reenactment of the capture of the slaves. When a private performance is held for an African American tour group, the Robinsons exclude whites (even though in other circumstances they might allow guests), on the not unreasonable basis that the African Americans are paying for the performance and feel more comfortable that way. The African American tourists understandably want to share the moment among themselves, as it is their historical experience. On other occasions the Robinsons do allow whites to participate.

"Through the Door of No Return—The Return" is a fascinating performance. After a tour of the castle the group assembles in the dungeon, where they hold hands, light candles, pray together, usually weep together, pour libation as a homage to the ancestors, and then pass through the door that the slaves went through to the slave ships that would take them to the Americas. After the slaves went through that infamous door, there was no return, and it was the beginning of diaspora history. In the Robinsons' reenactment, however, once the tour group gets to the other side, they sing "We Shall Overcome" and the Negro National Anthem, which are diaspora songs.[8] Then they reenter the castle, singing festive African songs and dancing to the beat of the drums to celebrate their joyous return to Mother Africa.

Another production company enacts a different "Through the Door of No Return." In this version by a Ghanaian tour operator in Accra, the performance ends after the participants go through the door; there is no reentry to the castle, or symbolically, no return to Africa. Thus, the African American production and perspective end with a return to Africa, while the Ghanaian production and perspective end with the slaves going through the door and not returning. The different performances and endings enact different versions of black history and dramatically reveal the disparate understandings of African Americans and Ghanaians.[9]

A further irony is that when African Americans return to Ghana, they find a kind of discrimination that they already have overcome in America. For example, if there is a long line of people waiting in a shop and a white person enters, the shopkeeper will frequently serve that white person ahead of the Ghanaians. A further complexity is that it was peoples of Ghana who captured the slaves and sold them to the Europeans in the castles, so from an African American perspective, one could say that the Ghanaians were not only brothers and sisters but also oppressors. Thus an African American tourist who meets a Ghanaian may secretly wonder, Did his ancestors sell my ancestors?[10] Some Ghanaians, on the other hand, seeing that diaspora blacks are prosperous and educated, feel they were in a sense fortunate that their ancestors were taken as slaves, because now they are economically well off and have a higher standard of living than the Ghanaians.[11] African Americans too may ask, What would my life have been like if my ancestors had not been taken as slaves but had remained in Africa instead?

Another view is that the African American interest in slavery and the dungeons focuses on one event and one time range in the past, as opposed to all the expressive aspects of contemporary African culture. In this perception the return should be multifaceted and fully open to the multiple dimensions of the present-day African experience. This concern is reflected in current scholarship about African Americans. Slavery was once treated as the central fact of African American history, but in the last twenty-five years scholars have studied many different aspects of historical African American life and culture. Richard Price (1983) correlates the Saramakas' statements about their past in slavery with ethnohistorical sources. David Scott (1991), however, is critical of this effort to verify an authentic past rooted in slavery, and proposes to change the problematic to ask how the figures of "Africa" and "slavery" are utilized by contemporary peoples to construct a history, to provide an identity, and to create narratives and practices. Rather than aim for an ever-more-accurate reconstruction of slavery, Scott shifts the problematic by asking about the meaning of slavery to contemporary peoples.

At the May 1994 conference in the castle, a prominent African American referred to Anthony Hyland, an architect working on the restoration, as a "white slave master." In Elmina a diaspora black person, after visiting the dungeons, physically attacked a Dutch tourist. One Ghanaian woman, who had seen the Robinsons' production of "Through the Door of No Return—The Return," told me that after viewing the performance she wanted to go out and strangle a white person.

After my return from Ghana, while writing this essay, I read a *New York Times* article written by Michael Janofsky titled "Mock Auction of Slaves Outrages Some Blacks" (1994). At Colonial Williamsburg, an enactment of a slave auction had been scheduled; four slaves were to be sold to the highest bidder. The performance had been organized by the African-American Department of Colonial Williamsburg, which includes thirteen black museum professionals.[12] The director of the department, a black woman, argued that open display and discussion was the only way for people to understand the degradation of slavery, a horror that had to be faced. She asked, If museums depict the Holocaust of Jews, why not a slave auction of blacks? But critics said the "slave auctions are too painful to bring to life in any form" (Janofsky 1994), and the Richmond branch of the NAACP reported that their phones were ringing off the hook in protest and outrage. The performance of the slave auction was canceled. The United States has not yet come to terms with slavery or its representation.[13]

Who Owns the Castles?

Aside from the issue of representation and interpretation, there is the question of who should control the castles and what narrative should be told. The Ghana Museums and Monuments Board is the designated custodian of all national monuments, but traditional chiefs also have a claim. In my meeting with the Council of Chiefs of Edina (Elmina), they noted that artifacts and furniture from Elmina Castle had been relocated to museums and sites elsewhere in Ghana, and they wanted the objects returned. The chiefs complained that when the African Travel Association brought five hundred travel agents and officials to the area, they did not even pay a courtesy call to the Elmina traditional chiefs, who felt embarrassed and offended. Further, they said that CEDECOM (Central Region Development Commission), the regional planning agency, does not inform them of its plans for tourism development even though that development is taking place in their area of jurisdiction. The chiefs also suggested that the land on which Elmina Castle is located belongs to them—to the stool, that is, the emblem of the traditional chiefs—so they should get royalties.

This very issue is what precipitated warfare between the British and the Ashanti after the transfer of the West African settlements from the Dutch to the British in 1872. The Ashanti claimed that Elmina belonged to them and that the British should therefore pay them ground rent. The British refused, so in 1873 the Ashanti attacked. The people of Elmina sided with the Ashanti, so the British demanded that the Elminas give up their weapons. When they refused, the British bombarded Elmina and destroyed the part located along the sea coast, adjacent to the castle. That section of Elmina has never been rebuilt, and it is now an archaeological site. Since 1873 all the residents of Elmina have lived on the other side of the Benya River, away from the castle. It could be said that the British military moved the local population away from the castle so the British and the Elmina people would be separated by the river.

The process of separation has continued to the present. Before the restoration in the area surrounding the castle there was a market with small stands and food stalls. All of these sellers and market people have been relocated away from the castle grounds (see fig. 15). Previously the market had served the needs of the local residents, but now the castle serves the tourists. In our focus group discussions there was no objection to the removal of the food sellers; in fact, the majority of Elminas approved of it. They understood that the castle area had to be cleared and cleaned for the tourists.

When I first went to Elmina Castle in June 1994, I was shocked to find a sign at the entrance that read, in English and in Fanti, THIS AREA IS RESTRICTED TO ALL PERSONS EXCEPT TOURISTS (fig. 16). The local people, the residents of Elmina, were not to go beyond the castle wall and were prohibited from entering the castle grounds. It was explained to me that this was to keep the locals from defecating in the area around the castle and on the beach and also to protect the tourists from being hassled. Elmina residents are able to enter the castle only as tourists—they are supposed to pay an admission fee of three hundred Ghanaian cedis (about U.S. $30), though the guides told us that not all do so. One Elmina resident refused to pay the entrance fee, stating that the castle and the land belong to the Elmina people. (Some African Americans also refuse to pay the fee, saying they didn't pay to leave here, so they shouldn't have to pay to come back.) The Elmina people have again been separated from the castle, their castle, which has been turned over to the tourists. The local people not only are excluded from their major historical site but have become objects of tourism themselves, for the tourists look at and photograph the people as well as the sites.

As one enters the grounds and approaches the castle at Elmina there is a second sign (fig. 17), a huge one that which lists the donors and agencies involved in the restoration project (the Monuments and Cultural Heritage Conservation project) as follows: United States Agency for International Development (USAID), United Nations Development Programme (UNDP), Shell (Ghana) Limited, Ghana Museums and Monuments Board, International Council on Monuments and Sites (U.S. Chapter), and Smithsonian Institution. Finally, in a smaller sized printing at the bottom, it states that the project is being implemented by the Central Region Development Commission and the Midwest Universities Consortium for International Activities (USA). The latter, MUCIA, includes my university, the University of Illinois.

These signs suggest that while the people of Elmina are restricted from entering the castle the project has been given over to a blue-ribbon group of international aid agencies and is controlled by their staff and hired consultants, of which I am one. The United States is mentioned on the sign three different times. The government of Ghana is not mentioned except through two of its agencies, which are themselves dependent upon USAID and United

15. Elmina Castle and surroundings, view from the town

16. Sign by the entrance to Elmina Castle

PPOJECT: MONUMENTS & CULTURAL HERITAGE CONSERVATION (ELMINA CASTLE)
DONORS: UNITED STATES AGENCY FOR INTERNATIONAL DEVELOPMENT (USAID)
UNITED NATIONS DEVELOPMENT PROGRAMME (UNDP)
SHELL (GHANA) LIMITED
IMPLEMENTING AGENCY:
GHANA MUSEUMS & MONUMENTS BOARD
COLLABORATING AGENCIES:
INTERNATIONAL COUNCIL ON MONUMENT & SITES (U S CHAPTER)
SMITHSONIAN INSTITUTION
THIS PROJECT WHICH IS PART OF THE TOURISM DEVELOPMENT SCHEME FOR THE CENTRAL REGION IS BEING IMPLEMENTED UNDER THE AUSPICES OF THE CENTRAL REGION DEVELOPMENT COMMISSION IN PARTNERSHIP WITH THE MIDWEST UNIVERSITIES CONSORTIUM FOR INTERNATIONAL ACTIVITIES (U.S.A)

17. Sign on the grounds of Elmina Castle

Nations money. So who owns the castle? Who has the power to represent one of Ghana's greatest historical monuments?[14]

Tourism as Commerce

Ghanaians generally welcome tourists, but in the focus groups I learned that some tourists were considered "ruffians," "dirty," and "drug addicts," and some of their behavior was considered "shocking." A forty-six-year-old female said some tourists are "really dirty," and some "look like madmen." A forty-four-year-old male said, "The way some of them dress, the way some of the men have their earlobes pierced, the very short dresses of some of the women which expose their private parts, are what I don't like about them." A nineteen-year-old female said, "Some are Rastafarians and I think they do not normally bathe. We don't like that." Some Ghanaians also expressed distrust. I quote from the transcriptions of the focus group discussions:

> Some are CIA agents, but come under the cover of tourism and help their government to deal with African governments. They normally help their government to overthrow African governments. Our government should watch these people very well. (male, age 36)

> My worry is that we are near the sea. And we receive a lot of foreign boats on our shores. And in these days of many stories about wars, we could be taken unaware by enemies. Before we could do anything, we would be surrounded by enemies. (male, age 18)

There are also aggressive acts toward tourists, mugging and stealing, to such an extent that the local government has assigned guards to protect the tourists. I heard over and over again about the need for protection of the tourists.[15] The district chief executive expressed the hope that the tourists coming to Elmina would register with the Ghana Tourist Board, which would then inform the assembly, which would then know of their coming so they could be guarded.

The term *protection* appeared repeatedly in our focus group discussions and interviews, so our research group probed for shades of meaning to better understand how the word was being used locally. We found three meanings: first, it means guarding the tourists against theft; second, it means guiding the tourists and helping them find their way in Elmina town; third, it means protecting them from harassment and from the annoyance of people coming up to them requesting money or a pen or an address. A protector, then, is not only a guard but also a cultural broker, a mediator between the citizens and the tourists. When a tourist walks through the town accompanied by a guard-guide-protector, then that tourist is much safer because the other residents of the community recognize the Elmina person serving as protector and do not disturb the tourist.

Above all other negatives, one behavior is the most offensive to the local Ghanaians.[16] The people of Elmina object strenuously when tourists take photographs without permission. This sentiment was frequently heard in the focus group discussions and interviews.

> I am ever ready to destroy the camera of any *obruni* who takes my picture without my permission. (male, age 40)

> One tourist at one time took a picture of a fisherman who was changing his clothing. This was not good. At that time I even called a police officer to intervene but he did not mind me. We wish this attitude of tourists should be checked because we blacks cannot take such pictures in Europe or America. (male, age 37)

> They take pictures without the consent of the people. Some intentionally take pictures of naked and badly dressed people. These pictures give a bad impression about us when they are sent abroad. (female, age 63)

> Some tourists take pictures without our consent. I once struggled with a tourist who took my picture without telling me. I seized the camera and removed the film from it. I had wanted to destroy the camera but I did not. We want them to make us aware before taking our picture so that we may charge them because in their countries, people pay for everything. (female, age 19)

There are two factors involved in the strong objections to tourists taking photographs without permission.[17] One concern is that tourists take photographs of naked children and dirty places, then return home displaying a very negative image of Elmina and Ghana. The issue here is the poor representation of the Elmina people, a derogatory image. The second factor is that the taking of photographs is not reciprocal. Citizens have complained that those taking the photographs return home and sell them for a profit, but the people of Elmina get nothing in return. The observation was made a number of times about local people traveling abroad and seeing pictures of Elmina people on calendars and postcards and in magazines. It was asked, If the photographers profit why shouldn't their subjects?

The Ghanaians' concern about photography is indicative, almost metaphoric, of the pervasive commercial nature of the transactions between tourists and locals in Elmina. Little children continually ask for money, as do many adults. One constantly hears the phrase, "Obruni, money money." Less-educated people ask for money directly, while educated persons request payment in a more subtle and indirect manner. Ghanaians resent the image of

African poverty reported by Westerners, yet the practice of begging for money from Westerners is widespread. The practice is possibly a consequence of the tremendous disparity in wealth between the tourists and the locals. Asking for payment may, however, be a cultural characteristic—in some situations, residents of Elmina ask for money from other members of their own community. Both a local elder and one of our Elmina research assistants had completed papers for their B.A. degrees at the University of Cape Coast. Their papers were on Elmina festivals and culture, and in both cases they had to pay for the information they received.

The consequence of this practice from the tourist perspective is that it exposes the commercial nature of tourism. Tourism is a business—indeed, an industry—and the tourists do have to pay for their experience, but the commercial aspect is frequently disguised.[18] When tourists go on organized group tours they usually pay for everything in advance, and thereafter no money changes hands except what is paid for drinks and incidentals. The touristic experience is bought, but there are few reminders of this on the organized tour. Individual budget travelers, too, hold to the myth that they do not pay for their touristic adventures, and they believe that they become friends of the local people. Many tourists believe the myth, encouraged by the tour operators, that they are guests and that the locals are their hosts. But if in Elmina tourists are constantly asked for money—for everything, including photographs—it reminds the tourists that they are not guests but paying customers. It destroys the illusion that the tourist is simply a visitor and an adventuresome traveler. For those African Americans who return to Africa for self-realization or to experience the slave dungeons, the commercial nature of the encounter may be especially disappointing, as it dramatically shatters their conception of themselves as returning home to their black brothers and sisters.

Our research team speculated further about the mercantile nature of tourist-local interactions in Elmina. One member brought up the point that politicians in Elmina pay for votes, and missionaries pay for converts—so why shouldn't tourists pay for photographs? After all, this is capitalism, and isn't tourism the commodification of social relations and experience? The citizens of Elmina may have it right—that tourism is a business based on exchange, so to trade money for photographs is appropriate and realistic.

There are other objections to the behavior of tourists. Locals are offended when tourists walk through the town in swimming suits, especially bikinis, and when they wear see-through clothing. Giving or receiving with the left hand is considered impolite in Ghana, yet tourists do it. We received some comments, especially from older people, that it was inappropriate for tourist couples to walk hand in hand or to touch or kiss in public. A Ghanaian woman usually walks behind her husband. But some of the Elmina youth did not object to this aspect of tourist behavior. They found themselves explaining to their elders that touching or kissing in public is just part of Western culture and that the Elmina folk should learn to understand it. Still others said that for couples to walk together and to touch each other showed affection, respect for one's partner, that it was better than the Elmina way, and that in this regard, the people of Elmina could learn from the tourists.

Cultural Revival

A final consequence of tourism is that tourist interest in Ghanaian culture has led to an increase in Ghanaians' own interest in their culture. As anthropologists know, most people in most societies take their culture for granted and do not ordinarily think about it. However, in times of change, controversy, ritual, or performance, people are led to examine their culture, and the coming of the tourists has a similar result. Especially in crafts and in cultural expressions such as dancing, drumming, and musical group performances, there is a revival due to the attention tourists pay to these long-standing "traditional" practices.

> Tourism has even made us more conscious about our culture. It has made us revive some of our cultural practices like dancing, drumming, dressing, and even our festivals. You know, most of the tourists express interest in these aspects of our culture. (male, age 38)

> Yes, these days, because of the tourists, the chiefs dress nicely and better than in the past. (female, age 19)

Tourism not only enhances Ghanaians' interest in their traditional culture, it also supports local festivals and enhances the display of the power of the chiefs, but this performance says little about the chiefs' political power. There is a vast literature in African social anthropology on the decline of the power of chiefs as a consequence of colonialism and modernization, and this is certainly true in Ghana.

The festivals of Ghana are among the main ritual performances and tourist attractions. I attended the 1994 Fetu Afahye, the annual festival in the Oguaa traditional area, in the town of Cape Coast. The activities of the *afahye* were spread over seventeen days, culminating on September 3 in a procession *(durbar)* with the *asafo* companies (military organizations) and the traditional chiefs marching through the town, ending in Victoria Park. *Asafo* membership is inherited patrilineally although the Fanti have dual descent. It would be beyond the scope of this essay to describe the festival other than to say that it serves many functions. It is a libation to the seventy-seven Oguaa gods for the harvest from the earth and from the sea, an opportunity for spiritual renewal for the community, a display of the traditional social organization, a period for renovation of the shrines, a time of family reunion, and a period of carnival and merrymaking—celebrated by boat races, a state ball, dances, political speeches, a masquerade, a church service, a beauty queen contest, a walking race, a concert, and a football (soccer) match. For a week there is singing, drumming, and dancing in the streets of Cape Coast. It is a festive occasion for the entire community, but it has not had unbroken historical continuity.

In 1932 the colonial government banned the festival and seized all firearms because of a clash between two of the military organizations. The *asafo* companies had always been competitive, but in 1932 the situation got out of hand. The Ghanaian government removed the ban in 1964, and the *afahye* has been conducted since that time. According to one history of the festival, told to me by Nana Awuku, a traditional chief and a business leader, the 1970s were the peak time for participation and energy in the festival.

Since the 1980s the festival at Cape Coast has been in decline. Fewer people attend and many appear to be losing interest. One factor has been the continued erosion of the authority of the traditional chiefs, which began with the treaty of 1844, when authority was transferred from the chiefs to the British. Since Ghanaian independence the government has taken over many of the functions previously performed by the traditional chiefs. President Kwame Nkrumah further transferred power from the traditional chiefs to the central government by requiring that the central government give its approval for the installation or removal of a traditional chief. The festival of Elmina, the *bakatue,* was not performed from 1979 to 1988, as there was no paramount chief.

Another factor causing the decline has been the charismatic Christian movement, which has been very powerful in Ghana. The Christians ask, How can one be Christian and believe in fetishism, spirits, and ancestor worship? During the height of the 1994 Fetu Afahye, a Christian group held a religious meeting in Cape Coast, in direct competition with the festival.

A third factor has been the economic one.[19] In 1993, only four traditional chiefs participated in the Fetu Afahye, primarily because of the cost. In a comparable festival held in Elmina, one chief spent 700,000 cedis (U.S. $700), and in the Cape Coast *afahye* another chief spent 1 million cedis (U.S. $1,000), an enormous sum by Ghanaian standards. The latter chief had to hire drummers and members of his retinue for the procession. A visitor might look with awe at the large following of the chief, at the adoration displayed, and might marvel at the display of African tradition. But these days, adoration and tradition have to be purchased. It cost one chief 250,000 cedis (U.S. $250) just to purchase a cow that was necessary to feed his "followers."

Chiefs and others can no longer afford the festivals, one of the most spectacular tourist attractions in the Central Region. In 1994, in order to encourage the participation of the traditional chiefs in the procession, CEDECOM provided a monetary subsidy to the chiefs, and the number of participating chiefs increased from four to nine. It is ironic that the agency of government specifically charged with change and development finds itself supporting traditional chieftaincy in order to encourage tourism. In a sense, CEDECOM is reconstructing the institution of the chieftaincy not as a locus of political authority, for that has long since eroded, but as display, as performance for tourism.[20] They see their task as one of supporting the Fetu Afahye without diminishing its character as an "authentic" celebration. Major support for the afahye is also provided by commercial sponsors, such as Embassy Cigarettes, Fan Milk, and Accra Brewery.

These governmental and commercial subsidies do not imply that the festival has become completely commodified or that it has lost its meaning to all the people. The festival still has traditional significance, rooted in indigenous social structure. The ritual and spiritual components, such as the pouring of libation and sacrifices at the shrines, are still performed by ritual specialists, even in places where the community-wide celebratory aspects of the festival are in decline.

Though charismatic Christians might not participate in the *afahye* in Cape Coast, many others do. Over time, the religious and societal aspects of the festival have been supplemented by new additions, such as the beauty contest and the town ball. And the carnivalesque features and the pure enjoyment are apparent. Once at the Fetu Afahye I found myself dancing in the street, and I looked across the road at an old woman selling in the market, who was also dancing in front of her stand, smiling at me. Ours eyes met. We both kept dancing separately but we continued to look at each other, as if dancing together, across the road. It was a joyous moment.

Final Thoughts

Gilroy, in his important book *The Black Atlantic,* distinguishes between the essentialist view of blackness and the more constructivist and synchronistic concept of an emergent black Atlantic culture, one that he calls a rhizomorphic, fractal, transcultural, and international formation that combines elements from Africa, the Caribbean, America, and Britain (1993, 4). I applied this distinction to my data. The Robinsons and many African Americans, while on tour in Ghana, proclaim a black essentialism in their discourse. The very name of the Robinsons' company, One Africa Productions, claims that all blacks are Africans—and though some live on the African continent while others live in the diaspora and may be African Americans, they are all one people, one Africa. The Robinsons focus on a common origin, on the essential unity among all blacks, and on historical continuity, thereby erasing hundreds of years of separate experience. This is what they say, but it is different in their practice, in their lives, and in their performances. Their ceremony, "Through the Door of No Return—The Return," starts with the tears of slavery in the dungeons on the Gold Coast, turns to American diaspora nationalist songs, and ends with festive contemporary African music; it is clearly a blend of historically disparate elements. It constructs a three-part narrative of initial horror, diaspora resistance, and joyous return. Thus, while the Robinsons' texts are essentialist, their practice is constructivist.

Ghanaians, on the other hand, do not hold an essentialist view of blackness, for although they are very aware of the similarity in skin color, that attribute is not, for them, the single overriding classificatory criterion for the sorting of human beings. They see the returning African Americans primarily as foreigners, as Americans, as wealthy, and as tourists. In my view, not to see African Americans solely as black provides a liberating corrective for an American society beset with racial problems, where race, defined solely by skin color, is widely perceived as a biological given that determines all else that is important about a person. Ghana provided me with a tremendous sense of elation because it rocked the foundations of the American schema of categorizing persons and provided a new way of seeing others.

So who owns Elmina Castle—the diaspora blacks who left as slaves, the Elmina citizens and the traditional chiefs who remained in place, USAID and the other international aid agencies that support the restoration and provide the interpretive perspective, or the tourists to whom the castle has now been dedicated? This is a rhetorical question because the castle has not simply been a passive place. Elmina Castle may have been built initially as a European colonial intrusion on the Guinea Coast, but subsequently it has made its own claims to power and monumentality. Dominating the countryside, a massive structure on the edge of a humble fishing village, the castle takes on properties of its own and imposes its own meanings on the surrounding area. Elmina Castle is a bastion of power, a site to be struggled over, a transition point in the passage of goods and people from the interior of Africa to Europe and the New World. By their very nature, castles are dominant localities that define boundaries, that tell us who has the right to be inside, within the center of power and in control, and who is outside, on the periphery. Castles are a dynamic presence, places that produce movement between home and abroad, sites for the construction of narratives of time and narratives of space. Old castles have long histories, stories of peace and battle, honor and degradation, beauty and cruelty, civilization and barbarism. Who owns the castles? Who has the right to tell their story?

PART TWO Competing Stories

4

Lincoln's New Salem as a Contested Site

PUBLIC PRESENTATIONS of the past in museums and at historic sites, national monuments, tourist attractions, world's fairs, art exhibitions, and archaeological reconstructions have lately been of interest[1] to anthropologists and historians for what they tell us about the construction of culture (E. Bruner, ed., 1984), the production of history (Lowenthal 1985), the invention of tradition (Hobsbawm and Ranger 1983), and the marketing of heritage (Dominguez 1986). *Construct, produce, invent,* and *market* are verbs that highlight the processual, active nature of culture, history, tradition, and heritage. No longer are these taken as merely persisting or as transferring mechanically from one generation to the next: anthropologists have problematized culture, history, tradition, and heritage, focusing on their emergent nature, on how they are made, and on the practices and processes involved in their coming into being. In this literature, museums and monuments may be seen as new "knowledge" that arises in relationships of power (Foucault 1980).

Power, however, is rarely monolithic and is usually contested. Despite the efforts of a nation or an organization to present a monolithic view of itself as integrated and unified, without dissent or internal conflict, such functionalist interpretations are more prominent in the pages of Emile Durkheim (1915) and A. R. Radcliffe-Brown (1952) than in social life and practice. Society and its agents of power may aim for the monolithic view, but it is something strived for rather than finalized or achieved. There are always dissident voices and challenging readings, and indeed, much of the new scholarly literature on public history and cultural displays may be seen as a critique of authoritative viewpoints. This literature is not just a tension between the official and the heretical or between the establishment view and its resistance; rather, it is one of multiple competing voices in dialogic interplay (Bakhtin 1981, chapter 6). The notion of resistance reduces polyphony to a dualism.

Although all the studies in this volume document how culture is invented and produced, this chapter focuses on competing stories and sees the production as a site of struggle. The chapter deals with New Salem Historic Site, a reconstruction of the village in central Illinois where Abraham Lincoln lived in the 1830s. New Salem depicts prairie village life in the 1830s and provides a representation of the story of Lincoln, one of the great American narratives. The 640-acre site is now an outdoor museum and recreation area attracting over a half-million tourists a year. New Salem consists of the historic village, with twenty-three reconstructed log houses furnished as they were in the 1830s, and a campground, a picnic area, and hiking trails.

Rather than dealing with Lincoln in the abstract as a decontextualized myth or text, I chose to study a given enactment of the Lincoln story at a specific historical moment at the site of New Salem in its prairie context, for it is only in the specifics of a particular performance that scholars may learn how the site and the story are actually produced and experienced (Bauman 1992). The emphasis on the particular is essential in my theoretical perspective, in part because disembodied decontextualized narratives have no politics, as there are no persons or interests involved. Without a specified audience, narratives have no meaning, because the meaning is only in the audience's reading. This privileging of the specific leads to a consideration of the complexity of forces and the multiplicity of voices and meanings at work. Audiences are not passive recipients of received wisdom and of official views; the challenge is to understand the interpretations of the audience in particular instances.

My thesis, based on my performative perspective, is that despite the efforts of museum professionals, historians, and the scholarly community to present an ever more "accurate" perspective of Abraham Lincoln and life in the 1830s in the village of New Salem, their scientific views are contradicted and suppressed by the way in which the reconstructed village is produced and by how it is interpreted and experienced by the visitors. In other words, New Salem is a contested site, not in the sense of a grand political conflict between, say, the colonial powers versus the colonized, or between state power versus revolutionaries, or between privileged social classes versus the oppressed, although the story of Lincoln contains all of these elements. The contest is between the museum professionals and scholars who seek historical accuracy and authenticity on the one hand, and the people's own popular interpretation of Abraham Lincoln's heritage as it is manifested in a given site in contemporary America on the other. New Salem is contested in a quiet sense. It plays itself out in what I call the soft struggle over meaning between the "official" interpretation of the site and how that official view is undermined by the processes of its own production.

Interpretive Themes

Most tourists who come to New Salem have at least a generalized knowledge about Abraham Lincoln, a prior story derived from the media, from school history courses, and from the wider culture. They know that Lincoln led the Union during the Civil War and that he abolished slavery, but they may not know how the story of Lincoln connects specifically to the site of New Salem. The reconstructed village became a historic site because Lincoln lived there for six years between 1831 and 1837, so the focus is on the young Lincoln of almost thirty years before the Civil War. The key interpretive theme is presented to visitors in several forms: in a handout distributed at the entrance to the reconstructed village, in a dramatic statue of Lincoln located adjacent to the parking lot, in written materials sold in the souvenir shop and the bookstore, and in a video shown in the orientation center.

The handout, from the Illinois Historic Preservation Agency, is titled "Lincoln's New Salem" and provides a map of the village and a description of the site:

> The six years Lincoln spent in New Salem formed a turning point in his career. From the gangling youngster who came to the village in 1831 with no definite objectives, he became a man of purpose as he embarked upon a career of law and statesmanship. . . . Strangely, the six years that Lincoln spent in New Salem almost completely encompass the town's brief history. The community was growing and thriving when Lincoln reached there in 1831, but in 1839, just two years after he left New Salem for Springfield to practice law, the county seat was established at nearby Petersburg. Thereafter, New Salem declined rapidly.

The key theme is that Lincoln spent his formative years at New Salem, that he was forged there, and that somehow, mysteriously, the village had existed for that divine purpose. New Salem is a site of transformation: Lincoln arrived as a poor youth, a "raw-boned lad," an unskilled common laborer, or as Lincoln later described himself, "a friendless, uneducated, penniless boy," and he left six years later with a law partnership in Springfield and a seat in the Illinois House of Representatives. The same theme of transformation is depicted in a striking bronze statue of Lincoln with an ax in one hand and a book in the other (fig. 18). An explanation of the message of the statue is given on the back of a postcard that may be purchased in the souvenir shop, which says that the statue "portrays Lincoln in the symbolic act of discarding the ax (frontier life) and taking up the book (study of law)."

The state park coloring book for children, also sold on-site, states that New Salem was to serve "a special purpose in its short life," that of providing a place where a young man with "less than a year of formal schooling would continue his self education, and start on the road toward the high place he was to occupy in national and world esteem. "By the time Lincoln left New Salem he had "found himself" and was on his way to "his great destiny." After his departure the village "strangely" declined, for it had served its "special purpose."

The film presented to the tourists at the orientation center expresses the same theme. The title of the film, "Turning Point," refers to the transition in Lincoln's career. The narrator says about New Salem that "something happened here that can't be quite explained." Lincoln arrived as "an uncouth country boy," became a statesman, and then left the community, and after that the village was deserted. It was "almost as if the village rose up out of the wilderness to meet Lincoln, and then faded away again once he was gone. Somehow this place changed the man. It changed the course of history."

Similar themes are found in the work of Carl Sandburg, who refers to New Salem as Lincoln's 'Alma Mater' (1954, 743) and his "nourishing mother" (1954, 55):

18. Lincoln statue

> In April he packed his saddlebags to leave New Salem where six years before he had arrived, as he said, "a piece of floating driftwood," being now a licensed lawyer, a member of the state legislature and floor leader of the Whig party. The hilltop village, now fading to become a ghost town, had been to him a nourishing mother, a neighborhood of many names and faces that would always be dear and cherished with him, a friendly place with a peculiar equality between man and man. . . . Here he had groped in the darkness and grown toward light. Here newspapers, books, mathematics, law, the ways of people and life, had taken on new and subtle meanings for him. (1954, 55–56)

New Salem is presented as the site where it all happened, the scene of a rural Midwest version of the familiar American rags-to-riches success story, a master narrative in American culture, though in this case the hero is a humble backwoodsman rather than an immigrant. When Lincoln arrived at New Salem he was not yet established, he did not own a house in the village but only boarded there, and he tried a series of occupations before settling on law and politics. During his New Salem years, Lincoln achieved what he did by hard work, study, and reading by candlelight. This is the great log-cabin-to-president myth,[2] the American dream, even the frontier hypothesis of Frederick Jackson Turner, for Lincoln was formed by his overcoming of the hardships of frontier life just as the United States had been formed by its conquering of the wilderness.[3] New Salem is a national shrine because it gave birth to the adult Lincoln.

The Scholarly and the Popular

Is this picture of New Salem historically accurate? Is it "true"? It is true that Lincoln went into law and politics at New Salem, but the emphasis on New Salem as the site of the transformation of Abraham Lincoln may be overdone. After all, Lincoln was twenty-two years old when he arrived at New Salem, already an adult; he had spent his truly formative adolescent years elsewhere. Lincoln announced his candidacy for the state legislature in 1832, only seven months after his arrival in New Salem, so it is reasonable to assume that he was already politically inclined before his arrival.

Academic historians would agree that the interpretation of the site presented in the brochures overemphasizes the importance of the New Salem years to the neglect of the earlier Indiana years and the time Lincoln spent at Vandalia, Illinois. Further, the historian Mark E. Neely (1982, 222) suggests that the importance of New Salem as a tourist attraction may have served to inflate the importance of the New Salem years in Lincoln biographies. Thus a touristic representation may have distorted the discourse of professional historians, which reminds us that tourism and scholarship are not as independent as might be assumed.

There is a tension, however, between tourism and scholarship, between the popular and the academic, and this tension represents an arena of conflict, a locale of contestation, for on the one hand the historians are influenced, sometimes unconsciously, by popular representations, but on the other hand they are engaged in a conscious ongoing argument against the mythic popular Lincoln. This may be seen in the titles of biographical studies that seek the "real" Lincoln (Luthin 1960), the man "behind" the myth (Oates 1984) or the "hidden" Lincoln (Hertz 1940), as if the historical scholar had to clear away the mythologies to get at the true Lincoln waiting behind and underneath the tangle of popular beliefs.

The tourists, however, are generally not aware that the New Salem years have been overemphasized, for the site is there. They can walk on the ground that Lincoln walked and touch the log houses; the physicality of the site lends credibility, power, and immediacy to the story (chapter 6). A visit to New Salem becomes an occasion for retelling, and both story and site become more real and believable as a consequence of their association. In the telling New Salem appears as a natural occurrence, a historical given, although the story of how the site came to be reconstructed is also told to the tourists, in the brochures and by the interpretive guides, and it is an important narrative in itself, a kind of subtext about the site. The fascinating reconstruction story illustrates how New Salem has moved in and out of history and tells how the local residents, the people of Menard County, have come to have a claim on the site as if they were overseers and owners.

After 1839 New Salem declined as the residents moved to nearby Petersburg, the new capital of Menard County. New Salem subsequently became a dead site, one of hundreds of villages established in Illinois in the nineteenth century and then abandoned. Between 1839 and 1860, New Salem was not marked, and it effectively passed out of history. In 1860, however, when Lincoln became the presidential nominee of the Republican Party, a series of campaign biographers and journalists returned to New Salem to inquire about Lincoln's early life in Illinois.

In the William Dean Howells's biography (1960, originally published in 1860) what emerged was not the objective story of Lincoln's life but a constructed political image of "Honest Abe" the "rail-splitter," the common man of the prairies, the man of humble origins from the rural backwoods. The biography speaks of "integrity without a flaw" (42), of a man "unblemished by vices" (46), and concludes that "God never made a finer man" (46). For political purposes the biography emphasized the New Salem years and not only downplayed the 1837–1860 Springfield years, but suppressed what Lincoln had become since leaving New Salem, a successful lawyer and man of influence and power who had married into a socially prominent family and who had a substantial income (Warner 1953). Howells stressed the 1830s Lincoln as the new man of the West to create a contrast to Eastern decadence, and not the 1860 Lincoln with his connections to the wealthy elite and to a world of power. The opposition between the common man and the aristocrats was part of the political rhetoric of the era. Lincoln himself used this image of his past as a political tool, and indeed, he contributed to its construction, for he referred to his humble beginnings.

After Lincoln was assassinated in 1865, he became the martyred leader, the Christ figure who had given his life so the nation might live. Warner (1953) has noted that wars are an effective context for the creation of powerful national symbols, and I think this is especially so for wars of independence, when a nation is created, and for civil wars, when the existence of the nation is threatened, for during these times the nation is not taken for granted but becomes problematic. Lincoln became the "second savior" who sacrificed his life for the Union. After the Civil War more journalists and writers came to Menard County and to Petersburg to interview the former residents of New Salem and to gather information about the early life of Lincoln.

In 1897 the local people formed the Chautauqua Association for the explicit purpose of restoring the site of New Salem.[4] This was thirty-two years after Lincoln's assassination, thirty-seven years after the first reporter had come to collect data about Lincoln for a biography, and almost sixty years after New Salem had been abandoned. Why, after so long, did they decide to restore the site? Possibly interest in the restoration was activated when most of the original settlers who had lived in New Salem were passing away, so that the restoration of the site was also an effort to preserve the memory of a way of life that was fast disappearing. Because some Petersburg residents in 1897 had parents or grandparents from New Salem, the original settlers were their direct ancestors. For others the old village represented the life of the pioneers who had first settled the land they now occupied, and they had great respect, even reverence, for these early pioneers.

Over time there arose in Menard County what Benjamin Thomas (1954, 143) calls the "Lincoln legend," and what Richard Taylor (1984) calls the "New Salem tradition." It consists primarily of stories, some true, some apocryphal, about Lincoln and about life in the village. Such narratives often take the form of morality plays—for example, as a store clerk Lincoln overcharges a customer and then walks miles to return the proper change. Local historians became custodians of this body of traditional lore. At first those who had known Lincoln were privileged informants and storytellers, but in time, as the original settlers died off, the privileged informant came to be not the person who had known Lincoln but the one who remembered what his father or his grandfather had told him about Lincoln. These stories are preserved in Herndon and Weik 1889, Onstot 1902, and Reep 1927; have become part of the oral tradition of the people of Menard County; were incorporated by Sandburg and others into their own writings; and, through these sources, have by now become part of American mythology and are known by every schoolchild.

Professional historians say that the New Salem tradition is unreliable, and they regard it with skepticism. When William Herndon interviewed the old settlers, they "spun yarns about Old Abe" and characterized him as an "Illinois Paul Bunyan . . . a prairie Davy Crockett," so that his book "brimmed with gossip, hearsay, and legend" (Oates 1984, 6–7). When the Old Salem Lincoln League gathered the elderly people to tell their stories in 1918, the village of New Salem had already been deserted for seventy-nine years! As Taylor (1984, 5) so aptly puts it, "The New Salem tradition relies heavily on memories recorded many years after the fact and stories handed down from generation to generation, but stories change in the telling and memories usually cloud with the passing years." People magnified their own or their family's connection to Lincoln, they exaggerated, and they cast Lincoln in their own image, as a pious Christian or a temperance advocate.

Possibly the most famous controversy surrounding Lincoln that arose from the New Salem tradition concerns his reputed romance with Ann Rutledge and his unhappy marriage to Mary Todd. The story, in brief, is that Lincoln met Ann in 1832 when he boarded at the Rutledge Tavern in New Salem and fell hopelessly in love with her. Then she died in 1835, and he was devastated. The event had a profound effect on his life, leading him to marry someone he did not love, Mary Todd, but driving him to greater heights in his political career (Neely 1982, 265). This bland telling does not do justice to the romance and fantasy that has captured the public imagination: a story of unrequited first love, with Ann cast as "the slender, blue-eyed, fair-haired Ann Rutledge" (Reep 1927, 128), and Mary as a "female wildcat," a "tigress," and "haughty" (from Herndon quoted in Oates 1984, 6).

Until recently, professional historians had agreed that there was not a shred of evidence to support the story, that it was simply gossip popularized by Herndon (Herndon and Weik 1889) and picked up by Sandburg, who devotes pages to a graphic and detailed description of a courtship that may never have occurred.[5] In Robert Sherwood's famous play "Abe Lincoln in Illinois," which was made into a movie in 1940, Lincoln's love of Ann Rutledge figures very prominently. That the Rutledge story is discounted by most historians appears not to affect the number of popular tellings, and I have heard many versions of the story in New Salem. Currently the grave site of Ann Rutledge is advertised as a tourist attraction in the Petersburg tourist brochure, and there is a prominent sign on the main highway at the entrance to Petersburg directing visitors to the grave site. On the tombstone is engraved a poem by Edgar Lee Masters, the last part of which reads as follows:

> I am Ann Rutledge who sleep beneath these weeds,
> Beloved in life of Abraham Lincoln,
> Wedded to him, not through union,
> But through separation.
> Bloom forever, O Republic,
> From the dust of my bosom!

Stephen Oates calls the poem "ridiculous" (1984, 12), yet he repeats the Ann Rutledge story, and Thomas (1954) devotes four pages to a description of the romance before he announces that the story has no basis in fact. What we have here is not only another example of the scholarly versus the popular, of academics confronting a widely held myth, but the fascinating phenomenon that by repeating the story, even if only to refute it, historians contribute to its perpetuation.

I sympathize with the predicament of scholars whose information about the historical Lincoln comes to them filtered through the images of the frontier hero and the martyred saint. Robert Johannsen (1989, xii) contrasts the legendary Lincoln with the historical one: "Lincoln remains, and probably will always remain, a challenge to the historian and biographer, for the crust of myth and legend that has enclosed Lincoln . . . has proved well-nigh impenetrable." Oates notes that we know Lincoln through the "mists of mythology" (1984, 15). But that has not diminished the productivity of Lincoln scholars. The sheer amount of literature has been staggering: David Donald (1948) estimated that from 1865 on an average of fifty books a year had been written about Lincoln. Thomas F. Schwartz, the director of the Abraham Lincoln Library in the Old State Capital in Springfield, Illinois, informs me that the library has ten thousand books and pamphlets in its catalog. This is an average of seventy-five books and pamphlets on Lincoln every year since the Civil War, more than one a week—and that number does not include journal articles; nor does it count Civil War books that discuss Lincoln.

Representations of Lincoln have changed with the times (Lewis 1957, Basler 1935), but Carl Sandburg most effectively captures what the historians call the mythic figure and what I call the popular, a combination of the folk hero and the saint. Oates writes, "Sandburg's became the most popular

Lincoln work ever written, as a procession of plays, motion pictures, novels, children's books, school texts, and television shows purveyed Sandburg's Lincoln to a vast American public, until that Lincoln became for most Americans the real historical figure" (1984, 7). The professional historians' evaluation of Sandburg is that his books are full of errors of fact and interpretation, that they repeat many folk tales about the young Lincoln, and that they are more poetic than scholarly, yet Henry Steele Commager, in what is certainly a direct acknowledgment of the tension between the academic and the popular, attributes Sandburg's popularity to his realization "that Lincoln belongs to the people, not to the historians" (from Neely 1982, 267). Taylor, Johannsen (1989, 280), and other professional historians see Sandburg as poetry that has "captured the essence of the American past" and has a "spiritual authenticity."

Many historians have framed their scholarship in reference to the popular image of Lincoln. With the publication of Gore Vidal's *Lincoln* (1984), exactly the same issues were raised in a series of letters in the *New York Review of Books.*[6] C. Vann Woodward states that whereas Sandburg's Lincoln is a hero, Vidal's is a crafty manipulator, Nixon-like; the two authors give us a Lincoln appropriate to each historical era (1987, 24). Woodward writes, "Much as they may deplore the fact, historians have no monopoly on the past and no franchise as its privileged interpreters to the public" (1987, 23). He further notes that people derive their conceptions of history from popular media, novels, stage plays, movies and television—and, I would add, they do so from historic sites like New Salem.

Surely part of the appeal of Abraham Lincoln as a national symbol, both for the American public and for the historian, is precisely the ambiguity and the mists of mythology within which Lincoln is embedded. There is an openness to interpretive possibilities inherent in the stories about Lincoln, for they may be read in so many different ways depending on the imaginative proclivities and ideological position of the segment of society doing the interpreting. In scholarly discourse historians aim to tell "what really happened." Menard County residents see themselves as preserving tradition; honoring their ancestors and the early pioneers; respecting the memory of the Great Emancipator, who lived among them; and also promoting tourism and defending their legitimate economic interests in New Salem. The tourists want to hear retellings of the great American dream, to celebrate America, to educate their children, to learn more about Lincoln and about frontier life on the prairie, to experience the site where it all happened, and to bring home photographs, souvenirs, and stories as memories of their visit. Each of the parties involved has its own interests.

New Salem Village as Performance

The conflict between the popular and the scholarly enacted in the media and in the rarefied pages of the *New York Review of Books* is also played out daily in the more humble context of New Salem as the site is enacted and performed. New Salem is a contested site because different interpretations and different interests are in competition. Let us now turn to the site to explore further how the struggle over meaning works out in performance, beginning with descriptive information about the site, then moving from history to ethnography, from text to practice.

There are two distinct historical zones at New Salem, an upper part consisting of a parking lot, a concession that sells food and souvenirs, a bookstore, a picnic area, campgrounds, an amphitheater, and an orientation center, and a lower part that contains the reconstructed village. A long wooden fence divides the two zones, separating the 1990s from the 1830s. There is no admission charge or entrance gate, so visitors come to the parking lot, go through the orientation center, and then follow the signs down past the fence to the old village. The tours of New Salem are self-directed; the tourists, individually or in groups, simply walk through the site, going from one log building to another (fig. 19).

Once within the village, tourists encounter guides in period dress, called interpreters, who answer questions and provide information (fig. 20). Some other historic sites that reproduce the past, such as Plimoth Plantation (Snow 1993), use the interpretive technique of living history, where the interpreters adopt first-person roles. Each interpreter at Plimoth plays the part of a particular individual from the 1620s, not only in dress but also in speech, and goes about everyday life in the community, which requires that the visitors ask questions and interact with the Pilgrims. In New Salem the interpreters are clearly identified as specific persons from the 1830s, but they do third-person interpretation in that they tell the visitors about the 1830s rather than enact the 1830s. In practice, however, third person interpretation frequently slips into first person, as the interpreters and the tourists play with the two time frames. When visitors come into a store, for example, the interpreter may ask, "What would you like to buy today? We have just received new bolts of cloth from St. Louis." The element of play is one of the more attractive features of New Salem as a historic site, providing entertainment and pleasure to both the interpreters and the tourists.

Although New Salem relies primarily on interpreters to communicate information within the village, the administration has a staffing problem. Their predicament is that as a public institution they have limited funding, and they have budgeted positions for only six paid interpreters, yet there are

19. Lincoln's New Salem. Photo by Illinois Historic Preservation Agency.

20. Interpreter in the Routledge Tavern. Photo by Illinois Historic Preservation Agency.

twenty-three buildings, and the park is open from 9:00 to 5:00 (or 8:00 to 4:00), every day, seven days a week, except for a few major holidays. Usually during the week only four or five buildings and the museum have interpreters, but even this requires a staff of more than six.

New Salem therefore does what many museums do when they are restricted by a limited budget—it uses volunteers. There are approximately two hundred volunteer interpreters at New Salem. They are asked to provide their own period dress, to work at least fifty hours per year, and to work at least four hours at a time. To help train the interpreters, a series of manuals has been prepared, one for each building. Each manual focuses on a different theme, which the interpreters are told to stress so that as visitors move to each new building they will receive new information. The training manuals, prepared by Richard S. Taylor and the staff of the Illinois Historic Preservation Agency, are clearly written, sophisticated presentations of mainstream Lincoln scholarship. The information provided to the interpreters is based on current historical scholarship and relies "on the best judgment of accepted scholars" (Taylor 1984, 6). There is a recognition of the tension between the scholarly and the popular and an understanding that many volunteer interpreters are from Menard County and are probably steeped in traditional Lincoln lore. The manuals acknowledge that the New Salem tradition is colorful and of interest to the visitors, but the interpreters are advised to use it critically and to introduce their statements with the qualifying clause, "according to tradition."

The Henry Onstot residence is located at the entrance to the village and is the first house the tourists usually visit. The first theme in the training manual for the residence is that New Salem was a commercial trading center and not an isolated, self-sufficient frontier village: New Salem in the 1830s was the hub of commerce and industry for the surrounding area, and many of the residents were businesspeople and merchants. In New Salem there was a saw and grist mill, a carding mill, a number of stores, a tavern, two physicians, and skilled tradespeople such as a blacksmith, a cooper, a hatter, a cobbler, and a woodworker. Area farmers came to New Salem to grind their grain, card wool, repair equipment, purchase supplies, and pick up their mail. The training manual points out that it is misleading to call New Salem a frontier village because by 1830 there were no Indians in central Illinois and the frontier had moved elsewhere. The term *frontier village* usually refers to a community of trappers, hunters, and squatters living on the edge of the wilderness. From the perspective of the surrounding farmers, New Salem was an urban center.

Tourists, however, do not want to drive down from Chicago to see another urban commercial center, even a nineteenth-century one. What is it then that many 1990s tourists expect from an 1830s site? One of the brochures says that New Salem "takes us back to a simpler time," and this captures touristic expectations. Many visitors have a romantic view of the past and see New Salem as an isolated, self-contained rural village where material possessions were produced locally and by hand. New Salem is, in a way, like Club Med, an antidote for civilization. The 1830s are viewed with nostalgia for a time when life was simpler, less cluttered, and more natural. According to this mind-set, the past was a time of honest values, quiet good humor, generosity, and inner strength, a time when a figure like Lincoln was not only heroic, but a prototype of society. Lincoln was hard-working, humble, fair, courageous, and a good neighbor who had learned how to get along with people. Tourists are not naive, and they are not fools. Most know that the way Lincoln is characterized is an exaggeration, the stuff of folk legends. Lincoln represents an idealized person in an idealized time. The old settlers and pioneers of the 1830s, the ancestors who settled the land, also were also Lincoln-like. The power of the Lincoln legend gives generalized support to the entire New Salem era.

How then does one reconcile the professional historians' view of New Salem as a commercial center and the popular view of New Salem as an isolated pioneer village? The two views are not reconciled; rather, they stand in opposition, for there is a dispute about significance, over how to interpret the site. What is most fascinating, however, is that the way New Salem is produced as a site subverts the main message of the professional staff who are the producers.

One approaches New Salem village through flat central Illinois farmland. To someone coming from Peoria, Chicago, Springfield, or any of the surrounding towns, the setting certainly looks rural and isolated. Then at the entrance to the park, amid a densely wooded area, there is a sign pointing to the "pioneer village," and many tourists blur the distinction between *pioneer* and *frontier*. Within the old village, the houses are not clustered together but are spread out, in an arrangement very unlike the neat grid pattern of homes in contemporary urban settings. The furnishings in the homes seem sparse, the rooms appear small, there is very little space, and visible possessions are few (fig. 21). To the twentieth-century eye, it is hard to envision New Salem as a commercial center.

About 80 percent of the volunteer interpreters are women, and during my visits the majority of them were engaged in some kind of craft activity. Thus, when the tourists enter a house, they see a woman sewing, quilting, spinning, or somehow occupied with her hands, which gives the impression of domesticity and self-sufficiency, not of commerce and trade. One weekend when I

21. New Salem interior. Photo by Illinois Historic Preservation Agency.

visited New Salem there were quilts in every cabin, on display for a special event coordinated by the New Salem Lincoln League. The event was called the New Salem Quilt Show, and it was described by the Springfield Convention and Visitors Bureau as featuring "quilt demonstrations and period crafts in the home." Other weekend special events sponsored by the New Salem Lincoln League include an art exhibit and summer festival, a "Prairie Tales" festival with featured storytellers, a traditional music and bluegrass festival, and a candlelight tour. The final event of the year, Christmas at New Salem, was described in the 1988 brochure as follows: "The austere charm of an 1830s Christmas includes 'villagers' in period clothing who do their chores, cook and scuttle through the log homes of New Salem. Watch a wide variety of pioneer crafts demonstrations and take a wagon or sleigh ride through the pioneer village where Lincoln once lived."[7]

New Salem celebrates crafts and rural traditions and has turned the historic village into a folk festival, and the visitors love it because it fits their prior image of an Early American Village. It presents an idyllic, peaceful, harmonious, neighborly community. The way the site is produced structures the way the site is experienced by the visitors. Even if the interpreters say that New Salem was a commercial trading center, and some do, these words are less effective than the more physical and visual way that New Salem is presented and experienced. The tension between the academic and the popular translates in part into a tension between the verbal on the one hand and the visual and experiential on the other, and the latter is more forceful.

Discussion

There are struggles over meaning between New Salem as the site of Lincoln's transformation and New Salem as craft festival, between the academic Lincoln and the popular Lincoln, and between New Salem as a commercial center and New Salem as an idyllic, self-sufficient prairie community. In addition, there are further layers of contestation between New Salem as a public park and recreation area with campgrounds and hiking trails, and New Salem as a historic site containing the reconstructed village. Well over ten thousand campsite rentals occur at New Salem each year, and the park has become a place to go to vacation and experience the wilderness.[8]

Sometimes the disagreements at New Salem are silent ones played out in their own separate discourses, but at other times the struggles becomes open and explicit, leading to socially disruptive direct confrontation. It is during these times of conflict that the core cultural values become exposed and are openly discussed and defended, as each side aims to protect its interests. In 1979, for example, a unit within one state agency proposed a master management plan for New Salem that emphasized preservation and ecological conservation, with the objective of returning New Salem to its original appearance. They proposed to move the main campsite, reroute a state road, and reduce the number of visitors to the reconstructed village. The local community opposed these measures so vigorously that public meetings were held, the area newspapers covered every move in the news section and in editorials, and the governor's office finally intervened. Governor Jim Thompson appointed a committee to investigate the matter, and eventually the plan was scrapped.

New Salem has multiple audiences with conflicting interests and values. One cannot look for the meaning of New Salem within New Salem itself, but must turn instead to the people's own interpretations of the site.[9] And individuals are not monolithic or constant, as their reactions to the site shift historically over the life span and even within the time frame of a single visit.

Although many contemporary visitors have a romantic view of New Salem and feel nostalgia for a pastoral past when life was simpler, many rural people, including local farmers from central Illinois, have a somewhat different perspective. They see the original New Salem residents as their ancestors, as pioneers who first farmed the land that they now farm, so when there are demonstrations at New Salem of baking bread, preserving vegetables, canning berries, making soap, spinning cloth, and other craft activities, the local people see a direct continuity. They are interested in the nineteenth-century technology as older solutions to the problems they confront daily in their own lives and on their own farms. They may note that their grandmother had a spinning wheel just like the one in New Salem, and they point to other historical continuities. They are pragmatic rather than romantic about the past, and they focus on the perceived similarities between the 1830s and the 1990s, noting, of course, how much harder life was in the earlier period.

At times there is an enhancement effect as members of different segments of society, all pursuing their own interests, find themselves converging on the same activity. The administration and producers at New Salem have placed an emphasis on crafts and have built into the site a blacksmith's shop with a blacksmith demonstrating his craft (fig. 22), a working cooper's shop, and a shoemaker's shop, and there are many demonstrations of crafts, including the making of brooms, candles, soap, and cloth. The New Salem management view is that a log residence with no activity is not as inherently interesting as a building featuring a craft demonstration, and their aim is to make the site more appealing and engaging to the visitors. They want to put on a good show, and the craft demonstrations provide a wonderful opportunity for the

22. Blacksmith shop. Photo by Illinois Historic Preservation Agency.

initiation of conversations between the interpreters and the visitors, initially about the craft activity, but then more generally about life in the 1830s. The dialogic interplay between the interpreters and the tourists is one of the more engaging features of the site.

The emphasis on crafts is magnified because of the interests of the volunteer interpreters. Most of the volunteers are people local to the area, most are women, and most are interested in crafts. Cyndi Voelkl (1980, 8) writes that "the volunteers are expanding the crafts program at New Salem." There are craft associations and classes at the site, and many participants become volunteers because they want to practice crafts and to play at being an 1830s person, to reproduce the world of their ancestors and of the hardy pioneers who first settled in central Illinois. In a region experiencing the loss of the family farm and migrations to the city, it may well be therapeutic or at least cathartic to dress up as an ancestor, relive better times, and explain one's past to the tourists (cf. Stewart 1988). To reproduce a life one never lived, a life even one's ancestors may never have lived, is to create a fantasy world, but as a volunteer interpreter at New Salem it is possible to enact that fantasy and to occupy that imaginary world for at least four hours a day—preferably on the weekends, in good weather.

In sum, the producers of New Salem, including the museum professionals and the staff, collaborate unwittingly with the volunteer interpreters to insert such a strong village craft emphasis in the site that they steal meaning away from Abraham Lincoln as well as from their own new social history view of New Salem as a commercial trading center. They also steal the meaning of crafts from the 1830s residents, because in the 1830s crafts represented the most modern technology of the day, utilized the most sophisticated techniques of the era, and formed the basis of commerce and survival. In Lincoln's New Salem the problem is how to present 1830s meanings to 1990s visitors, to show that 1830s crafts were not quaint activities to be viewed within a frame of nostalgia and romanticism. How to understand the past in the present is, of course, the universal problem confronting the producers of any heritage site, and is indeed the basic problem in the writing of history.

Historians don't own history, and they have some powerful competition in interpreting the past. Fortunately, no one group can impose an interpretation on the early Abraham Lincoln or on New Salem, and it is precisely in the struggle over meaning in historic sites, museums, and tourist attractions that the diverse segments of a democratic society are able to express their interests and stake their claims. For students of society the social dramas enacted in the silent struggles over meaning provide an ongoing metacommentary about American culture and about ourselves.

5

Abraham Lincoln as Authentic Reproduction
A Critique of Postmodernism

POSTMODERN WRITERS SAY that in hyperreality the reproduction is better than the original; for example, a museum diorama is more vivid and effective than the scene it represents (Eco 1986, 8). Jean Baudrillard writes that Americans construct imitations of themselves and that the perfect definition of the simulacrum is when the reproduction is "more real" than the original (1988, 41; see also Eco 1986, 18). Meaghan Morris writes that once we have a simulacrum, "the true (like the real) begins to be reproduced in the image of the pseudo, which begins to become the true" (1988, 5). Umberto Eco contends about America that "the past must be preserved and celebrated in full-scale authentic copy; a philosophy of immortality as duplication" (1986, 6). Eco takes us on a "journey into Hyperreality in search of instances where the American imagination demands the real thing, and, to attain it, must fabricate the absolute fake" (1986, 7).

Is this just postmodern gibberish? Are the writings of Baudrillard and Eco simply the babblings of a long series of Europeans who have rediscovered an America of the Continental imagination?

Baudrillard (1983) writes that in this postindustrial era, we have entered a new stage of history, an electronic one marked by changes in information flow and patterns of reproduction. In the Renaissance we had originals and counterfeits; in the industrial period we had the serial repetition of the same object; but in this postmodern phase we have simulation, without origins, referential values, or beginnings, where the simulacrum becomes the true. For Baudrillard and for Eco, America is hyperreality. "America cultivates no origin or mythical authenticity; it has no past and founding truth. . . . It lives in a perpetual present. . . . It lives in perpetual simulation" (Baudrillard 1988, 76).

My objectives in this chapter are to examine critically the postmodern perspective of Baudrillard and Eco; to develop a view of historical reproduction that is based on a constructivist position that sees all culture as continually invented and reinvented (E. Bruner, ed., 1984); and to argue for transcending such dichotomies as original/copy and authentic/inauthentic. My interest is in a critique of postmodernism, but because that term is used so loosely and in such diverse contexts—from architecture to the arts to scholarship to popular media—in the interest of clarity I take it to refer specifically to the writings of Baudrillard and Eco, two of its more prominent practitioners, and even more narrowly to their work on copies and originals in America. Lest the focus seem too narrow, it should be noted that the theory of simulacra is an essential component of many different postmodern positions.

I argue also that despite Baudrillard's and Eco's theoretical arguments against origins, in their work about America there is an implicit original, and it is Europe, for they see America as essentially a satellite of Europe (Baudrillard 1988, 76). I will show also that not only Baudrillard and Eco, but scholars such as Dean MacCannell and Richard Handler, in their writings on authenticity, retain an essentialist vocabulary of origins and reproductions. Jacques Derrida (1974) has taught us that these either/or binaries are built into Western metaphysics and that not only are such oppositions well-established, but one term is privileged at the expense of the other.

In order to examine these issues, I turn to an ethnographic example, Lincoln's New Salem, a historic site in central Illinois, and to the museum professionals in charge of producing it. A historic site is a good place to gather data on issues of reproductions, originals, and authenticity[1] because museum professionals struggle with these issues daily. The working practitioners who take responsibility for the staging of the site, they continually construct and reconstruct New Salem as they change exhibits, develop new story lines, and train interpreters and guides. Among historic sites, New Salem is a particularly appropriate place to study because the literature at the site calls it an "authentic reproduction"—an intriguing oxymoron, as one is thus not sure whether New Salem is an original or a copy. The meaning of this phrase needs to be explored.

Although Baudrillard and Eco do not deal with the significance of historic reproductions to tourists and visitors except by implication, this chapter does reject some of their postmodernist generalizations. In the concluding section I present an alternative reading of the significance of New Salem that contrasts with the views of Baudrillard and Eco. My alternative view is derived from fieldwork with the tourists themselves, although my research also focused on the understandings of the museum professionals. While this segment of the chapter is admittedly speculative, it contains the seeds of a revisionist position focused on the visitors' construction of meaning. My hypotheses are that the tourists at New Salem are (1) learning about their past, (2) playing with time frames and enjoying the encounters, (3) consuming nostalgia for a simpler bygone era, and simultaneously (4) buying the idea of progress, of how far our society has advanced. Finally, they are also (5) celebrating America, which at New Salem means the values and virtues of small-town America. These experiences go well beyond a search for authenticity. The New Salem experience provides visitors with a sense of identity, meaning, and attachment.

In the conclusion to the chapter I apply what has been learned about New Salem to postmodernism and to the literature on the invention of tradition, authenticity, and historic sites in the United States. Rather than more grand theorizing about the postmodern condition, this chapter offers an alternative perspective based on a specific case study utilizing the methods of ethnography and the concepts of performance and practice.

New Salem

New Salem Historic Site[2] is a reconstructed village and outdoor museum located in Illinois at the place where Abraham Lincoln lived in the 1830s (Thomas 1954). Most Americans know that Abraham Lincoln was U.S. president during the Civil War, that he freed the slaves, and that he was assassinated in 1865. Lincoln is arguably the greatest American folk hero; his life is an embodiment of the American success ideology.

Carl Sandburg's famous biography calls New Salem "Lincoln's 'Alma Mater' " (1954, 743) and refers to the site as Lincoln's "nourishing mother" (1954, 55). Implicit in Sandburg's story is the frontier hypothesis of Frederick Jackson Turner: he suggests that just as the United States was formed by its overcoming of the obstacles of the wilderness, so too Lincoln was formed by his overcoming of the hardships of frontier life. Also implicit is the notion that America is an open society, that the American dream of success can be achieved by anyone willing to work hard by day and to study by night. New Salem, then, is a national shrine of America's civil religion because it is the locality of the transformation that gave birth to the adult Lincoln. Lincoln's story is the story of America, the rags-to-riches, log cabin–to–White House American narrative.

The premier tourist attraction in Illinois, drawing over a half-million visitors a year, New Salem Historic Site is a public facility owned by the state of Illinois. The village consists of twenty-three log houses, and in most of the houses there are interpreters in period dress who greet the tourists (fig. 23), discuss aspects of life in the 1830s, and engage in craft demonstrations

23. A volunteer interpreter in period dress

24. Cooking demonstration in Routledge Tavern

(fig. 24). New Salem is one of a number of reconstructed prairie villages in the Midwest, and indeed, as Baudrillard and Eco point out, there are many reconstructed historic sites in the United States (J. Anderson 1984).

Authenticity, Copies, and Originals

Ada Louise Huxtable writes, "It is hard to think of a more dangerous, anomalous, and shoddy perversion of language and meaning than the term 'authentic reproduction' " (1992, 24). She is writing about Colonial Williamsburg, but the term is used at many other historic sites as well,[3] including New Salem. What does *authentic reproduction* mean? As anthropologists know, the meaning of any expression is not a property inherent in its wording or in its dictionary definition, but rather is dependent on the context in which it appears and on the perceptions and practices of those who use it. To learn how *authentic reproduction* is used, we turn first to the discourse produced by museum professionals, by the staff and the interpreters at New Salem.

By using the term *authentic reproduction,* the museum professionals acknowledge that New Salem is a reproduction, not an original, but that they want that reproduction to be authentic in the sense of giving the appearance of the 1830s. Most aim for what Richard Taylor and Mark Johnson (1993) call "historical verisimilitude," making the 1990s New Salem resemble the 1830s New Salem. *Authentic* in this sense means "credible and convincing," and this is the objective of most museum professionals: to produce a historic site believable to the public, to achieve mimetic credibility. This is the first meaning of *authenticity.*

Some museum professionals go father and speak as if the 1990s New Salem not only resembles the original but is a complete and immaculate simulation, one that is historically accurate and true to the 1830s. This is the second meaning of *authenticity.* In the first meaning, based on verisimilitude, a 1990s person would walk into the village and say, "This looks like the 1830s," as it would conform to what he or she expected the village to be. In the second meaning, based on genuineness, an *1830s* person would say, "This looks like New Salem," as the village would appear true in substance, or real. I found that museum professionals use *authenticity* primarily in the first sense, but sometimes in the second. Richard Handler and William Saxton (1988, 242) write that for all living-history practitioners authenticity is an exact isomorphism, following the second meaning; but I found at New Salem that this was so only for some practitioners some of the time. In order to achieve authenticity, the museum professionals rely on historical scholarship and on scholars' and experts' interpretations of such sources as archeological finds, deeds, court documents, diaries, letters, newspaper accounts, recorded statements and memories of older settlers, and comparative evidence of other 1830s villages in the Midwest.

There are at least two other meanings of *authenticity*. In the third sense it refers to the original, as opposed to a copy; but in this sense all reproductions are inauthentic by definition. New Salem Historic Site, however, claims to have some original objects and one original building,[4] so the aura of authenticity in the third sense pervades the 1990s site, as if the luster of the few originals has rubbed off on the reproductions. In the fourth sense, *authenticity* refers to what is duly authorized, certified, or legally valid; in this sense New Salem is authentic, as it is the authoritative reproduction of New Salem, the one legitimized by the state of Illinois. There is only one officially reconstructed New Salem, the one approved by the state government. This is a fascinating meaning because in this sense the issue of authenticity merges into the notion of authority. The more fundamental question to ask here is not whether an object or site is authentic, but rather who has the authority to authenticate—or, to put it another way, who has the right to tell the story of the site. This is a matter of power.

This question emerged late in the nineteenth century when the term *authenticity* first appeared in New Salem discourse. After William Randolph Hearst purchased the site in 1906 and donated the land to the local Chautauqua Association, the movement to reconstruct New Salem appeared poised to achieve its objective; the reconstruction of New Salem had become a real possibility. But a question emerged: What did the 1830s New Salem look like? The village had been abandoned in 1839, and by 1906 it was simply a barren plot of ground on the top of a hill with no remaining buildings or markers. Local historians, journalists, politicians, entrepreneurs, businesspeople, descendants of the original settlers, and residents of the surrounding Menard County who had an interest in the reconstruction all voiced their views and their interests, and authenticity committees were formed. Thus the concern with authenticity originated even before any museum professionals or scholars became involved in the reconstruction. Questions surfaced such as: Where should the buildings be located? Should they be built with one story or two? What were the original details of construction? Which material objects should be in which houses?[5]

From the late nineteenth century to the present, experts have given different answers to these questions, reflecting their own understandings and concerns. Even before the site was turned over to Illinois in 1919, the reconstructed New Salem was contested. The layers of contestation—scholarly versus popular views of Abraham Lincoln, various descendants of the original settlers defending their family names, New Salem as a public park versus New Salem as a historic site, the Lincoln message versus craft activities, and historical versus business interests—have hovered over New Salem like the dark clouds of a thunderstorm engulfing the Illinois prairie.

Because of conflicting interests and the struggle over meaning at New Salem, the fourth sense of *authenticity*—and the question of who has the authority and the power to authenticate—is always present in the background, at least for museum professionals, insiders, locals, and scholars, and at times of open dissent it becomes even more prominent. However, most tourists are not aware of authenticity in this fourth sense unless a particular dispute over interpretation becomes a public issue.

The museum staff rely on the authority of professional and local historians, and frequently the scholars do not agree. Because the state of Illinois owns the site and provides the funding, some (e.g., M. Wallace 1981) might expect the site to reflect the interests of the dominant classes and the elite, but the administrators at New Salem report that in practice state officials interfere rarely, and then only when an issue has become openly politicized. The problem is not one of the establishment versus the people, but rather one of multiple competing voices, even within what may appear to be homogeneous blocs, such as the scholars, the people, the locals, or the establishment. There are many different views, and the question is who has the authority to decide which version of history will be accepted as the correct or authentic one. This issue of who constructs history is a familiar one in our age of multiculturalism.

The problem with the term *authenticity*, in the literature and in fieldwork, is that one never knows except by analysis of the context which meaning is salient in any given instance. My aim was to understand the different meanings of authenticity as employed in social practice rather than to accept at face value the usually unexamined dichotomy between what is and what is not authentic. Thus far, I have identified four meanings of *authenticity*,[6] which I label verisimilitude, genuineness, originality, and authority. Museum professionals at New Salem accept the first and strive for a New Salem that resembles the 1830s and is credible to the visitors; they occasionally lapse into the second and speak of an accurate simulation; they tend to ignore the third as New Salem is an acknowledged reproduction, except for the presence of a few originals; and they cannot avoid the fourth, the question of authority.

The staff at New Salem use the term *authenticity* consciously and frequently, and they want to work toward the approximation of a believable simulation, if not an accurate one, in part because their reputations and their professional identities depend on it. They are defined by others and define themselves as experts on the 1830s. I ask, then, Have the museum professionals achieved authenticity at New Salem in either the first or the second sense? Is New Salem either a credible simulation or true to the 1830s original? How well do the museum professionals achieve their objectives? I begin with some trivial examples and then move to deeper levels, from the explicit to the implicit, as we penetrate the unexamined and the taken-for-granted.[7]

The Site

One day the superintendent of New Salem saw a gasoline can exposed to public view in the cooper shop, and he requested that in the future it be hidden from the visitors. If the gasoline can was needed, he said, it could be retained, but it should not be visible. On another occasion, one of the interpreters constructed a flower bed outside the Sam Hill house on a patch of bare ground that had been getting muddy in the rain, causing tourists to track mud into the house. When the assistant superintendent saw the flowers she said they looked "ridiculous" and were not "authentic" as there were no flower beds in the 1830s, and she promptly replaced the flowers with less obtrusive wood shavings. Although one could raise questions about the shavings, the point here is that in these two cases items considered inappropriate, a gasoline can and flowers, were replaced or removed from the tourists' view. Authenticity in either the first sense, of credibility, or the second, of genuineness, cannot be taken for granted; there is backsliding, and the site needs constant monitoring and editing.

At New Salem there are many conscious compromises of authenticity. Some were necessary for the creation of the site, and some are required for its longevity, while most others are designed to make the visitors' experience more enjoyable. These compromises are the little white lies of historical reconstruction. They make the reconstructed New Salem better than the original, at least for contemporary tourists.

Here are examples. Gutters are constructed on the log cabins to channel rainwater. In the past the animals would roam free, but now they are fenced in so animal waste is not scattered throughout the village and so visitors are protected. Fences within the site are made to look as if they were original, but they are designed to direct the flow of tourist traffic. Unobtrusive restrooms have been built with drinking fountains on the side, a convenience not found in the 1830s. Benches have been placed along the path so visitors may sit and rest. The road is now paved so when it rains the tourists do not have to walk in the mud.

In the 1830s the schoolhouse was located a mile and a half away from the village, but it has been reconstructed inside the compound for the convenience of the visitors. The carding mill is supposedly operated entirely by animal power, by oxen moving in a circle, but it has a hidden motor. The

Rutledge Tavern and the First Berry-Lincoln Store have electric heaters that are placed where they cannot be seen by the tourists. The caulking between the logs on the sides of the cabins is made of cement, but in the 1830s cement had not yet been invented. There is a disguised security gate around the entire village to protect against vandalism, as well as a security system and alarm boxes that the tourists never see. At one time New Salem's buildings included devices that allowed visitors to listen to recorded commentaries as part of a self-guided tour. These devices have since been removed, but there are still small wires sticking out from some of the houses.

Because the houses are old, they periodically need renovation. In one case over 50 percent of a house was renovated, so the state building code required that a ramp be built for persons who use wheelchairs. A flagstone ramp was constructed as required, but it is kept covered up with leaves and dirt so it will be less conspicuous. At New Salem the lawn is mowed. I asked the superintendent if they mowed in the 1830s, and he replied that they probably did not, but added that if you do not mow your lawn in central Illinois now you are not regarded as a good citizen. Many more examples of conscious compromises of a believable or precise replication could be presented, but now I turn to more subtle factors that are at work.

The houses at the 1990s New Salem represent the original 1830s houses; thus they are weathered to look old so that they will be more credible, as the original houses existed 160 years ago. The 1830s houses, however, actually looked much newer, as the village of New Salem was founded in 1829 and abandoned by 1839, only ten years later. The 1830s houses were not occupied long enough to look aged, hence the 1990s houses at New Salem appear older than the originals. This example shows that there is a tension between the first and second meanings of *authenticity.* To the degree that the houses look old and weathered, they are more credible to the visitors but are a less accurate reproduction of the 1830s. The houses also look more respectable than those of the original village, as all are substantial log houses; there are none of the cabins, shacks, or flimsy structures that may well have existed in the 1830s village. Thus the 1990s New Salem presents a more suburban version of history that is built into the construction of the houses and the site. Again, it makes the site more believable to 1990s tourists, but less true to the 1830s original.

During the ten years the town was occupied in the 1830s, the residents cut down the surrounding trees to obtain lumber for building and for firewood; but in the reconstructed New Salem, the trees have been allowed to grow and hence the foliage is more dense and lush. In the 1990s the thick stand of trees at New Salem gives the village a much more rural and rustic appearance than it had in the 1830s.

The interpreters are in period dress, but they have a special problem with eyeglasses. The volunteers and the staff do wear their own eyeglasses, which they need, but some have bought small round "granny" glasses because they think these look more old-fashioned. The costumes in general present a dilemma, as no one really knows about the dress of the original occupants of New Salem. There are no specific records about attire.

A June 19, 1936, newspaper account from the *Peoria Journal* reads as follows: "Four guides at the village wear jeans jackets and trousers, linsey-woolsey shirts and leather boots as part of their costumes, to portray the role of the original residents." Although jeans, wool shirts, and boots may have been an acceptable version of 1830s dress for the 1930s, this is no longer the case in the 1990s, as most students and many other visitors themselves now wear jeans. There has to be some difference in attire to distinguish between the tourists and those who play the parts of the original residents. What was proper 1830s dress in 1930 is not proper in 1990; in terms of the concepts developed in this chapter, what was considered authentic, in the sense of credible, in one historical era has changed in the course of sixty years. Standards change, and the consciousness of what is authentic changes with them. The museum professionals at historic sites realize that they need to be aware of the public's sense of what is believable. This is a complex problem because there are many publics; because some persons are more aware, knowledgeable, or skeptical than others; and because the professionals' and the public's view are interdependent—each shapes and is shaped by the other, in dialogic interplay.

When I began my research at New Salem in 1988, there was little discussion of the interpreters' costumes; but this changed during the summer of 1990. At that time some of the staff made the criticism that too many interpreters dressed the same, that all the costumes seemed to be derived from the television series "Little House on the Prairie," that everyone wore work clothing, and that they all looked like farmers. Some original residents were not farmers, and there were differences in wealth in the community. As the accuracy of the costumes was called into question, an internal dialogue began among the staff about authenticity. As Lionel Trilling (1972) notes, authenticity becomes an issue only after a doubt arises.

The debate about clothing reminded me of Victor Turner's concept of social drama, and it illustrates the constructivist process at work by showing how the culture at New Salem is continually reinvented. At first the style of clothing was simply accepted and was neither examined nor discussed. The critique of clothing practices emerged as an abrupt breach, as a rupture of accepted custom leading to a period of doubt, wide discussion, and mounting crisis. Alternative clothing styles were explored, and experts were consulted. New dress patterns were devised and the issue was at least temporarily resolved. The dispute was less about what genuinely existed in the 1830s New Salem, which no one knew, and more about the issue of credibility, about what was currently acceptable 1830s dress. In all probability, the issue will arise again in the future and the cycle will be repeated.

During the discussion about clothing, someone made the point that costumes should reflect class distinctions. It was argued that because the residents of the Sam Hill house were rich, as Hill was a successful merchant, and those of the Burner house were poor, they should have different costumes. Current views of class disparities may have been projected into the past. The interpreters at the Hill house, for example, were to wear upper-class clothing, and those at the poorer Burner house were to wear working-class dress—except for Mrs. Hinsley.[8] She was a volunteer interpreter assigned to the house of the Galihers, known to be a poor 1830s family. In the new vision, Mrs. Hinsley was expected to wear working-class clothing; but she was interested in clothing, had nice outfits of her own design, and wanted to dress well, so she wore what was considered to be inappropriate rich clothing. Mrs. Hinsley was a point of resistance, and no one could change her. She expressed her individuality in dress.

Authenticity is a struggle. From the point of view of the professional staff, whose goal is to make New Salem a believable or genuine reproduction, one constantly has to be aware of possible inauthenticities. But there are even more fundamental problems, as inauthenticity is built into the fabric of New Salem, into the details of construction and into the social practices of the production at the site.

Each log house is named for its most prominent resident, and when the visitors come, the interpreters tell the story of the occupants of that particular house. For example, there are the Rutledge Tavern, the Onstot house, the Hill house, and so forth. In the 1830s, however, many of the buildings were occupied by a series of families, and the Onstots lived in three different residences, as did others. The First Berry-Lincoln Store was a store for only a few months, but because of the importance of Abraham Lincoln and the widely known story that he was a shopkeeper, the Berry-Lincoln name has been given to the residence. With this practice New Salem has fixed history, solidified and simplified it.

The story told about the single resident family for each dwelling is one of transitoriness: of when the family arrived, what they did at New Salem, and when they departed from the community. Although these narrative histories are not necessarily inaccurate, they do not appear to be the stories the 1830s residents would have told about themselves, at least not in their finality, for at the end of each story the family leaves New Salem, and the narrative is finished. Each thus contains a complete cycle of transition, beginning with the family's arrival and ending with its departure. Clearly such stories could not have been told until at least 1839, after the village was abandoned. This retrospective perspective serves to reinforce the master narrative of New Salem, Abraham Lincoln's transition from common laborer to educated lawyer and politician in preparation for his life work of leading the nation in the Civil War and saving the Union. If New Salem is seen as a site of transformation for its hero, Abraham Lincoln, then the individual story of each family replicates the larger narrative structure.

Not only is each house given the name of just one former resident, but in a concession to the limited state budget, in each house there is only a single interpreter. The visitors move from one house to the next, and in each one the interpreter provides information about one or another aspect of life in the 1830s. There are no groups talking and visiting together, no scenes of farmers from the surrounding area coming to town with their families to sell grain, repair tools, see a doctor, or buy supplies. New Salem is thus presented as a village of autonomous homes and isolated individuals, without any sense of group or community activity, with the consequence that the 1990s representation provides a distorted view of 1830s life. There are special events at New Salem, like craft and quilt shows, but even then the visitors move serially through the displays, visiting each booth in sequence. The result is that 1830s life is presented as devoid of its group character and as much more like suburban life in 1990s America, where neighbors live in their individual homes and are socially isolated from one another.

Taylor and Johnson (1993) note that New Salem does not have any interpreters representing the frontier toughs called Clary's Grove boys, or the carousing, gambling, cockfighting, hard drinkers who were part of 1830s pioneer life in New Salem. The roughnecks have been left out of history. This concession to middle-class sensibilities is similar to Colonial Williamsburg's ignoring of blacks, the "other half" of Williamsburg life (Gable, Handler, and Lawson 1992). Colonial Williamsburg recently corrected that omission; there is, however, no current movement to represent the frontier roughnecks in New Salem.

New Salem is an outdoor museum, and like all museums, the way it is apprehended by the visitors is primarily visual. The tourists do hear about the 1830s from the interpreters inside the homes, generally in the form of oral narratives, and there is conversation, but primarily they move through the site and they look. They almost never hear two or more interpreters talking to each other. However, the 1830s may well have been more of an oral than a visual culture, characterized by the exchange of information, by talking, gossiping, and telling. As this dimension is less dominant in the 1990s New Salem, the way the village was experienced and the sensory mode through which it was perceived in the two eras may be fundamentally different.

Thus, it is impossible to make a historic reproduction accurate in every regard, especially with limited knowledge and resources; the best one can hope for is a representation that the tourists are willing to accept. Even if the log houses of the 1990s prairie village were an exact physical replica of the original 1830s houses in every detail, another question could then be raised: How does one make authentic the sensory mode of experiencing and indeed the very meaning of the site?

There are truly enormous differences between the 1830s and the 1990s. One difference, almost too obvious to mention, is that most persons in the 1990s New Salem are tourists, while in the 1830s there were no tourists, although there were visitors, travelers, and traders. Also, the 1990s New Salem is an idealized community that leaves out the conflict, tension, and dirt of the 1830s. New Salem in the 1990s is presented as an idyllic, peaceful, harmonious village.

Many of the craft activities in the 1830s New Salem were considered to represent the most modern and advanced technology of the time and were designed for efficiency and survival, but in the 1990s the same handicrafts represent nostalgia for an earlier period when the stuff of material culture was made by hand and locally produced. The meaning of *craft* was completely different in the two historical eras. In the 1830s, New Salem was a commercial trading center, and when Lincoln migrated there he probably regarded the town as an urban center; but in the 1990s, New Salem is, for many, rural, isolated, self-contained, rustic, and folklike (cf. Whisnant 1983), in opposition to the commercialism, materialism, and fragmentation of twentieth-century America.

The 1990s New Salem features Abraham Lincoln—indeed, the site is called Lincoln's New Salem, and an official in the state tourist bureau told me, "What we sell in Illinois is Lincoln"—but Abraham Lincoln was not that prominent in the 1830s village. Lincoln left New Salem in 1837, and in 1839 the village was abandoned when the county seat was moved to another location. Thereafter, from 1839 to 1860, New Salem was unmarked and effectively out of history. Then in 1860, when Lincoln became the presidential nominee of the Republican Party, campaign biographers and politicians constructed the political image of Abraham Lincoln as Honest Abe, the railsplitter, the common man of the prairies, the man of humble origin who stood in opposition to the Eastern establishment. After Lincoln was assassinated in 1865, he became the martyred leader, the Christ figure who sacrificed his life for the Union. Thus arose the mythic Lincoln, the great American folk hero celebrated in novels, songs, poems, plays, biographies, and textbooks and known by every schoolchild in America.

The present-day restoration of the 1830s New Salem attempts to reconstruct the historical and the mythic Lincoln, but this history and myth did not yet exist in the 1830s, for it emerged only after 1865. This disjuncture is illustrative of the many built-in paradoxes, ambiguities, and ironies at the New Salem historic site.

Two Stores

The challenge in this anthropological analysis is to transcend the opposition between the authentic and the inauthentic. In considering the 1830s and the 1990s, there is no need to prioritize, to define one as better than, more real than, more basic than, or more authentic than the other, nor does such a qualitative comparison typically occur to visitors at historic sites. There is the 1830s New Salem and there is the 1990s New Salem. The 1830s village was historically prior, it came first, whereas the 1990s New Salem came later and conforms to 1990s sensibilities, allowing visitors to attribute their own meanings to the site. I develop the implications of this point by examining two New Salem stores.

The First Berry-Lincoln Store (fig. 25), where Lincoln worked in the 1830s as a storekeeper, has been reconstructed as a store selling souvenirs to the visitors, unlike the other reconstructed stores in New Salem, the Second Berry-Lincoln, the Hill-McNeil, and Offutt's, which do not have items for sale. The First Berry-Lincoln Store, with volunteer salespersons in period dress, is operated by the New Salem Lincoln League for profit. It is quite successful, and the proceeds are used to support the activities of the site. When the store first began, the New Salem Lincoln League formed an authenticity committee to check on each item sold; but these early efforts met with limited financial success. The league eventually hired a professional manager for the store who had an eye on the bottom line. The new manager selected the inventory to sell, and the authenticity committee no longer met.

It is instructive to examine the inventory of the First Berry-Lincoln Store. It has become a gift shop, with many handmade items, including pottery, baskets, quilts, rugs, stuffed dolls, brooms, large wooden ladles, copper pots, products of the cooper shop such as small barrels and tubs, pattern books of early American clothing, coonskin caps, and candles. I was told that many tourists come asking for objects made in the craft shops of New Salem, but

25. The First Berry-Lincoln Store

my observation was that they do a brisk business in all items and that the shop is frequently crowded with tourists. When I asked the volunteer if their inventory was representative of the items sold in the 1830s store, the answer was that they want everything they sell to be "authentic to the era," which means that the items could have been made in the 1830s. This is authenticity in the sense of credibility. When I inquired whether tourists ask for authentic items, the reply was that the question rarely comes up.

The setting of the store is a log cabin; the storekeepers are dressed in 1830s clothing; the objects sold look "old-fashioned," "country," or "folk"; and my interviews suggest that the tourists accept them as such. To the degree that the museum professionals are successful in adhering to the goal of creating a credible reproduction based on verisimilitude—that is, a historic site believable to the visitors—the probability is greater that the tourists will be satisfied with what they find at the site. This turns the discussion from the museum professionals to the tourists. It would be a mistake to assume that tourists necessarily make the same distinctions about authenticity that the museum professionals do . Museum professionals are the producers, whereas tourists are the consumers and do not approach the site in the same way. Tourists know, of course, that the objects they purchase are not from the 1830s and that many are not even reproductions of 1830s objects, and they may realize that no store in the 1830s ever had an inventory like that of the present First Berry-Lincoln Store. They are buying souvenirs, mementos of their trip to New Salem, gifts for those back home, and not necessarily authentic objects or even objects that are authentic reproductions.

Historians have no direct knowledge of the inventory of the First Berry-Lincoln Store in the 1830s at New Salem as no records have been found, but other stores on the prairies in that time period stocked items such as varnish, shellac, paint ingredients, dyes, spectacles, spices, knives, axes, tools, pens and ink, hardware, thread, buttons, needles, jewelry, liquor, china, books, textiles, hats, window glass, tin pans, nails, gunpowder, door locks and hinges, and foodstuffs such as coffee, tea, sugar, flour, rice, cheese, and molasses (Atherton 1939; Kwedar, Patterson, and Allen 1980). There were fashionable goods from Eastern wholesalers, manufactured items, and products from Europe. Tourists in the 1990s are not interested in these 1830s items, or if they are, the items are better purchased somewhere other than the New Salem craft shop.

Given the inventories of the 1830s and the 1990s stores, it is clear that each stocked items that met the needs of their clientele. The older store sold items necessary for the survival of the 1830s prairie pioneers, while the contemporary store with its handmade crafts sells souvenirs to the 1990s tourists. Each store was meaningful in its era, and I do not see what is gained by privileging one at the expense of the other. It is the postmodernists and the social theorists who make such judgmental evaluations.

Discussion

My argument about authenticity and reproductions is different from the postmodern one presented by Baudrillard and Eco and is also different from the position taken by such theorists as MacCannell and Handler in their writings about tourism, authenticity, and historic sites.[9] For Baudrillard and Eco, the simulacrum becomes the true; the copy becomes the original or even better than the original. In postmodern hyperreality, all we have are pure simulacra, for origins are lost or are not recoverable or never existed; there was no original reality. As Baudrillard says, "it is always a false problem to want to restore the truth beneath the simulacrum" (1983, 48). This is the postmodern condition, he argues, one specific to our electronic era. I argue instead that this is the human condition, for all cultures continually invent and reinvent themselves. In the 1830s during the development of New Salem, there was a prior image, the cultural knowledge of how other prairie villages in central Illinois were built in the 1820s. It could be said that the 1830s village was a copy based on a model of 1820s villages, adapted to the conditions of the 1830s, modified in accordance with the particular situation of the New Salem locality, and subject to whatever creative modifications were devised by the

New Salem residents. We all enter society in the middle, and culture is always in process (Turner and Bruner 1986).

This perspective, which I have been advocating for decades (e.g., E. Bruner 1973a, 1984b, 1993a), has sometimes been known as the constructivist position. Recently it has been called the "invention of culture" tradition, and it has produced important studies (e.g., Babcock 1990a; Borofsky 1987; Handler and Linnekin 1984; Hanson 1989; Hobsbawn and Ranger 1983; Hymes 1975; Wagner 1975). But the roots of the perspective are really very old, going back to Wilhelm Dilthey, John Dewey, George Herbert Mead, and the American pragmatists; to the 1920s writings of the great Russian literary scholar Mikhail Bakhtin; to Roland Barthes and the poststructuralists; and to performance theory (cf. Bauman 1992).

The constructivist view that culture is emergent, always alive and in process, is widely accepted today (Lavie, Narayan, and Rosaldo 1993). All proponents of this view concur that the meaning of the text is not inherent in the text but emerges from how people read or experience the text. They all agree that socialization is at best an imperfect mechanism for cultural transmission and that each new performance or expression of cultural heritage is a copy in that it always looks back to a prior performance, but also that each is an original in that it adapts to new circumstances and conditions. As Richard Handler and Jocelyn Linnekin argue, "All genuine traditions are spurious . . . all spurious traditions are genuine" (1984, 288); or as Clifford Geertz says, "It is the copying that originates" (1986, 380). The 1990s New Salem is an original because each reproduction, in the process of emerging, constructs its own original—or better yet, as I advocate in this essay, the distinction between the original and the reproduction could just be abandoned.

In our era both the 1830s New Salem and the 1990s New Salem are continually being constructed in an endless process of production and reproduction. All that is known about the 1830s is what we can learn from a few artifacts, archeological remains, old records, stories, and mental models of the old prairie village, models that may exist vividly in the imagination of the public and the historians, but that are ever changing. The 1830s New Salem is continually being reconstructed as history is rewritten history to fit the present era, just as we rewrite Abraham Lincoln (e.g., Basler 1935). The twentieth-century New Salem has changed many times and has been totally rebuilt at least twice. A 1918 restoration of the village was razed to the ground in 1932, and a second restoration occurred in stages during the 1930s. Periodically the log structures receive additions and modifications, as do the interiors. In the 1990s a new visitor and orientation center was opened, the location of the store was changed, and a restaurant was built at the entrance to the park.

It is not just that the 1990s New Salem and the 1830s New Salem are always in the process of construction, but also that the 1990s New Salem influences our conception of the 1830s town. In other words, what is called the copy changes our view of the original. This is a problem that haunts Michael Taussig's book, *Mimesis and Alterity* (1993). Academic historians would agree that the 1990s New Salem, by its very presence, overemphasizes the importance of the 1830s New Salem in the early life of Abraham Lincoln, to the neglect of the formative influences of his earlier, Indiana years. Lincoln was twenty-two years old when he arrived at New Salem, already an adult. A twentieth-century touristic representation may have distorted the discourse of professional historians and hence our understanding of the 1830s.

In their work on authenticity, hyperreality, and the simulacrum, Baudrillard, Eco, MacCannell, and Handler all are making a critique of the culture of the West and of America. MacCannell (1976) makes the claim that tourists are so dissatisfied with their own culture that they seek authentic experiences elsewhere. His work was rooted in the 1960s and repeated the old nineteenth-century critique of Western civilization, that of alienated man in search of self.

Handler and Saxton have a similar position. They write, "For living-history practitioners, as for many of us, everyday experience is 'unreal' or inauthentic, hence alienating. Practitioners seek to regain an authentic world, and to realize themselves in the process, through simulation of historical worlds" (1988, 243). For MacCannell, tourists seek authenticity in another place, in a tourist site; for Handler and Saxton, it is in another time period, in a historic site. Authenticity for Handler has to do with our "true self" (1986), and he and Saxton contend that "an authentic experience . . . is one in which individuals feel themselves to be in touch both with a 'real' world and with their 'real' selves" (Handler and Saxton 1988, 243), which assumes that we do not experience our everyday worlds as real or authentic. In the work of MacCannell and of Handler and Saxton, the quest for authenticity is doomed, or, as they point out, it is a failed quest, because the very search destroys the authenticity of the object, which before the quest was presumed to be pristine and untouched. These authors thus assume an original pure state, an authentic culture in the third sense, like the ethnographic present, before contact. It is as if history begins with tourism, which then pollutes the world.[10]

MacCannell and Handler say that tourists are looking for authenticity, but it may be that these contemporary intellectuals are the ones looking for authenticity and that they have projected onto tourists their own longings. The museum professionals who say that a historic site is an authentic reproduction use *authenticity* in the first and second senses, not the third.

The question is, Who are the ones seeking authenticity? Trilling's (1972) insight again is that authenticity emerges to consciousness when a doubt arises. Those in central Illinois in the early twentieth century who found themselves in the predicament of having to reconstruct an 1830s New Salem without adequate knowledge became concerned with authenticity. In our era, anthropologists, museum curators, historians, serious collectors, and art dealers, as well as some tourists, acknowledge that they are seeking authenticity. I agree with Arjun Appadurai (Appadurai, ed., 1986, 44–45) that authenticity today is becoming a matter of the politics of connoisseurship, of the political economy of taste, and of status discrimination; beyond that, I would claim, it is a matter of power, of who has the right to authenticate.

The concept of authority serves as a corrective to misuses of the term *authenticity*, because in the raising of the issue of who authenticates, the nature of the discussion is changed. No longer is authenticity a property inherent in an object, forever fixed in time; instead it is a social process, a struggle in which competing interests argue for their own interpretations of history. Culture is seen as contested, emergent, and constructed, and agency and desire become part of the discourse. When actors use the term authenticity, ethnographers may then ask what segment of society has raised a doubt, what is no longer taken for granted, what are the societal struggles, and what are the cultural issues at work. These are ethnographic questions, empirical questions, requiring investigation and research. Grand theorizing thus gives way to ethnography.

There are two fundamental problems with the essentialist vocabulary of originals and copies, of the authentic and the inauthentic. One is that, despite claims to the contrary, there frequently is an implicit original, an authenticity in the third sense. For the postmodernists the original is Europe, and America is a satellite. Baudrillard (1988) says that he knew all about America "when I was still in Paris" (5), claims that America "was born of a rift with the Old World" (10), asserts that "the truth of America can only be seen by a European" (28), and contends that America is "the only remaining primitive society" (7). If for the postmodernists the original is civilized Europe, then for MacCannell and Handler the original is what was before alienation; it is the pure state, located elsewhere, around the bend, beneath or behind the touristic or the historic site.

The second problem with essentialist vocabulary is its built-in bias that designates one side of the dichotomy as better so that the other side becomes denigrated. It usually implies that originals are better than copies. When postmodernists Baudrillard and Eco seemingly say the exact opposite, they mean that it is the Americans who value the copy more than the original; this is, in effect, their critique of American culture. The net consequence of the project of Baudrillard, Eco, and MacCannell (and Boorstin [1961]) is to diminish historical sites like New Salem because they are seen as inauthentic, as pseudo, as surface, as plastic, as simulacra, as hyperreality, even as fakes. Essentialist vocabulary also implies that copies are based on originals, but from a constructivist perspective, the process may not be that simple. Sometimes an object is constructed in the contemporary era and then an older form is somehow "discovered" and is employed as a hypothetical original to add historic depth and legitimacy. To label one form a copy highlights the features that are similar to the supposed original and may not adequately take account of the differences or of the variations in the societal contexts within which the originals and the copies were produced. The vocabulary of origins and reproductions and of the authentic and the inauthentic may not adequately acknowledge that both are constructions of the present.

Conclusion

Let us turn now to my hypotheses about the tourists. If the tourists are not buying into scripts of postmodern hyperreality or authenticity, then what are they buying into at New Salem? In their writings, Baudrillard and Eco make grand generalizations about America, without nuances. They use homogenizing monolithic language when they write about Americans, and they do not differentiate among the many kinds of tourists at historic sites. They also fail to recognize the constructed nature of the meanings of historic sites.

In the view argued here, the meanings of New Salem Historic Site for tourists are constructed in the performance of the site, as visitors move through the village and as they interact with the interpreters. Experiencing the site gives rise to meanings that might not have been predicted before the visit, so in this sense the site is generative. It is not that all meaning is individual and idiosyncratic—for of course there are cultural patterns, as I will demonstrate—but that meanings are generated in a social context. An ethnographic perspective is needed to examine the social organizational settings within which New Salem is experienced. Baudrillard and Eco reflect none of this complexity.

Here are some examples of differences among the visitors to New Salem. Many visitors to theme parks come as family groups, not as isolated individuals, so the family becomes the basic social unit for processing the touristic experience, and therefore the visit frequently assumes an educational focus (Willis 1993). When school is in session, busloads of schoolchildren arrive with their teachers for class outings at New Salem. One day there were forty different busloads, and the educational function was quite explicit. Another time a group of immigrants from Chicago, students in a citizenship training class, spent a hurried two hours rushing through the site. In these cases parents or teachers were explaining the meaning of New Salem, emphasizing the role of Abraham Lincoln in American history to different groups of learners.

I have shared the New Salem experience with a troop of seven- and eight-year-old Girl Scouts who were on an all-day outing with their scout leader and a few parent volunteers, and the main attraction appeared to be cooking beef stew for lunch in a wood-burning fireplace. It seemed to take hours for the stew to cook and everyone was hungry, so the conversation centered on the life of the early pioneers who settled in central Illinois, and particularly on the difficulty of that life, a recurrent theme among many of the visitors. It was a learning experience for the Girl Scouts.

One Illinois farmer entered a log house where one of the interpreters was spinning wool. The farmer stated that when he was a child there was a spinning wheel in his home very similar to the one at New Salem, and he recalled images of his grandmother sitting at the spinning wheel and telling stories about her early life on a family farm on the prairie. His experience of New Salem provides a very evocative example of what many tourists do when they visit the site: they make associations between what they see at New Salem and their personal lives. The meaning of New Salem is thus emergent in the social context of the visitor's experience of the site.

A judge told me how he loved to come to New Salem very early on snowy winter mornings so that he could walk in solitude the same hallowed ground that Abraham Lincoln had walked. The judge had practiced law in the same district as had Lincoln. He had a bronze bust of Lincoln in his office, he had played the part of Lincoln in local theatrical productions. He was tall and thin, he physically resembled Lincoln, and he had clearly made a personally meaningful identification.

Visitors to New Salem include Lincoln buffs, antique collectors, retired people making their way through the theme parks of America, sophisticated urbanites from Chicago on a visit to the "rural" hinterlands, and university professors entertaining foreign visitors. It is indeed a varied audience. Tourists are not monolithic, and neither is the meaning of the site. There are many New Salems (Bodnar 1992). Tourists construct a past that is meaningful to them and that relates to their life and experience, and this is the way meanings are constructed at historic sites.

What encourages the local production of meaning is the format of dialogic interaction between the interpreters and small groups of tourists who move from house to house. As each interpreter tells about Lincoln or about the 1830s village or about the history of the original residents, the tourists have an opportunity to ask questions and to interact with the interpreter. Although the main message of the museum professionals, that of New Salem as the site of Lincoln's transformation, has been presented to the tourists in the orientation video and the brochures, the tourists' relationship to the interpreters has a more personal and immediate quality. The interpreters, too, have received the official messages of the site, primarily in training sessions and in manuals, but they frequently depart from the official scripts and move off in their own directions,[11] and the tourists bring their own concerns and interests to the interaction. The result is a very open format, more like a discussion than a lecture, one that allows for improvisation and that facilitates the constructivist process.

I found many instances of a playful quality to the interaction, whereas much of the literature emphasizes the seriousness of the tourist quest and experience.[12] The interaction between interpretive guides and visitors at historic sites may be oriented to enjoyment as much as to discovery of historic fact. For example, one time when I was on the reconstructed Mayflower in Plymouth, a site that does first-person interpretation, I saw a woman guide in period dress. She told me that it was a long and arduous journey across the ocean, that she had lost her husband on the voyage, and that she felt so lonely in this vast new country. Then she looked me straight in the eye and winked, and I could not tell if it was a 1620s wink or a 1990s wink. Interpreters at New Salem often engage in light banter and joking behavior with the visitors. A woman storekeeper in period dress will say to the assembled tourists, "What have you come to purchase today?" Such an inquiry, an example of slippage from third to first person, will lead to humorous conversation about the goods sold in the store or about the 1830s prices, noting how low they were compared to today's prices. In these settings, many tourists play with time frames and experiment with alternative realities; it is a good way to learn about the past. Visits to historic sites have a strong entertaining and playful quality.

In the course of my fieldwork I often remained in one location and noted how the topic of conversation changed with the arrival of each new group of tourists. Also I followed some groups from house to house and noted how the discourse and even the roles changed as persons moved through the village. The roles of tourist and interpreter are not fixed. A mother who had come as a tourist began to explain New Salem to her children, and at that point she was, in a sense, becoming an interpreter, switching roles. Subjectivities and motives change, even within one individual and even in the course of a single visit.

Although individuals construct their own meanings, I found that recurring patterns and generalizations clearly emerged. In reporting on what I learned about the meaning of New Salem to the tourists, I acknowledge that my findings are hypotheses and that they are my own constructions of meaning, open to further study and testing. That said, in addition to learning about the past and enjoying the historic site, I noted the following three major themes.

First, some tourists to New Salem are consuming nostalgia, the handcrafted and the locally produced, in opposition to Machine Age materialism. Many tourists to New Salem view the village with a sense of longing for a vanished past, for an imagined time when life was simpler, purer, and more natural—a Midwestern equivalent of the Garden of Eden. Many see in New Salem the image of early pioneer life in the prairies, a return to the first settlers in central Illinois. For these tourists New Salem is an Illinois origin myth, a prairie pastoral.

Second, as visitors walk through the village they are also buying the idea of progress, of how far our nation has advanced, for the one question the interpreters repeatedly ask is, Would you like to live back in the 1830s when life was so hard? The answer is invariably no. The theme of progress is prominent in New Salem discourse. The emphasis is on the contrast between the hardships of the 1830s and the conveniences of the 1990s.

These first two themes may seem to be in conflict because whereas the first focuses on the simplicity of life in the past, the second focuses on the severity of that life. In the first technology is seen as evil; in the second it is seen as progress. Yet many visitors hold both views simultaneously. In their imagination they yearn for a simpler life, but they are not alienated beings; they want modern 1990s conveniences, and they would not be willing to give up their 1990s lives in exchange for the life of the 1830s.

Finally, many tourists are also buying a commemoration of traditional America, of honest values, good neighbors, hard work, virtue and generosity, the success ideology, and the sense of community in small-town America. The tourists are seeking in New Salem a discourse that enables them to better reflect on their lives in the 1990s. New Salem and similar sites enact an ideology, recreate an origin myth, keep history alive, attach tourists to a mythical collective consciousness, and commodify the past. The particular pasts that tourists create or imagine at historic sites like New Salem may never have existed. But such sites do provide visitors with the raw material, experiences, with which to construct meaning, attachment, stability, and a sense of identify. In the America of Baudrillard and Eco, copies refer only to themselves, no origin myths pertain, and no collective reality is invoked. This, however, is an America of their own imaginations and not an America of everyday practices.

Following Jack Zipes (1979), New Salem can be read in two fundamental ways. There is the pessimistic view (Haraway 1984; M. Wallace 1981), which sees museums and historic sites as exploitative and deceitful, as strengthening the ruling classes, creating false consciousness, and manipulating the imaginations of already alienated beings. Or there is the optimistic view, which focuses on the utopian potential for transformation, offers hope for a better life, says people can take charge of their lives and change themselves and their culture. The story of Abraham Lincoln is, as Zipes writes, the "folk tale motif of the swineherd who becomes a prince" (1979, 119), and there is revolutionary potential in this fantasy, for it can be heroic and can lead to greater—not less—engagement with social life. In this respect fantasy, art, and historic sites have a similar function.

In postmodern writings, contemporary American tourist attractions tend to be described in ways that replicate elements of postmodern theory, emphasizing the inauthentic, constructed nature of the sites, their appeal to the masses, their imitation of the past, and their efforts to present a perfected version of themselves. This is a narrow and distorted view that fails to account for the popularity of such sites and the number of them on the American landscape, that begs the question of the meaning of the sites to the participants, and that by its denigration of these sites and of popular American culture imposes an elitist politics that is blind to its own assumptions.

6

Dialogic Narration and the Paradoxes of Masada

Edward M. Bruner and Phyllis Gorfain

OCCASIONALLY A STORY BECOMES so prominent in the consciousness of an entire society that its recurrent tellings not only define and empower storytellers but also help to constitute and reshape the society. Such a story is the 1,900-year-old account of the first-century siege, resistance, and defeat at the mountain fortress of Masada on the shores of the Dead Sea.[1] The dramatic Masada narrative and similar cultural texts are particularly significant because they frequently tell national stories and rarely remain monologic. They serve to integrate the society, encapsulate ideology, and create social order; indeed, the story may become a metaphor for the state, and poetic means may be used for political purposes. But because these narratives are replete with ambiguity and paradox, an inherent versatility in interpretation arises that allows for conflicting readings and dissenting, challenging voices. Despite the forces toward authority and monologic certitude, the semiotic openness in the Masada narrative, as in all great stories (see Rabkin 1967, 13–28), creates the potential for contradictory explanations of world order and generates an arena for ideologies at war.

An ongoing discourse emerges from the exchange of authoritative and challenging tellings and, in turn, supports a historically situated debate over the interpretation and uses of the story. Authoritative voices attempt to fix meanings and stabilize order, whereas challenging voices question established meanings and tend to be deconstructive. Taken together, the various tellings and interpretations lead to what we call a process of dialogic narration.

Many of our ideas about dialogic narration are derived from the powerful insights of Mikhail Bakhtin (1981). In using this terminology, we argue that a story cannot be viewed in isolation, as a monologic static entity, but must be seen in a dialogic or interactive framework; that is, all stories are told in voices, not just in structuralist oppositions or syntagmatic functions of action. A story is told in a dynamic chorus of styles that voice the social and ideological positions they represent. Stories are polyphonic—they voice the narrative action, the reported speech of characters, the tellers' commentary, evaluative remarks, interpretive statements, and audience acknowledgments. This dialogic freedom creates in storytelling a field for the contesting of views and the play of power. For us, the term *dialogic* is not restricted to describing a two-way binary interchange but calls attention to multiple languages, to plural voices, and to the heterogeneity of speech acts, genres, and styles.[2]

Bakhtin holds a similar view of language as the interaction of formal givens and spontaneous utterances. He points to the interactive embeddedness and dialogic orientation of every utterance and story:

> It is entangled, shot through with shared thoughts, points of view . . . enters a dialogically agitated and tension-filled environment of alien words, value judgments and accents, weaves in and out of complex interrelationships, merges with some, recoils from others, intersects with yet a third group: and all this may crucially shape discourse, may leave a trace in all its semantic layers, may complicate its expression and influence its entire stylistic profile. The living utterance, having taken meaning and shape in a particular historical moment in a socially specific environment, cannot fail to brush up against thousands of living dialogic threads, . . . cannot fail to become an active participant in a social dialogue. (1981, 276)

Bakhtin writes primarily about language, which for him is alive. He writes of an "uninterrupted process of historical becoming that is characteristic of all living language" (1981, 288) and says that there is no static representation of reality. Further, language is stratified and heteroglot, and there are "socio-ideological contradictions" between different historical epochs and between various contemporary groupings. For Bakhtin there is no such thing as a language, but rather many overlapping, intersecting, contradictory languages: "All words have a taste of a profession, a genre, a tendency, a party, a particular work, a particular person, a generation, an age group, the day and hour. Each word tastes of the context and contexts in which it has lived its socially charged life" (1981, 293).

We take Bakhtin's ideas about language and apply them to narration. As we focus on the play of voices in the Masada tradition, our concept of dialogic narration recognizes that no story is "a" story or "the" story, but rather each story is a dialogic process of many historically situated particular tellings. In our theoretical perspective narration refers to a process rather than to an entity; to a discourse rather than to a text; to interpretation and feeling rather than to an abstract sequence of events. Narration includes voice, point of view, and the positioning of the narrative within a discourse. In sum, we do not conceive of narration as monologic in voice or monolithic in structure since we find that within any narration the elements of style, rhetoric, point of view, plot, interpretation, evaluation, and performance choices are not necessarily concordant or isomorphic. At the end of a story, for example, one may have incomplete and unresolved styles and points of view, as expressed by dialogues among characters, even if the plot itself is totally resolved (see Bakhtin 1981, 349).

Relationship to Other Narrative Studies

Identifying ourselves with the work on narration and performance, style and power currently being advanced by folklorists and anthropologists such as Barbara Kirshenblatt-Gimblett, Richard Bauman, Dell Hymes, Barbara Meyerhoff, Victor Turner, Clifford Geertz, and others, we reconceptualize the narrative process in a way that extends the discussion beyond the narrow confines of structuralism on the one hand and pure emergence on the other. The difference between our more processual and contextual approach and the extremes of structuralism and pure emergence may be seen if we examine the relationship between a basic story and its variable manifestations (Genette 1980; Chatman 1978).

Some approaches to narrative privilege the basic story as the primary object or goal of research. Historicism, for example, analyzes a series of stories or tales in space and time to reconstruct an archetype or urtype; the basic story is conceived of as the single original source of all later versions and variants. Structuralism also isolates a basic story, but as an ahistorical deep structure, a model of the underlying relationships that produces the various surface manifestations through a set of transformational rules. The difficulty with historicism and structuralism is that as they isolate "the story" they also strip away all the uniqueness and spontaneity of narratives and their cultural-historical relevance to individuals and societies. A narrative core becomes monolithic; stories become static artifacts with rules unto themselves. In reaction to these paradigms other approaches to narration (e.g., Herrnstein-Smith 1980) focus so intensely on the presentness of the narrative act and on the responsiveness of form to situation and speaker that they end in pure emergence, thereby diminishing the importance of history and tradition. Our perspective, on the contrary, acknowledges that a story may exist prior to any narration—Masada does refer to a series of incidents and a configuration of recurrent themes—but we also insist that a story can only occur in a particular situated telling.

Authority and Power in Dialogic Exchange

Bakhtin's notions of hierarchy in language and of authoritative voices are especially significant for understanding dialogic processes. The "authoritative," in this view, is inherent not in some authoritative version of the story, but in the authoritative positions of tellers within a community, in the interaction between a performance situated within a locus of power and one offered on the boundaries of public structures. In Bakhtin's words, the "authoritative" is the "already uttered"; it is "prior discourse" backed by legal, political, and moral authority. Authoritative tellings of national stories thus enjoy a privileged position: they dominate official public performances. Challenging voices must make their utterances through the channels available to them and must employ different genres and forms, such as questions, interruptions, back-channel commentary, or argumentation in underground publications. Authoritative tellings occupy the dominant positions and sound like the words of fathers, adults, leaders, and teachers; they represent the "official line" and are sponsored by or associated with the state. The authoritative voice expresses the established position and sees itself as giving the correct interpretation. The challenging voices cannot be so easily characterized, however, for they remain individualized and bear a metaphorically "marked" quality; they are "other" and are always uttered in reaction to the dominant tellings.

In one sense the power of authoritative versions is derived from the power of the state, but in another, deeper sense each authoritative telling of a national story constitutes the power of the state. It follows that each critical, challenging telling may be perceived as an attack on the authority of the state, on the authority of the official tellers, and on the authority of "the story." The dialogue of idiolects and ideologies embodies more than a conflict over power; it also tests the way power is defined, displayed, recognized, and changed—through narration. Every performance, then, not only expresses power but creates it. This treatment of power is derived from Foucault's (1978) idea that power is constituted from the bottom up rather than emanating in some divine manner from the top down.

For many stories, no authoritative version exists or assumes dominance through state sponsorship. In the case of Masada, however, this kind of dominance does obtain. When an official government function, such as a formal military induction, is held at Masada and the story is told or referred to by government officials, this is an authoritative telling in our sense. When the

National Parks Authority, a state agency, issues tourist literature on the meaning of Masada, this is also an authoritative version.

Bakhtin writes that speech is basically polemical. So it is with narration. Authoritative and challenging tellers constantly struggle for supremacy over the interpretations and uses of a story, over the rights and powers of narration. Every dissident telling may be seen as an invasion of the establishment position, every commentary on the authoritative version as a critique. Competition emerges for narrative space in the discourse (Foucault 1973), for the right to tell one's story.[3] Just as speech is shaped in dialogic interaction, so is the narrative process.

Three Levels of Dialogic Narration

In dialogic narration the interaction among voices occurs in at least three domains. First, a story may be dialogic with itself, insofar as the story generates inquiry and resists a single definitive interpretation. Some stories, of course, are more dialogic than others, but we suggest that great national stories tend to be more open-ended, ambiguous, and paradoxical than others and hence more inherently dialogic. They raise questions about themselves for which no obvious resolution can be found.

Second, stories may be dialogic with culture and history. Any given telling takes account of previous and anticipated tellings and responds to alternative and challenging stories. The Freudian narrative (see Schafer 1980), for example, is dialogic insofar as it developed historically in response to the alternative methods of psychiatric treatment of its era, as well as to direct challenges and criticisms. Serious literature and parental choices in the twentieth century were vastly changed by this Freudian narrative tradition. In this second sense of *dialogic,* every telling responds to and helps to condition its cultural and historical context.

Third, in any given telling there is a dialogic relationship between self and society. Tellers and listeners do not take passive roles in a superorganic process of storymaking but actively engage in an interpretive act to make "the story" meaningful to themselves and relevant to their own life situations. In this third sense, there is a dialogue between autobiography and history as each person is aligned with the prevailing cultural tradition; or, to put it in other terms, the national self is constituted through national stories. If we ask where the dialogic is located, the answer is that the dialogic is located in the discourse about the story, about society, and about the self.

Our aim, then, is to develop the concept of dialogic narration, to contribute to narrative theory by introducing a processual perspective, and to root the narrative process in society without reducing it to a mere reflection of society. Let us turn now to the story of Masada, and then to further discussion of the three dialogic domains of the intrinsic, the historical, and the experiential.

Masada

It should be relatively easy to give an account of Masada, the mountain fortress near the Dead Sea (fig. 26), as there are so many occasions for tellings. Masada is simultaneously a tourist attraction (MacCannell 1976), a pilgrimage site (Turner and Turner 1978), an archaeological excavation (Yadin 1966), the idiom of political debate (Alter 1973), the topic of a novel (Gann 1981), a scholarly dissertation (Zerubavel 1980), a television spectacular (Cultural Information Service 1981), and, for some, a national symbol of the state of Israel. New recruits to the Armoured Corps of the Israel Defence Force take their oath of allegiance at the top of the fortress and repeat the words of the poet Lamdan: "Masada shall not fall again." Israeli schoolchildren visit Masada as part of their school curriculum, families from Israel and other countries hold bar mitzvah and bat mitzvah ceremonies at the synagogue on top of Masada, and there is a Masada stamp and even a commemorative coin, the "Official Israel Masada Medal." On all these occasions the story is told or referred to. Which one shall we tell here?

In scholarly articles one usually tells a story by presenting a plot summary, a supposedly objective kernel narrative based on the facts of the case. Here is such a version of the Masada tale:

> The Jewish revolt against Roman rule led to the conquest of Jerusalem and the destruction of The Temple in A.D. 70. However, a group of 960 Jewish zealots continued the fight from the fortress at Masada built years earlier by King Herod. In A.D. 73, after a three-year siege, the Roman Tenth Legion advanced up a stone ramp to the mountaintop only to find that the zealots had committed mass suicide.

One of the difficulties with this account is that it adopts a rhetorical stance of assumed objectivity, as if the facts were established, which is not the case. Also, it is told in such a flat style that it makes one wonder about the point of the story!

How about this version, excerpted from the guide to a television series (Cultural Information Service 1981):

> In the first century A.D., Palestine was part of the vast Roman Empire. . . . Sporadic uprisings by the populace against Roman oppression were held in check until the year A.D. 66 when a large-scale revolt broke out. Rome sent the famous general Vespasian to quell the rebellion. Victory seemed assured when,

26. Masada. Photo courtesy of Israeli Ministry of Tourism.

> in A.D. 70 his son Titus conquered Jerusalem, burning the Second Temple. . . . One group of freedom fighters escaped across the desert to Masada. From the mountain fortress, these zealots conducted raids on Roman camps. In A.D. 72 the Roman Tenth Legion under the command of Flavius Silva marched on Masada. In A.D. 73, 960 Jewish men, women and children made their last stand against 5,000 Roman soldiers. . . . The Jewish leader, Eleazar, presents the alternatives to his followers, "The choice is yours. You can choose to fight them in the morning. They'll kill you or enslave you. You can choose to hide from them. They'll find you. Or you can choose to take their victory from them. They will remember you." The next morning when the Roman commander Silva discovers that all the Jews have committed suicide he says, "The victory—we have won a rock. In the middle of a wasteland. On the shore of a poisoned sea."

Or this telling, from a tourist advertisement in the *New York Times Magazine* (April 26, 1981, p. 83):

> You're standing on a massive mountain of stone, some 1300 feet above the Holy Land. It's an awesome sight with a breathtaking view of the Dead Sea and the sweeping sands of the Judean desert. You feel a sense of power standing high among the remains of King Herod's palace. Are there ancient spirits here?

> Or is the wind playing a game with your imagination? Perhaps it's the fearless Eleazar ben Yair shouting commands to his courageous band of Jewish patriots. It was on Masada that 960 men women and children fought off the mighty Roman Tenth Legion. It was on this very spot 1900 years ago that these freedom fighters took their own lives—choosing a death of glory to a life of slavery.

The television version makes the home audience a spectator to a historical and narrativized conflict between the two generals, the Roman Silva and the Jewish Eleazar, the heroic protagonists. The tourist ad places the lone reader at the abandoned site and suggests the kernel stories the reader as tourist will hear as dim memory at Masada itself.

So which story should we tell in order to tell "the story of Masada"? With Derrida we find that any telling forces us "to choose among several interpretative"—and we would add rhetorical—"options" (1980, 55). A story, he writes, forms "an open and essentially unpredictable series . . . an account without edge or boundary" (1980, 73).

Our tellings thus far are derived from American, as opposed to Israeli, accounts and from popular, as opposed to scholarly, literature. If there were sufficient space, we would analyze the tellings of the Masada story by the first-century historian Josephus Flavius or by the Israeli archaeologist and army general Yadin, as well as those by religious and political critics. The vast literature on the subject testifies to the extensive discourse generated by the story. Our purpose in this chapter, however, is to demonstrate how all these tellings, including ours, are dialogic. And so we turn to our first domain, the story itself.

The Intrinsic Dialogue

Authoritative tellings view the mass suicide at Masada as a courageous act, a symbol of freedom (Livneh and Meshel ca. 1970, 2). But using the story to celebrate freedom and continued life, when the events end in death, produces a paradox. The meaning of death must be taken in the Masada narrative as a victory over death. Suicide is paradoxically hailed as a victory over external forces, as an assertion of determination. As Israelis tell the story of Masada, they manipulate the paradox; in recalling the story of mass suicide they bring it to life, to avoid the ending of the story in death. They tell the story in order to say, "Never again." But such a telling cannot be so monologically directed, and it raises semiotic and interpretive dilemmas (Syrkin 1973).

With the Masada story, no telling can fully ignore the question, even if it suppresses it: How is mass suicide to be interpreted? Was it heroism or madness, an acceptance or denial of reality? As a definitive and irrevocable act, so obviously an absolute choice, suicide forces others to consider alternatives. Multiple possibilities arise, yet the meaning of suicide remains ambiguous, and our cultural and social judgments often ambivalent. Freedom of choice in living and in interpreting stories becomes all the more evident when viewed against the final act that precludes all such choices.

Audiences can ask about alternatives: Could the zealots have escaped from Masada? Was accommodation with the Romans possible? Could the besieged have fought to the last and still have been as heroic? In the made-for-TV movie, Eleazar is portrayed in his final speech as saying in a kind of reflexive way, "They will remember us"—in effect asking his compatriots to exchange life for memory, for the construction of a story. This is only one of many arguments Eleazar uses in the movie and in the novel. In Josephus's first-century account, the eloquent Eleazar concludes, "Let us therefore make haste, and instead of affording them so much pleasure, as they hope for in getting us under their power, let us leave them an example which shall at once cause their astonishment at our death, and their admiration of our hardiness therein" (1936, 853–54).

The aim of mass suicide, like all acts of martyrdom, is to leave a message, to communicate meaning and stimulate exchange. The zealots' choice was death in exchange for remembrance. Israelis choose to use that remembrance in alternative ways. Jewish rabbinical tradition ignored or suppressed the Masada story for twenty centuries because the commentators disapproved of suicide and the secularity of the story's values (Zerubavel 1980, 95–116). Suicide may take control over death and leave a legacy of memory, but suicide cannot control the uses of that legacy—the interpretations or evaluations of the action, or the response of future generations of readers. Ironically suicide, like authoritative readings, attempts to fix meaning but produces inquiry instead, a story full of implication and one that remains intrinsically open-ended. Paradoxically no act seems more final than suicide, but the act itself confounds finality: mass suicide may end life, but it cannot end the story.

Paradox generates dialogic meanings because of its self-contradictory structure. As Colie writes, paradox equivocates: "It lies, and it doesn't. It tells the truth, and it doesn't" (1966, 6). Paradox speaks with two voices; it always exists in two universes of discourse. In a failed paradox one truth becomes evident, one voice predominates. But in a true paradox one meaning must always be taken "with respect to the other," so that paradox produces meanings in dialogue, "infinitely mirrored, infinitely reflected, in each other." Paradoxes involve reflexivity in their self-referentiality (Babcock 1980, 5); they "play with human understanding" (Colie 1966, 7) and comment on themselves for what they ultimately refer to is the interpretive process itself.

Precisely because in paradox one meaning is not dominant, interpretation not singular, and truth not apparent, paradox operates as a figure of thought which foregrounds the multiplicity of meaning, interpretation, and truth.

Even as suicide poses a semiotic problem about endings, it also generates a problem of beginnings, a question about authoritative sources—an epistemological enigma. By eliminating its own protagonist, a suicide story precludes any definitive account. Who is left to tell the tale and how do we know what actually happened? Even suicide notes fail to explain the choice fully or to describe the final act, for they are written, however close to the end, at a distance from it. If there were witnesses we wonder, Why did they fail to intervene? The problems multiply with tales of heroic last stands. All last-stand stories must have a source, and nearly all of these narratives derive from "a lone survivor" (Rosenberg 1974). But these accounts strike us as necessarily suspect and partial, for questions emerge about lone survivors: Why didn't they die with the rest? Were they insufficiently courageous or did they lack full solidarity with the group?

In the case of Masada, Josephus claims, the story comes to us from one person among a small group of survivors, two women and three children. They supposedly hid at the bottom of a dry well, in the conduits that brought drinking water to the zealots. The waterwork technology responsible for the remarkable survival of the zealots in the desert becomes a new means for survival—now against the forces of both suicide and invasion. The semblance of burial in an underground well creates parallels between the return to life and the telling of the story. Both emergence from the well and the telling of the story become resurrections, yet both feats remain merely symbolic restorations. The emergence from the grave is not from actual death, only its likeness; the story is not the redemption of the dead, only the symbolic means for that redemption through the creation of memory. The neatness of the concordance between survival and storytelling adds power to this story, but it also makes the artificiality more evident. The symbolic relationship between survival and narration is thus both causative and analogic. This doubling qualifies the tale as a possible fabrication; at the least it highlights it as a construction, whatever its truth. Such artful narratives move us, but they may also remind us how they stand at a remove from the shadowy events they illuminate.

Our sense of the fictionality of Josephus's account is further enhanced when we examine his biography, for Josephus epitomizes the unreliable narrator. He did not witness the events at Masada, and he wrote the account years later when he, a Jewish general who had defected to the Roman side, composed his history of the Jewish wars in Rome while under the protection of the emperor Titus.

A further question arises about his motives, for in an earlier incident at Jotapata, Josephus, then a commander, had participated in a suicide pact following the defeat of his forces. In that incident Josephus chose not to commit suicide but to become, eventually, a storyteller. After forty of his comrades died at Jotapata in a procedure similar to the one he describes for Masada, he chose not to take his own life; he betrayed his pledge and turned himself over to the Roman conquerors. The contrived plan for suicide and the casting of lots to determine who would die last appear in both cases. Josephus invented this device at Jotapata, and its reappearance in his account of Masada suggests that he laminated his personal story over that of the zealots. We could argue that he did so both to expiate his own offense by valorizing their bravery and to excuse his own cowardice (which he admits to in his autobiography) by denigrating the zealots' act, as he does in some of the rhetorical exchange.

We do not aim to criticize Josephus, only to highlight some of the enigmas that produce an epistemological dilemma about the authority of the text. In the case of Masada, the problems about suicide, endings, and Josephus produce an ongoing dialogue. The literature is vast and the resulting Masada discourse is reflexive—a stance that is also dialogic, since reflexivity speaks in two voices, just as paradox does. Reflexivity paradoxically requires the subject to look at itself as object, the speaker to speak about the process of speaking (Babcock 1980; Ruby 1980). Any narration of Masada must, at some level, not only tell the Masada story but also address the narrative process, even if indirectly: How does one know the story? How does one understand and use the story?

Performances of legends—narratives that purport to be true accounts of real events—abound in claims to authority and authenticity. Authenticating devices such as voices quoted, speech reported, and narrator commentary create a fictive and dialogic quality that betrays the inherent problems of belief in storytelling. The play of uncertainty in narrative is what accounts for the elasticity in the readings.

Every story can be reinterpreted at a later date or retold in a different context, and new meanings will emerge. In all narration an inevitable gap opens between the original event and the telling, but here we refer to something more specific. We claim that the story of Masada, because of its incidents of resistance and suicide, is especially riddled with paradox, reflexivity, and inquiry. There is no guarantee, of course, that the story will necessarily be told. Narration depends on historical circumstances. But once the Masada narrative is told, we suggest, the potential for variable interpretation is inherent.

The Historical Dialogue

The cultural and historical aspects of the Masada story crystallize in a struggle over meaning that takes place between authoritative and challenging versions in Israeli political and moral discourse. In the current heroic version, Masada represents militancy, resistance, freedom, and an ancient claim to the land. Such tellings see the zealots surrounded by the mighty Roman legions as in the present Israel is surrounded by hostile Arab neighbors. For General Yadin, Masada is an inspiring story of the resistance of the few against the many, a story of David fighting Goliath. This biblical narrative, used by Yadin and others in analogy to Masada, is used elsewhere in the Middle East to characterize a variety of asymmetrical contests.

Establishment stories emphasize the martyrdom of the zealots, who gave their blood in the desert for the freedom of Zion. They are seen against a tradition of Jewish martyrdom that stretches from the time of the Babylonian captivity to the death of the first Israeli national hero, Yosef Trumpeldor, whose defeat produced the national motto, "It is good to die for our country" (Zerubavel 1980, 182–216). Whatever the analogy, the Masada story is seen in relation to other known stories and narrations. In this interaction of tellings, the dialogic quality of the story is heard against history and its characterizations in narrative.

For the youthful generation in Israel during the 1930s and 1940s the zealots were seen as Jewish militants who defied the religious and political majority to fight the Romans vigorously, cleverly, and indefatigably. At that time, Masada served as a challenging narrative set against the traditional image of the Eastern European Jews who maintained tradition through the Diaspora, but only, according to the folk idea, by means of prayer, study, accommodation, and retreat (Benjamin Hrushovsky and Dan Ben-Amos 1982, personal communications). After World War II, the apparent failure of assimilation and piety led young people to turn away from their European heritage with its honored folk image of the Jewish male as Talmudic scholar who finds fulfillment through knowledge. Further setting themselves against the alternative of emigration to America, youthful Israeli idealists saw themselves as choosing the rigors and perils of pioneering a new, besieged, collective society, like the zealots who together survived the rigors of desert life instead of choosing to live in the cities under Roman occupation.

In the challenging political reading "from the left," Israel is seen as a fortress state, isolated from the rest of the world, creating its own doomed Masada. The story is retold to warn of the outcome of such absolutist and isolationist choices. Orthodox religious readings "from the right" question the glorification of suicide. These critics chafe against the defiantly secular embrace of Masada and its lesson of fighting, rather than prayer, as the method for Jewish survival. Both types of criticism call into question the authority of Josephus, undermine the archaeological evidence that is used to support his story, and employ scholarly, religious, historical, and other texts to counter the authoritative readings. The challenging readings introduce into the dialogic discourse a multiplicity of other texts, voices, and alternative authorities. Both challenging tellings emphasize the ending of the Masada story, the mass suicide, whereas the establishment tellings emphasize the middle of the story, the heroic resistance (Zerubavel 1980).

Professor Yehoshafat Harkabi writes that those leaders who dragged Judea into futile military struggles two thousand years ago were irrational, as the ancient Jewish state was destroyed in the process and a terrible price was paid in human life and suffering. Harkabi warns that in glorifying Masada and the Bar Kochba revolt "we are forced into the position of admiring destruction and rejoicing over a deed amounting to national suicide." Yehoshua Sobol, a dramatist, claims that under the Romans the Jews "were given much more freedom and autonomy than we give the Palestinians today in the occupied territories." Through the idiom of the Masada story, Harkabi and Sobol argue against the present Israeli government policies and against such contemporary nationalistic-religious groups as Gush Emunim, which they equate with the zealots of the first century (all quotes from the *Jerusalem Post Magazine,* August 7, 1981, p. 9).

The authoritative version claims that stability exists in narration, as if the 1983 interpretation of Masada is the same as the A.D. 73 interpretation. It tells the story as objective truth, tries to stabilize meaning, and uses poetic and inspirational rhetoric. These tellings tend to be monologic—one voice, one story, one truth. Challenging versions present alternative interpretations, locate tellings within history, and claim to be more realistic. They characterize establishment versions as romantic, political, mythical, poetic, and so on (Alter 1973). Alternative versions set the voice of Josephus in his autobiography against the voice of Josephus in his historical writing; they discriminate between archaeological fragments and archaeological inference. Their tellings tend to be deconstructive and delegitimizing. Indeed, in order to place a different interpretation on Masada, they first must attack and unhinge the authoritative account. They do so by explicitly exposing the constructed nature of storytelling. In the process of the attack, critical tellings are metacommunicative, for they openly question the act of narration as they attempt to reconstitute the sites of power.

Although we stress the distinction between authoritative and challenging tellings, they are not two independent stories but rather multiple stances toward a story told in dialogic relationship. The authoritative story as the dominant narrative (E. Bruner 1986b) provides the social matrix for dissident voices and secondary tellings.[4] There may be a struggle over meaning, but one meaning is always taken with reference to the other. And all interpretations derive from the paradoxes, enigmas, and ambiguities inherent in the Masada story.

We need to clarify the distinction between dialogue and that which is dialogic, for the two are not the same. First an example of dialogic exchange in the form of a dialogue: When one of the present authors (Bruner) was at Masada, the tour guide told the standard story, the one from the tourist literature. One member of the tour group, which was made up of professors, asked, "How do we know that Josephus was correct?" The guide replied, "The archaeologists have proved it. Everything that Josephus wrote was absolutely correct." Another question: "Were the zealots like terrorists today?" "No, they were freedom fighters," answered the guide. This interplay, a dialogue between separate speakers, was also dialogic in that the story was being told in response to mildly challenging voices.

Now an example that shows dialogic exchange but not dialogue: Before going to Masada, the same group of professors had visited other tourist sites, including the Museum of the Holocaust, which conveys the message, "Let us never forget," and the Museum of the Diaspora, which demonstrates that many kinds of Jews in the world have survived and preserved Jewish tradition. These metonymic sites on a guided tour stand in a dialogic relationship to each other in that they create a multivocal discourse about the fate of Jews and the alternatives available to them in different historical eras and cultural contexts. No face-to-face dialogue occurs, however. When taken together, Masada, the museums of the Holocaust and the Diaspora, and other sites are more than mere tourist attractions. They form a larger dialogic story that the Israelis choose to tell about themselves.[5]

Dialogic narration is not simply a dialogue or a debate but a polyphonic discourse based on tellings, retellings, or references to important cultural narratives. Any particular telling of the Masada story then resonates against previous and future tellings, against its own past centuries of silence, against metonymic sites, against analogic stories of Jewish resistance (that of the Warsaw Ghetto, for example), and against stories that embody alternatives. The stories of alternatives become particularly fascinating from our theoretical perspective because alternatives to the Masada story almost never appear in the authoritative texts but are present in the consciousness of Israelis and remain an inherent part of the Masada discourse.

At the time of the destruction of Jerusalem in A.D. 70, when the zealots were in the fortress at Masada, Rabbi Johanan ben Zakkai asked the Romans for permission to establish an academy of learning at Yavneh. He realized the helplessness of the struggle against Rome and founded the academy to preserve traditions in the absence of a functioning priesthood in Jerusalem.

Today, ben Zakkai is called the Savior of Judaism, and frequently in Israeli discourse Masada is opposed to Yavneh in a duel set of metaphors for the two types of response they represent. Authoritative tellings take such alternative stories into account but do not necessarily voice them. From an examination of the text itself, one would never appreciate the cultural significance of the alternative stories.

Yet such alternative stories figure implicitly in dialogic narration and become explicit when critical voices tell the story. For example, such accounts claim that the present-day Israelis are not descendants of the zealots who died, but of those, like the people of Yavneh, who made peace with the Romans and lived. The two stories, Masada and Yavneh, serve as alternative guides for Israeli policy and also offer alternative social roles—the warrior versus the scholar. Thus, in their lives as in their stories, the Israelis live out a dialogic reality (Don Handelman 1982, personal communication). Their stories resonate not only against Israeli political options in the Middle East but also, more broadly, against Jewish historical experience throughout the world. In their stories they formulate basic questions about their past and their future.[6] Shall we follow the people of Masada or of Yavneh? Fight or accommodate? Resist militantly and in nationalistic terms or survive culturally by preserving traditions?

Having established more clearly the distinction between dialogue and the dialogic, we note the remarkable dialogic narration in the poem that renewed the Masada story. The famous motto "Masada shall not fall again" derives from the poem "Masada," written by Isaac Lamdan in 1923–1924 after he had migrated to Palestine from postrevolutionary Russia. In the first part of the poem he contrasts four options available to Jews in the bloody aftermath of the Russian Revolution. These options appear dialogically and polyphonically in the poem, for they are spoken by four different, unnamed persons. Each alternative is really the voice of an ideology. The first option is to seek vengeance; the alternative of Masada is only a fiction for this speaker. The second option is to be passive, to wait for the end; the alternative of Masada is only an illusion. The third option is to embrace communism, to join the revolution and make a new world; the alternative of Masada is a "ruined fortress" that failed against Rome in A.D. 73 and will fail again. The fourth option, which Lamdan selects, is Masada, which now represents a commitment to Zionism and to a new life in Palestine.

Lamdan's poem, written long before the Holocaust and the establishment of the state of Israel, places the Masada story among the alternative courses of action available at a particular historical moment. Moreover, because Masada is viewed in a variety of ways—as fiction, illusion, a ruined fortress, the promised land—the poem gives voice to the choices inherent in the Masada story. Yudkin (1971) asks why Lamdan chose to write about Masada, a mass suicide, a "symbol of defeat," to celebrate a new life in Palestine, rather than selecting another story from a more successful period in Jewish history, such as one from the biblical era. In this very question and in the poem itself we see aspects of the intrinsic dialogue—what are the options?—and the experiential dialogue—how does this relate to Lamdan's personal vision and life situation?

In its historical dialogic dimension, the Masada story has furnished multiple uses and many variant readings. The discourse about Masada has evolved over time and has moved in and out of history. After Josephus, with a few scattered exceptions, the story dropped out of Jewish literature for 1,800 years. The Josephus account remained intact, of course, but the story was rarely told by Jews, and the location of the site was forgotten until it was rediscovered in the nineteenth century. The Masada story was resurrected with the rise of Jewish nationalism, with Lamdan's poem, with youth movement expeditions to the site, and later with the official 1963–1965 archaeological excavations. In a sense, the dialogic narration of Masada frames the state; its beginning commemorates the destruction of the old Jewish state in A.D. 73, and its resurrection foreshadows the emergence of the new Jewish state in 1948.

Masada may have reached its peak significance in Israeli society by the 1960s, for some observers now see a shift to the Western Wall as a favored symbol (Shargel 1979). The Western Wall stands as the last remnant of the Temple in Jerusalem, which was destroyed in A.D. 70. It signifies Israel's continuity with the past. In the words of one Israeli, "Even the mighty Romans couldn't knock the Wall down completely." The Western Wall has become associated with Jewish spiritual resistance and with the Israeli claim to the disputed city of Jerusalem. As a site it offers something different from the double-edged sword of Masada: it is a more hopeful and optimistic symbol, better suited to the present government's expansionist claims, which are based on both nationalistic and religious grounds.

We see, then, how a dialogic discourse changes over time with changing circumstances and with the evolving relationship between what stands as authoritative and what stands as challenging. Masada was once the challenging story, opposed to the European narratives. Now that story is under attack.

We might instructively compare Masada with the Alamo to see how such stories change. If the story of Masada has begun to decline, the story of the Alamo has declined so far that it has lost much of its resonance in the contemporary world, primarily because the history of Texas is resolved, at least with regard to Mexican and U.S. boundary claims. When the Roman hegemony was complete, the Masada story was over, only to be resurrected when it was needed in a new historical context. If lasting peace were to be established in the Middle East and no threats to endanger the security of Israel or Diaspora Jews, then Masada might become a historical relic. What keeps the story alive is that the survival of the present state of Israel is not yet resolved. In 1942, after the Japanese attack, a popular song told us to "remember Pearl Harbor as we did the Alamo." In times of upheaval, dialogic stories such as Masada and the Alamo achieve renewed prominence.

Not only do the Masada and Alamo stories possess similar historical dialogic qualities, they also have similar intrinsic features. They cite a defeat in order to incite victory. Masada and the Alamo serve as national shrines and tourist attractions, both marking the locations of heroic last stands. The defenders of Masada and the Alamo died for freedom and for the creation of a memory. The mottos of the two are similar and both are paradoxical. Both were sites of resistance to authority. The zealots were marginal to the Jewish defenders as a whole. William Travis acted against official orders to destroy the Alamo, and the Alamo's defenders were not part of the regular army, Travis being the only person in the fortress who wore an army uniform. In both Masada and the Alamo, marginal revolutionaries became national heroes, but only retrospectively. The defenders of Masada and the Alamo subverted not only the authority of the Romans and the Mexicans, but also the authority of their own governments' resistance to their enemies. Only later did history redeem their subversion.

In both cases ambiguities arise over the authenticity of the "original" event. If you visit the Alamo today, for example, you see a display about the defender James Butler Bonham, including both descriptive information and a picture. Under the picture a small inscription states that this is not really a picture of Bonham but rather a portrait of his nephew, who "resembled" Bonham, presented so viewers may know the "appearance" of the man who died for freedom. The original is known by a representation of a representation. At the Alamo a Bowie knife is prominently displayed, but the curator does not claim that the knife now placed under glass is the original; it is only a reproduction, a representation, to show what the Bowie knife used in the original event looked like—it is a presence to mark an absence. During a visit to the Alamo we also learn that the story of the Alamo comes from Moses Rose, the lone survivor, who escaped from the fort on March 3, 1836. A plaque relates his account of the events of the Alamo defense, but it also explains that this is not really Moses Rose's account. We learn instead that Rose stayed with the Zuber family, to whom he told his story, and that they produced an account that was not published until 1873, a full thirty-seven years later. The plaque is an account of an account of an account, a story without edge or boundary. Shades of Derrida!

Historic last stands offer magnificent examples of dialogic narration because they present problems of authority, closure, and interpretation. The ambiguities and paradoxes inherent in the original serve to make the story versatile and powerful; the story responds to shifting cultural and historical contexts; and meanings reside not in the original but in present tellings. Because the inevitable gap between the event and its tellings becomes so apparent in these narratives, the constructed nature of all narrative processes is exposed.

The Experiential Dialogue

The fluidity of interpretation and the elusive meaning of Masada are attached to the most solid of sites, to an immovable mountain, an eternal fortress. Masada is massive—1,300 feet high and twenty-nine acres in area on top. The attachment of such a mutable story to such an immutable site makes use of the mountain as a device to fix meaning, to lend stability to authority and interpretation. On the other hand, though Masada is a mountain fortress located in the Judean desert, the dialogic narration is used for mobility. Masada becomes all of Israel, A.D. 73 becomes all time, and an ambiguous mass suicide becomes a universal symbol of freedom, events in history thus attaining meaning beyond their context.

At the same time, the context is given meaning by the story. Whereas the names of sites provide coordinates in space, stories about sites provide coordinates in both space and time, giving sites a historical as well as a geographic alignment. Stories about the landscape identify persons and time—and allow the imagination to rest and wander, to become a stage for memory or a bridge for making connections. Still, at Masada, the attachment between story and site gives the legend the permanence of the mountain, as if the Masada story itself were unchanging.

The physical products of archaeological excavations—artifacts, utensils, coins, and other objects that can be seen and displayed—serve a similar function. It is not simply that scientific archaeology proves Josephus correct, as the tour guide claimed, but that the sheer materiality of the results of archaeology confers credibility on the authoritative interpretation, as if the story itself could be touched and handled. In effect, Yadin excavated the site to find the artifacts to authenticate meaning, as if digging in the ground, digging deep, would reveal the true original meaning of Masada. The height of the site lends awe; the depth of the excavation supplies symbolic verification. Both are used to enforce belief, finalize meaning, produce knowledge, and make knowledge itself appear as if it were an artifact.

An El Al airline advertisement touts Masada as "the mountain that will move you." The story is transformative, processual, and moving to the extent that it is experienced by persons traveling processually through the site. How can we experience a story? We can resurrect that buried past by visiting the setting, by seeing artifacts belonging to the characters, and by participating in the discourse. Many tourist-pilgrims who go to Masada climb up the Roman ramp, roam the mountaintop with the zealots, and then take the Israeli cable car down the other side. The story of Masada is thus simulated in the tourist-pilgrim experience, not passively contemplated from afar, and dialogic narration occurs on site. We move through the story as we move through the site, using all channels of communication—we hear the story, read the literature, talk about the story with other tourists, and see the site, photograph it, and touch it. More hardy souls—groups of young people and members of the military—climb or run up the winding snake path to the top of Masada, an exhausting two-hour trek best started in the early hours to avoid the desert heat—and arrive at the summit in time to witness the sunrise. The physical exertion maximizes the experience.

Stories, like ritual, are transformative insofar as they are experienced and performed (Turner 1982). Just as a story is never actualized except in a particular telling, the full power of a story is never felt unless it is realized in an experience. The interpretive process works in a similar way. We are never just the passive recipients of an interpretation that is mechanically transmitted. Interpretation requires that an active self engage in it. At Masada tourists climb the mountain; pilgrims celebrate Hanukkah; members of the Armoured Corps are inducted; adolescents engage in rites of passage; and schoolchildren, office groups, and families enjoy outings together. For religious retreat and camp groups Masada becomes theater, where children and young people take the parts of Romans and zealots and reenact the story.

What is so crucial about the experiential aspect of dialogic narration is that I return home not just with *the* story of Masada but also with *my* experience of Masada. An event is personalized and made relevant to our own life situation. The story of Masada becomes utterly present, fresh, and unique. A historical narrative is transformed into a personal narrative as we gain the right to tell the story. The consequence is to align individual biography with tradition and to incorporate national stories within the self. Meaning is individualized; culture becomes autobiography.

Narration, then, is not just dialogic with reference to texts or storytellers. It is equally dialogic with reference to readers of the texts or listeners to the story. As the story of Masada is told and retold, it reverberates not only through history and society but also through ourselves.

Conclusion

We advance the concept of dialogic narration as a contribution to narrative theory to show that stories are responsive to and interactive with themselves, with communities and their histories, and with listeners' selves. This perspective enables us to examine the narrative process in three domains: intrinsically, as the polyphony of voices and ideologies within a text; historically, as the dialogue between the text and its contexts; and experientially, as the alignment of self and history. We do not view stories as monologic entities reducible to a basic formula, as do some structuralists; instead, we see narration as ever changing, without edge or boundary. However, our readings do not end in the nihilism of radical relativity, with no meaning possible; rather, we see any given telling as situated in the real world, in a particular context, told in a voice that takes account of other voices by suppressing, denying, acknowledging, or responding to them. Our perspective does not have an a priori conception of privileged referents—Israel as Masada; youth as zealots; resistance as doom or as Israeli indomitability. Rather, we let indigenous voices tell us what is important and how meanings are chosen and how they compete. We focus on narration as a process, always in production, always in dialogic interplay, emergent and indeterminate, which exists in and helps to create a social world of virtuality, potentiality, and inquiry.

PART THREE Tales from the Field

7

The Balinese Borderzone

INTERNATIONAL TOURISM is an exchange system of vast proportions, one characterized by a transfer of images, signs, symbols, power, money, goods, people, and services (Lanfant 1989; Smith 1977/1989). The tourism industry is aggressive in ever seeking new attractions for its clients, so there are tours not only to Bali, which has been a tourist destination for over seventy years,[1] but also to places that formerly were difficult to access, such as Kalimantan, New Guinea, the Amazon, and even the South Pole. Tourism has no respect for national boundaries, except in those few countries that for one reason or another restrict tourism (e.g., Myanmar, Albania, Bhutan). Wherever ethnographers go or have gone, tourists have already been or are sure to follow. And wherever tourism establishes itself, our traditional anthropological subject matter, the peoples and cultures of the world, becomes commercialized, marketed, and sold to an eager audience of international tourists.

International mass tourism has precipitated one of the largest population movements of all time, in which literally millions of temporary travelers from the industrialized nations seek in the margins of the Third World a figment of their imagination—the exotic, the erotic, the happy savage. Bali, for example, is depicted in the tourist literature as a tropical paradise of haunting beauty, an unspoiled beach, a place of mystery and enchantment, an exotic South Seas island of dreams, where the people live untouched by civilization, close to nature, with a culture that is artistic, static, harmonious, and well integrated.[2] Here is the trope of the vanishing primitive, the pastoral allegory, the quest for origins (Clifford 1986; E. Bruner 1993a). This romantic characterization not only suppresses the true conditions of Balinese life; it also depicts a culture that never existed (Boon 1977, 1990; Picard 1992; Vickers 1989). The excesses of the descriptions of Bali and many other Third World tourist sites echo Orientalist discourse and anthropological monographs based on a hypothetical ethnographic present. Indeed, the "happy primitive" image was a means of colonial control, one that was in part constructed by ethnography itself.

Tourism occurs in a borderzone physically located in an ever-shifting strip or border on the edges of Third World destination countries. This border is not natural; it is not just there, waiting for the tourists to discover it, for all touristic borderzones are constructed. Most tourists, and certainly those on group tours, do not just visit a country, they visit selected tourist destinations located within a borderzone. The concept of borderzones used in this chapter differs from the usage of Gloria Anzaldúa (1987), Guillermo Gómez-Peña (1993, 1996), Emily Hicks (1991), and Coco Fusco (1989), who theorize on the basis of the fixed U.S.-Mexican border, which is a site of migration between two national states. Touristic borderzones are fluid, they may shift over time, and almost by definition there are no immigrant tourists, but rather a recurring wave of temporary travelers, an ever-changing moving population.

The tourists are always present. They are always "there," but are always in motion, and they change constantly. The category and the presence of tourists are permanent, but the actual individuals come and go, flowing across the border like each new freshman class in college, from an ever-renewing source. The native or resident population is more or less permanent, but as I visualize the touristic border, the natives have to break out of their normal routines to meet the tourists: to dance for them, to sell them souvenirs, or to display themselves and their cultures for the tourists' gaze and for sale. The touristic borderzone is like an empty stage waiting for performance time; this is so for both the audience of tourists and for the native performers. The natives too, then, move in and out of the touristic borderzone. But the perceptions of the two groups are not the same, because what for the tourists is a zone of leisure and exoticization, for the natives is a site of work and cash income.

What is advertised as unspoiled and undiscovered in the touristic borderzone has actually been carefully manufactured and sold. The Balinese and other Third World peoples recognize the touristic thirst for the exotic and the unpolluted, so they present themselves and their cultures in a way that conforms to the tourists' image of them. From the outside tourists come to see the primitives; from the inside—from the native perspective—tourism is a route to economic development and a means of livelihood (Lanfant, Allcock, and E. Bruner 1995). The predicament is that the more modern the locals, the less interesting they are to Occidental tourists, and the less they can derive income from tourism. Intellectuals and artists like Anzaldúa and Gómez-Peña theorize about the U.S.-Mexican border, but the situation is very different for those who are the object of the tourist gaze in the underdeveloped Third World, for if peoples like the Balinese step out of their assigned roles in exotica, they may lose their major source of income. What most native peoples in this situation do is to collaborate in a touristic coproduction; it is a strategic essentialism. Tourism is not a passive agent either, but must also collaborate with the locals and accommodate to the local situation.

Renato Rosaldo writes that "borderlands should be regarded not as analytically empty transitional zones but as sites of creative cultural production" (1989, 208)—and, I would add, as sites of struggle. The touristic borderzone is a creative space, a site for the invention of culture on a massive scale. It is a festive, liberated zone, one that anthropology should investigate, not denigrate. To ask how the culture presented for tourists compares with the culture we ethnographers have traditionally studied is to ask the wrong question, one that leads to a theoretical dead end in the never-never land of nostalgia. The tourists are the ones who desire the uncontaminated past,[3] the so-called pure culture, so versions of that hypothetical past are invented and presented for tourist consumption. In this volume I collect some of my studies of the recent construction of "authentic" culture for a tourist audience; I do not intellectualize that construction of culture or judge it or criticize it as yet another Derridian instance of lost origins. Tourists do not travel to experience the new postcolonial[4] subject, the emerging nation in the process of economic development; they yearn for the story of the colonial past.

From the perspective of the geographies of identity the Western elite travel to the margins of the Third World, to the borderzone between their civilized selves and the exotic Other, in order to explore a fantasyland of the Western imaginary. Curiously, the Other, the postcolonial subject, has already traveled in the opposite direction, for the Jamaican, the Pakistani, the Malay, the Algerian is already established in the centers of Western power (Buck-Morss 1987). Paradoxically, then, the Western elite spend thousands of dollars and travel thousands of miles to find what they already have.

Many Western peoples of all social classes make a desperate effort not to "see" the Third World presence in their midst, for they segregate themselves in safe and exclusive neighborhoods or move to the suburbs if they can afford to do so or insulate themselves by alternative means. When they do see the Third World people who surround them, it is often with a very selective vision emphasizing poverty, drugs, crime, and gangs to the neglect of those Others who have become middle class; or the Others who are performers, entertainers, athletes, servants, or small-scale entrepreneurs. Western people enjoy ethnic restaurants and performances as long as they are in their proper space and place.

Although the elite may try to avoid the Other in First World cities, making a conscious attempt to overlook them or not to see them—an absence of sight—they go to the touristic borderzones with the specific objective of looking, for in tourism there is voyeurism, an overabundance of seeing. The Other in *our* geography is a source of disgust; the Other in *their* geography is a source of pleasure. In *our* place the Other is pollution; in *their* place the Other is romantic, beautiful, and exotic. In *our* geography the Western elite pay not to see the Other; in *their* geography, the Western elite pay for the privilege of viewing and photographing. There is a racialization at home and a primitivization over there in exotica.

I have consciously exaggerated the differences for emphasis, but I do understand that First and Third World people intermingle and circulate in each other's spaces and I do understand that there is upward mobility. For a large segment of the Western elite, however, the essential paradox remains—in First World cities the Other is a social problem; in Third World places the Other is an object of desire. At home the industrialized peoples of the First World avoid the very peoples they pay enormous sums to see and photograph in Africa or Indonesia. This is actually an old phenomenon, at least a century old in the United States, where Native Americans on their reservations become exoticized and romanticized, whereas the very same people as urban neighbors are often considered drunks and undesirables.

In Third World space, the Other becomes domesticated; reworked for the tourists; frozen in time or out of time, in past time or no time; performing a Western version of their culture essentially as entertainers. In First World space the Other is dangerous, associated with pathology and violence, bad neighborhoods and crime. Western people fail to see the joy and beauty of the Other in First World space, just as they fail to see the poverty and suffering of the Other in Third World space.

For the Western tourist the Orientalist stereotype is dominant in Third World space, and tourists go there to collect souvenirs and photographs to show to their friends at home. They go for adventure, for experience, for status, for education, and to explore and collect the image of the exotic Other. But the Other is already here at home, in the flesh, outside on the street, in a neighborhood across town. Tourists bring back a disembodied, decontextualized, sanitized, hypothetical Other, one they can possess and control through the stories they tell about how the souvenirs were purchased and the photographs taken. Tourists place the postcolonial subject in a new narrative frame, in stories in which the tourists become the traveling heroes and the

Other becomes the object of their search. Narrative mastery is the mechanism by which to fix meaning, to encapsulate and control the Other, to stop motion and time, to exert power.

Approach

This chapter explores cultural production in the touristic borderzone, to learn how the Balinese and other Indonesian peoples respond to tourism, and to study how American tourists experience Indonesia. James Clifford asks the right questions, "How do different populations, classes, and genders travel? What kinds of knowledges, stories, and theories do they produce? A crucial research agenda opens up" (1989, 183).

In order to investigate these matters, as I explain in the introduction, I decided to become a guide on a tour of Indonesia, primarily for methodological reasons (Cohen 1985a). Tour groups assemble in their area of origin—in, say, San Francisco or London. They travel together, see the sights together, and eat their meals together, becoming a tightly knit unit, then disband at the end of the trip. It is thus difficult to penetrate a tour group from the outside at a midpoint in its voyage. Since the tour group is a traveling social unit, I felt that the best way to study tourism would be to travel with a group and to share the adventures of the common journey. As a guide I would be an insider, and I would be there to observe and record the tourists' reactions, behaviors, and interpretations. I wanted to learn whether tourists buy into the hyperbole of tourist advertising; whether they play at reality (Cohen 1985b); and whether they really are on a quest for authenticity, as Dean MacCannell (1976) claims, or have given up the quest and become posttourists (Urry 1990).

The agency that hired me as a tour guide advertised that their tours were led by "noted scholars," and it distributed a reading list to group members in advance of each trip. The front page of the tourist brochure for Indonesia presented a biographical sketch that included my academic qualifications, stressing that I was an anthropology professor who had conducted three years of fieldwork in Indonesia and spoke the language. This was a tour with a tour guide professor and tourist students, ostensibly there to learn. University alumni associations and museums often organize such tours with faculty lecturers; indeed, the frequency of alumni tours is growing. It might be said, then, that tourism is co-opting ethnography. Many anthropologists have led such tours, but few mention it and even fewer write about it or incorporate the experience into their academic discourse.

A sociological profile of the travelers on the Indonesia tours I guided shows that they were clearly older and more affluent than most tourists. Almost half were retired, and many were divorced or widowed women traveling alone. All except one had a college education, everyone had taken previous tours, and most had careers in business or the professions. There were physicians, executives, a lawyer, an engineer, and two professors. If, as MacCannell (1976) says, tourists are alienated beings who lead such shallow lives that they have to seek authenticity elsewhere, one would never know it from these tourists. Successful and affluent persons who were quite secure about their identity, they were traveling at a stage in their lives when they had the leisure and the income to do so. Tourism for them was consumption, and a tour of Indonesia was an expensive status marker (Bourdieu 1984).

An Incident in Bali

In addition to taking the tour group to the standard *barong* and *kecak* dances that are on all the tourist itineraries, I had arranged for them to go to an *odalan,* or temple festival, a ceremony that the Balinese enact for themselves.[5] These events are not ordinarily on the tour schedule, for one is never entirely sure when they will begin, so the local tour agencies are reluctant to include them. I, however, had lived near the temple in the village of Batuan a few years previously and knew the area. We arrived at the temple at about 4:00 p.m. The tourists, dressed in the appropriate ceremonial sash, sat together in a group along the temple wall and observed the scene, as I had instructed them to do. The Balinese do not appear to object to the presence of tourists at their temple ceremonies as long as they are respectfully attired and well behaved. We seemed to be the only tourists there except for one couple, dressed very casually, who stood off by themselves.

As the crystal sounds of the gamelan music pervaded the early evening glow, I looked across the temple compound and saw Hildred Geertz, the personification of Balinese ethnography, resplendent in full ceremonial Balinese dress (figs. 27 and 28).[6] I knew that Hilly was doing research in Batuan, for I had written to her in advance, informing her that after my work with the tour group was completed I intended to return to Bali, and that I looked forward to visiting with her at that time. Although I realized that Hilly was working in the area, I was surprised to see her at this festival.

I crossed the compound to say hello to Hilly, whom I had known for over thirty years, and her response was an astonished "I didn't expect you until next month." I replied that indeed I was returning the following month, and I offered to introduce her to the tour group. She responded, "Don't introduce me to those tourists, but after your tour is over, be sure to come to my house."[7] As Hilly later recalled the incident, she was "rather busy and didn't want to get involved in polite conversation with people I didn't know" (letter, August 5, 1991). As I interpreted the event, Hilly had welcomed Ed

27. The gamelan orchestra at the temple festival in Batuan, with Hildred Geertz seated across the compound, right rear

28. Hildred Geertz at the Bautan festival

Bruner, ethnographer, but had chosen to keep her distance from Ed Bruner, tour guide. After an awkward moment I went back across the compound to sit with the tour group. To ethnography, tourism is indeed like an illegitimate child that one chooses not to recognize.

Unexpectedly, Hilly came over to our group after a brief interval and asked if we would like to visit the studio of a nearby Balinese artist. I introduced everyone, and the tourists readily agreed. On the way to the artist's house, I asked Hilly why she had changed her mind. She replied that she was working on the life history of Ida Bagus Madé Togog, a Balinese painter, then an old man (and since deceased), who had been an artistic consultant for Gregory Bateson in the 1930s (fig. 29). Possibly Togog could sell one of his paintings to the tourists, she explained, and her reason for escorting us was to help the painter, not the tourists. The tourists didn't buy any of his paintings, but I did: a picture of the *barong* dance, which I have on the wall in my bedroom. It was Togog who had suggested to Hilly that she should bring her "friends" to buy his pictures. She wrote, "I had already brought a California artist friend, a New York psychiatrist, several anthropologists, an Australian historian, an American composer, and a whole bunch of Harvard students, just to mention a few" (letter, August 5, 1991).

As we walked to Togog's house, I could not help reflecting that here was I, ethnographer qua tour guide, with a group of tourists, and all of us being guided by Hildred Geertz, a tour guide guiding a tour guide, to the home of a Balinese artist who in his youth had himself been involved with tourism—with Gregory Bateson and the production of tourist art—and who now in his later years was even more involved with tourism. Togog had been Bateson's research consultant, but in a sense Bateson had been Togog's tourist. While we walked to the painter's studio, Hilly pointed to the house that Gregory Bateson and Margaret Mead had occupied during their research in Batuan in the 1930s, and all of us, the tourists and I, stopped to take pictures.

This scene, I said to myself, is paradigmatic: Ed Bruner's version of a Balinese cockfight, a scene to be commemorated, a postmodern pastiche, a meeting of the First and the Third Worlds in the postcolonial borderzone, a site of in-betweenness, of seepage along the borders. In this event, how does one distinguish between ethnography and tourism, between the center and the periphery, between the authentic and the inauthentic? These faded binaries seem so dated, no longer relevant to the work that ethnographers are actually doing in the field.

What arises in ethnography enters into tourism, but the reverse is also true; what arises in tourism enters into and is legitimated by ethnography (Picard 1992; Vickers 1989). Balinese do paint and dance for tourists, but at a later date many of these creative expressions enter into Balinese social and cultural life. In Batuan in the 1970s, for example, a cultural performance called the frog dance was devised for tourists. At the time of its creation, there was no "authentic" counterpart of the dance located elsewhere in Balinese culture; the dance was a commercial invention specifically designed for a tourist audience. It was an example of creative cultural production in the borderzone. Over a decade later, while I was living in Batuan in the 1980s, the organizers of a Balinese wedding asked a dance troupe to perform the frog dance at their wedding. What began in tourism had entered Balinese ritual, and might eventually be included in an ethnographic description of the culture. Further, dance dramas and other art forms constructed by Westerners have been adopted by the Balinese as their own and have been incorporated into their artistic repertoire. When President Ronald Reagan visited Bali in 1986, a *kecak* dance, one created by the German artist Walter Spies and some Balinese dancers in the 1930s, was selected as emblematic of Bali and was performed in Reagan's honor.

Balinese culture is performed worldwide, not just on the island of Bali. Balinese dance dramas are exported to the concert halls of Sydney, Paris, and New York and have become part of the international art world. As early as

29. Ida Bagus Madé Togog in his home studio with the painting of the *barong* purchased by the author

1931, a *barong* dance was performed at the Colonial Exhibition in Paris and was probably seen by Antonin Artaud there (Picard 1990, 58). If the Balinese perform at a temple, it is traditional culture and is described in ethnography; at a hotel, it is tourism; and on a concert stage, it is art, according to our Western categories.

From the Balinese perspective, however, these are not closed systems. The Balinese, of course, know whether they are performing for tourists, for themselves, or for the gods. They are very aware of the differences between audiences, and indeed they have public debates about the impact of tourism on their culture. The Balinese try to keep some sacred performances exclusively for themselves, but their language does not distinguish between sacred and profane, and in practice, over time, there is slippage.[8] Ethnography, tourism, and art as discourse and practice are porous at the borders, and cultural content flows from one arena to the other, sometimes in profound though subtle ways. Cultural innovation that arises in the borderzone as a creative production for tourists, what anthropologists formerly called "inauthentic" culture, eventually becomes part of Balinese ritual and may subsequently be studied by ethnographers as "authentic" culture.

For example, the *barong* and *rangda* performances involving trance (figs. 30 and 31) fascinated early Western visitors and residents more than any other Balinese dance form (Bandem and de Boer 1981, 148). Vicki Baum, in her novel *A Tale from Bali,* explicitly documents this Western infatuation with the *barong* (1937, 282). The gifted group of intellectuals and artists who lived in Bali in the 1930s, including Spies, Miguel Covarrubias, Jane Belo, Colin McPhee, Bateson, and Mead, were captivated with the *barong* and, in collaboration with the Balinese, commissioned new forms of the *barong* dance. The famous 1937 Bateson-Mead film, *Trance and Dance in Bali,* which is usually regarded as an early photographic record of a Balinese ritual, was actually a film of a tourist performance for foreigners commissioned and paid for by Bateson and Mead. As Ira Jacknis (1988, 167–68) and Belo (1960, 97–98, 124–27) document, the *barong* ritual filmed by Bateson and Mead was not ancient but had been created recently during the period of their fieldwork, and the story performed had been changed from the *Calon Arang* to the less dangerous *Kunti Sraya,* which, after various transformations since the 1930s, is being performed for tourists to this day.[9] Further, Bateson and Mead changed the dance for the film by having women rather than men hold the krisses, and they commissioned the dance to be performed during the day, when the light was good for photography, rather than having the performance in the evening.

The interest of these influential foreigners enhanced the prominence of the *barong* performances in Balinese life to such an extent that the *barong* has become the preeminent tourist performance and is now paradigmatic of Bali in Western discourse (Vickers 1989). The dance is so popular that it is performed for tourists by three different troupes simultaneously every day in the village of Batubulan and occasionally by dance troupes in other places as well (e.g., at Singapadu). The *barong* performance that was shaped by foreign fascination in the 1930s entered ethnographic discourse most prominently in the 1960s, in Clifford Geertz's influential "Religion as a Cultural System" (1966), in which he takes the *barong* and the *rangda* as illustrative of his generalizations about religion. Balinese culture, after all, has been shaped for decades by performances for foreigners, so it is not unexpected that the *barong* dance that an earlier generation of ethnographers helped to construct is described by a more recent ethnographer as the incarnation of "the Balinese version of the comic spirit" (C. Geertz 1973, 118) and as emblematic of Balinese religion. Even the Balinese themselves are not entirely sure what is "authentic" and what is touristic, and such scholars as Picard (1992) doubt that such a distinction makes any sense to the Balinese. To overstate the case for emphasis, the Balinese became what ethnographers studied in that Western interest in the *barong* led the Balinese to modify their culture so that the *barong* became more prominent in their performances.[10]

30. The *barong,* from a tourist performance by the Denjalan group at Batubulan

31. *Rangda,* the witch, from the Denjalan Batubulan performance

The Tourist Response

To return to the meeting between the tour group and Hildred Geertz, I ask, How did the tourists react to this incident in Bali? One woman said it was "thrilling," and another that it was the high point of the Indonesia trip. I eventually saw color slide shows presented at home in the United States by two tourist families, and both included photographs of the Bateson-Mead house, which in itself is not very striking. Slide shows are an occasion for a narrative summary of the tour, a means to personalize a group experience, and an opportunity to tell stories of travel and adventure. From the perspective of these tourists, the presence of Gregory Bateson and Margaret Mead, and of Ed Bruner and Hildred Geertz—collectively, to them, the epitome of scientific authority—gave them the validation that they, although mere tourists, were in the presence of professors who knew the "real" Bali.

In a sense, the tour agency's inclusion of an academic lecturer is a marketing ploy to have a built-in authenticator; thus I, and also Hilly, had become, like the Balinese, tourist objects (Morris 1995). Complexity is multiplied in a many-layered reflexive voyeurism, in a thick touristic description: the tourists were looking at the Balinese, the ethnographers were looking at the Balinese as well as the tourists; the tourists were looking at the ethnographers; and of course the Balinese were looking at everyone. One ethnographer, Bruner, was studying the other ethnographer, Hilly, who later, after she had read a draft of this paper, stated, "This is the first time I've ever been an ethnographic object." The tourists were also looking at the other tourists because the tour group for them was their basic social unit, the group they traveled with and discussed the sights with on a daily basis. I want to emphasize here not just the voyeurism, the tourist gaze, but also that all parties—the painter Togog, the ethnographer Geertz, the tour guide Bruner, and the tourists—were not just passive beings, looking or being looked at, but also were active selves interpreting their worlds.

Balinese painting is a flourishing art form on the island. It usually depicts scenes of Balinese life, ritual, and sacred beings, and one genre includes tourists. I offer as an example a portion of a painting by I Wayan Bendi of Batuan (fig. 32) that is doubly reflexive. The artist explained to me that the Balinese in the foreground doing the painting is himself, I Wayan Bendi. He is surrounded by scenes from Balinese daily life, including three tourists with cameras. The tourists are photographing the artist who is painting the tourists, indicating the degree to which tourism has become embedded in Balinese culture, as well as the ironic reflexivity of this artist.

I later learned that Hilly had selected Batuan as the site of her research precisely because the Balinese craft of painting for tourists had begun there in

32. Painting of Balinese life by the artist I Wayan Bendi, showing tourists

the 1930s (H. Geertz 1994). She was as much involved in the study of tourism and the borderzone as I was, and we had a similar postmodern perspective. She wrote to me in her letter of August 5, 1991:

> I was by no means "embarrassed" by the entry of your tourists into my Balinese world, for they were, and had been for some years, a common part of it. There was hardly a day in Batuan when foreigners had not been around. I had long ago clarified to myself the presence of "other tourists" as a part of my own research or, at least, had learned to live with it. The Balinese never let me forget that I was just one more tourist among the others.

Hilly graciously gave me permission to write about our meeting in Bali, although she felt uncomfortable that she did not have more of an active voice in the presentation of her own views.

Between Tourism and Ethnography

I found aspects of the tour guide role uncomfortable and ambiguous. As an ethnographer my aim was to study how the tourists experienced the sites, but as guide my assignment was to structure that experience through my commentary. My talk mediated their experience, so in a sense I found myself studying myself. I felt like the Kaluli shamans who create the meaning they discover (Schieffelin 1992) as I constructed for the tourists the meaning of the sites and then studied that meaning as if I had discovered it. Ernst Cassirer has noted that when we think we are exploring reality we are merely engaging in a dialogue with our own symbolic systems (see E. Bruner 1986b, 150).

"Tourist" and "ethnographer" are roles that one plays and manipulates. At times, when our tour group approached a new site, the Indonesians would behave toward me as if I were another tourist, and I could rupture that attribution by speaking the Indonesian language, which in effect said, "Don't confuse me with these tourists," or I could choose to remain silent and to accept the designation. At other times, by emphasizing my role as a working tour guide, I could identify with the Indonesian performers and locals, saying, in effect, that we are in the same situation, catering to tourists, who are our source of income. I stressed to the Indonesians that we were on the same side, as it were, in opposition to the tourists, but I was never sure whether the Indonesians accepted this alignment.

More disturbing was that during the journey I would slip back and forth between the touristic and the ethnographic, for I could not always keep them straight. I truly enjoyed these hardy tourists, who were, like me, older, college-educated, and of either professional or business background. At times I felt myself becoming a tourist, gaping in awe at Borobudur, rushing from the bus to take photographs, enthralled by breathtaking scenery in Sulawesi, luxuriating in the hot showers but complaining about the meals at the hotel in the evening. At other times I felt myself to be a straight ethnographer, making detailed observations of the tourists' behavior, dissecting their conversations, and writing my field notes late into the night. Balinese *barong* performers wear masks, but so do ethnographers.

As a tour guide I felt that what tourism needed was not another sojourn among the exotic savages of the mysterious East or more clichés and stereotypes, so I tried to demystify traditional tourism, to deconstruct the romantic images of the Indonesians, and to reveal the mechanisms of production of tourist performances. But the more I did so, paradoxically, the more I contributed to traditional touristic romanticism. For the tourists I became the heroic ethnographer, a regular Indiana Jones, Kurtz penetrating the heart of darkness, the true interpreter of the sites and enactments on the tourist itinerary. The tourists were proud that their tour had its own authentic ethnographer as tour guide, in contrast to those other, more touristy tours, the superficial ones that didn't have their own professor as a lecturer. In the eyes of the tourists, the more I revealed the artificiality of the constructed tour, the more I became the authentic ethnographer. I found myself in the position of authenticating the experience for the tourists at the same time I was deconstructing the Balinese cultural performances.

Authenticity and Verisimilitude

In Yogyakarta, the heart of central Javanese culture, the tour agency scheduled a supper and performance at the home of Princess Hadinegoro, a relative of the sultan. We arrived in the early evening, were the only tourists there, and were served drinks in the living room of the home. We then moved to the dining room, were seated at tables, and enjoyed a buffet supper while a gamelan orchestra played in the courtyard. After supper we moved to the courtyard and watched a Ramayana ballet, a performance of the old Hindu epic (fig. 33). The performers were in colorful costumes, their bodily

33. The Ramayana performance at the home of Princess Hadinegoro

movements were slow and controlled, and the presence of children peering over the courtyard wall added to the ambiance of the evening.

Afterward, when I asked whether they had enjoyed the event, the tourists replied that it was absolutely lovely. I then explained that the invitation to the home of the Javanese princess was a gimmick because it created the impression that they were guests which disguised the commercial nature of the attraction. Actually they were paying customers who had, in effect, gone to a restaurant. The princess ran a business to produce income, and she had tour groups to her home an average of twenty days a month. Further, I explained, although the Ramayana ballet was presented as if it were an ancient classical dance, this was not the case. The ballet is not a Javanese genre, and the Ramayana ballet was created in 1961 as a performance for tourists (Seminar Sendra Tari Ramayana Nasional, 1970) with support from the central Indonesian government of President Sukarno.[11]

The Javanese Ramayana, like the Balinese frog dance, is an example of new cultural production in the borderzone. At the time of its construction, it was somewhat of a theatrical event in Java because it brought together the best of the performing artists from Solo and Yogya and from two distinct court traditions and because the ballet was performed at the Prambanan temple.[12] As a dance for tourists, the Ramayana at the time of its construction did not use the Javanese language because foreigners could not understand it; the pace was made fast and the length short to hold interest; and the gestures were exaggerated to communicate a story line across wide cultural chasms. Since then the artistic standards have further declined and the ballet has been shortened and adapted to a number of tourist settings. Relative to other Javanese dances, the Ramayana was reduced and simplified so that it could be incorporated more readily into a Western system of meaning. In a sense, I told the tourists, the Ramayana is a caricature of a Javanese dance, a postmodern construction in the borderzone, an ancient Hindu epic reworked for foreign consumption.[13]

"Well," I asked the tourists, "what do you think of the evening now, knowing that the setting and the dance were not as authentic as you had assumed?" All of them responded that nothing I had said detracted from their enjoyment of the evening, that it was still absolutely lovely! "What did you like?" I asked. They replied that it was a good show, that they were the only persons present, that it was stimulating being in an Indonesian home and seeing all the old Dutch and Javanese pictures and memorabilia, that the food was fine, and that the performers were superb.

After this discussion, the performers, dressed in their street clothes, came out to meet the tourists as I had requested. We learned that the male lead, a history major at Gajah Mada University, had joined the troupe as a part-time job. His wife of six months was a student at the dance academy of the university, and she hoped to become a professional dancer. The tourists asked questions about the dance and contemporary life, I translated, and the session ended with the taking of group photographs. My idea was to remove the performers from roles in the timeless Hindu past and to show them as modern Indonesians who could interact with the tourists on a more direct and personal basis.

After leaving Java we flew to Bali to stay at the Bali Hyatt Hotel, a large resort complex on the beach in Sanur that caters primarily to tour groups. The next evening the hotel advertised a rijsttafel dinner with a performance of the Ramayana ballet at a cost of twenty dollars per person plus service fees. I suggested that our group attend as it was an opportunity to see the same performance in two settings on two different islands. I explained that following the creation of the Ramayana ballet, the Balinese had copied the dance drama in 1962 and had adapted it to their own culture. After the dance I again asked the tourists how they had enjoyed the evening. One replied that it was too much like Honolulu, then another corrected her and said it was more like Miami Beach. Everyone shared this negative view, and I inquired why. The answer was that they were in a room with three or four hundred other tourists, that one Hyatt hotel is like any other, that it was too crowded, that the buffet lines were too long, that there was no feeling of intimacy, and that they were too far from the performers to take good photographs. "But," I protested, "this is a Balinese version of the same Ramayana that you enjoyed so much in Yogya. The performers are a diverse group put together by a local producer, but they are good dancers, and the gamelan orchestra is hired as a troupe from one of the villages, so it is the same group that you might hear performing in a temple festival." Despite my arguments, they did not like the performance of the Ramayana ballet at the Bali Hyatt.

The next day in Bali was *Nyepi,* the one day in the calendrical cycle when all activity stops on the island, and the tourists could not leave the hotel. I felt it was an appropriate time for some extended discussion with the tourists, so I booked a seminar room for our meeting. Our topic was authenticity, an issue we had discussed in Java, and I rather liked the idea of holding a seminar on authenticity at the Bali Hyatt Hotel, a world-class hotbed of international tourism.

When I probed further into the differences between the Javanese and the Balinese versions of the Ramayana, it was apparent that for the tourists the context was the crucial variable: the atmosphere of a home for just our group as opposed to that of a tourist hotel with many groups. In Java the audience, the gamelan orchestra, and the performers were situated at the same level, whereas in Bali there was an elaborate raised stage for the performers and another separate area for the orchestra. There was even a raised platform labeled "photo point," where the tourists could go to take pictures. Both the performances were commercial, but in the first the commercial dimension was disguised, whereas in the second it was transparent.[14]

These upscale tourists did not object to the fact that a performance was constructed for tourists, but they demanded that it be a good performance—and they had their aesthetic standards. They were not romantics. They were concerned with the artfulness of staged theatricality, not with issues of authenticity. They said that authenticity might be an issue in the literature on tourism, but it was not an important issue for them. They pointed out that while the Ramayana ballet might be recent, it was still Indonesian. They did recognize that they might be responding to the "authenticity" of the setting, for the differences in the two performance contexts were striking. They stated that the Javanese setting was more exclusive, more high-class, held in the home of Javanese royalty; and these tourists were, after all, trying to secure an exclusive tourist experience, of which I was a part. But the Javanese version was also a better show than the Balinese one. The tourists appreciated my historical perspective on the dance and my data on the processes of its production, but my information did not detract from their enjoyment of memories of the evening on Java. I understood their position, and I believe they accurately characterized the views of many other tourists.

We had seen a Balinese *barong* trance performance by the Denjalan group at Batubulan the previous day, and it did not take much to realize that it was a dance for tourists, not Balinese. After all, the performance began at precisely 9:00 a.m. each day; only tourists and no Balinese were in the audience; admission was charged and souvenirs sold; and the performance lasted for precisely one hour, after which everyone returned to the tour buses. I said to the tourists, however, that the Denjalan group had two *barongs,* one of which was a consecrated *barong* with *sakti* (power); that the man in white sprinkling holy water on the stage, playing the part of a Balinese priest, was a Balinese priest, not an actor, and that the water he sprinkled was holy; that they sacrificed a chicken on stage as an offering; that the performers recited mantras before the performance; and that the dancers reported that sometimes they did go into trance. For the Balinese the gods are always present. I agreed with the tour group, however, that this was a dance staged for tourists. The tourists, in turn, accepted what was presented to them and had no inclination to look beyond the staged authenticity of the Denjalan performance for the "real" *barong.*

The seminar convinced me that the basic metaphor of tourism is theater and that tourists enter into a willing suspension of disbelief. The key issue for students of tourism, then, becomes the mechanisms by which a tourist production is made convincing and believable to the tourists, which in effect collapses the problem of authenticity into the problem of verisimilitude (Cohen 1988; chapter 5). What makes a theatrical or tourist production credible? This is the old anthropological question of how people come to believe in their culture (Crapanzano 1986).

It is not just that the Ramayana in Java had fewer tourists and the Ramayana in Bali had more tourists and was more touristy, which is the dimension the tourism literature has emphasized. When there are fewer tourists, it is easier to suspend disbelief, to lose oneself in the event or site, or to imagine oneself as an adventurer or explorer in a distant land. The performance becomes more believable. Nor is it a question of the authenticity of a performance, which implies the presence of another performance that is more genuine or truer to life. The Ramayana ballet is not a simulacrum; it has no counterpart elsewhere in the culture. Even if there were an original, it would not be of primary concern to the tourists. The problem of focusing so narrowly on the quest for authenticity is that one is always looking elsewhere, over the shoulder or around the bend, which prevents one from taking the Ramayana and the *barong* as serious performances that deserve to be studied in their own right.[15]

Clearly what MacCannell wrote in 1976 in his classic book about touristic authenticity was not relevant for the tour groups I took to Indonesia, but his 1990 comments on the ex-primitives and the postmodern tourists staging the touristic enterprise as a coproduction, as a kind of social contract, seems very provocative, as do Erik Cohen's (1985b) view of tourists' playful self-deception and John Urry's (1990) notion of the posttourist. The question emerges of whether the recent writings of MacCannell, Cohen, and Urry seem relevant because the world has changed or because for the first time scholars are beginning to understand touristic phenomena. The results of my studies of Indonesian tourism suggest that the issue of authenticity has been overdone in the tourism literature, that tourists are not primarily concerned with authenticity, and that it would be more productive to pursue the metaphors of theater and of borderzones than to study touristic verisimilitude.

Conclusion

With this essay I have tried to shed some light on what Taussig calls the epistemic murk of the anthropological predicament and what Hildred Geertz calls the great semiological swamp that we all live within. Postmodern complexities occur not only in the centers of Western power but also in postcolonial borderzones on the periphery, in what used to be the pure, authentic preserve of ethnographic science. Indeed, the border between ethnography and tourism is clouded, porous, and political. Tourism not only shapes Balinese culture but is now also part of Balinese culture; it could even be said that tourism is Balinese culture (Errington and Gewertz 1989; Picard 1992). Balinese born since the 1930s have lived their entire lives as tourist objects, and in some areas, such as Batuan, any adequate ethnographic account of Balinese economy or ritual would have to take account of tourism.

Balinese performances are exported to the centers of Western power, and they are also enacted every day in a shifting touristic borderzone on the edge of the Third World, a zone of interaction among natives, tourists, and ethnographers. Tour agents are always looking for new products to present to their clients, for new temples or new islands to discover and to "touristify." The Balinese, the Javanese, and other Indonesian peoples in the tourist zone are themselves always experimenting, creating, and playing with new expressive rituals, constantly devising new performances for the tourists. And the new Indonesian culture does not remain forever fixed in the zone in which it was created. Old ceremonial forms are reworked for tourists, culture produced for tourists enters Balinese ritual, what arises in tourism or ritual may be exported to the concert stages of the West for an international audience, and what was at one historical period touristic at a later period becomes ethnographic.

Anthropology has always recognized that peoples and cultures move, for concepts such as diffusion and migration have had deep roots in the discipline from the beginning, but we may not yet have taken account of the particular nature and the full extent of the movement of peoples and cultures in the postmodern world. The old anthropological metaphor of place, where one culture belongs to one people who are situated in one locality, is being challenged by the new metaphors of diaspora, travel, tourism, and borderzones (Appadurai 1988; Clifford 1989). I see the challenge as a continuation of the emphasis on practice, performance, movement, and process that has become so prominent in anthropology since the 1960s (Ortner 1984), and I welcome it. It makes ethnography more dynamic, more exciting.

8

Taman Mini
Self-Constructions in an Ethnic Theme Park in Indonesia

ANY GIVEN PERFORMATIVE EVENT should be viewed in its larger political and societal context. Here I view three ethnic theme parks, in Indonesia, Kenya, and China, in terms of what I call the social demography of the nations within which they are located. Tourist attractions are constructed not only in response to the requirements of international tourism but also in terms of internal domestic politics. This is especially so with these three parks, as all cater primarily to a market of domestic rather than foreign tourists and all serve national political purposes. I specifically consider alternative ways of interpreting Taman Mini in Indonesia, where, as at New Salem and Masada, local people operating within an official state-sponsored site impose their own meanings and social practices, make the place their own, and undermine the official interpretation of the site.

Comparative Perspective

Ethnic theme parks are an excellent setting for anthropological inquiry as they are sites where the ethnic diversity of the nation or the region is represented for the visitors in a single locality in one panoptic sweep (Anagnost 1993; Stanley 1998). Each park is a copy of a nation presented in an open air museum that charges an admission fee and has entrance gates and clear boundaries. In the sites I have studied in Kenya, Indonesia, and China, selected aspects of culture are exhibited and no effort is made to present the ethnic culture as a whole. What is displayed tends to be visual and experiential. Typical house types are a dominant feature, along with ethnic costumes, aspects of indigenous arts and culture, dance performances, and, in some cases, regional food.

Ethnic parks display living people in native costume who are on stage performing for tourists. Whereas ethnography reduces living peoples to writing and museums usually reduce them to artifact, ethnic parks continue the late-nineteenth- and early-twentieth-century tradition of world's fairs in that the objects on exhibit are real people (Kirshenblatt-Gimblett 1998). Saloni Mathur argues that the "living ethnological displays" of world's fairs constituted "perhaps the most objectionable genre in the history of anthropology's signifying practices" (2000, 492). There have been many critiques of displays of living people at world's fairs,[1] yet these practices have been recuperated in present-day ethnic theme parks that are constructed by modern nation states. No one seems to object. Whereas world's fairs in Western nations often imported people from the colonies for exhibit, nations with modern theme parks recruit their own citizens to be members of performance troupes where they become government employees on display for contemporary domestic tourists.

Although both world's fairs and ethnic parks are recreational, they are also seriously political. They symbolize centralized power. Cultural heterogeneity is put in its place—fixed, aligned, domesticated—and turned into recreational exhibition. The late-nineteenth- and early-twentieth-century world's fairs are frequently seen as demonstrating the power of empire over the colonies (Benedict 1983, 52). The ethnic parks discussed here, in Kenya, Indonesia, and China, are also created, owned, and operated by the government and are often seen as a vehicle for nation building.[2] To historicize these forms, world's fairs displaying living people were products of late colonial empires; ethnic theme parks arose during the 1970s era of nationalism in new states—Bomas of Kenya was opened in 1973, Taman Mini was begun in Indonesia in 1975, and the parks in China are products of the post-Mao era, reflecting a change in government policy toward minorities (Oakes 1998; Ren 1998).

Ethnic theme parks are paradoxical because they display difference yet promote unity. Their focus is on the distinctiveness of the various ethnic groups, on how they differ from one another rather than on what all the groups within the nation have in common, even though the ultimate aim is to promote nationalism. Theme parks place each ethnic group in its own discrete area within a performance space that emphasizes its distinctive cultural features. Thus, ethnic theme parks present a revivalist essentialism. Each culture is presented as unique, separate, and fixed, and this ironically is happening at the same time that the world (and anthropology) is moving toward mobile subjects, border crossings, and vast population movements.

Displays of living people in ethnic parks, what Andrew Ross (1994, 43) calls "ethnographic tourism," are interpreted differently by an audience of domestic tourists than they are by foreign tourists.[3] The opposition between domestic/foreign is also a play upon the local/global, insider/outsider binaries so familiar to anthropologists. While most visitors to Taman Mini are locals (R. Wood 1997, 14; Hitchcock 1998, 125), possibly the extent of the imbalance has not been acknowledged. On a visit to Taman Mini in 1986, I was informed by the public relations officer[4] that on Sundays and holidays they have thirty to forty thousand visitors, with about 3 percent of them foreigners and 97 percent Indonesians, mainly from Jakarta and West Java.

At a similar ethnic complex in southwest China, the Xishuangbanna National Minorities Park in Jinghong, located in a frontier area on the Mekong River bordering Burma and Laos, there were, in 1998, 48,200 foreigners who were visitors to the Xishuangbanna region and 2,211,200 domestic tourists, a ratio of 2 percent to 98 percent.[5] At other ethnic theme parks in China there appear to be somewhat more foreign tourists. Nick Stanley and King Chung Siu (1995, 35–36) report that at the Shenzhen Folk Culture Villages in Guandong province 80 percent of the visitors are mainland Chinese, whereas the other 20 percent, many of them also Chinese, are from Hong Kong, Taiwan, Macao, or elsewhere. In East Africa at Bomas of Kenya, outside Nairobi, I observed that an overwhelming majority of the visitors were urban Kenyan tourists or schoolchildren (chapter 2). Ethnic villages tend to be located near capital cities with large population concentrations and thus are accessible to local people.

Ethnic parks around the world differ in significant ways, mainly, I believe, because of the social demography of each nation. Kenya has forty-two ethnic groups, with the largest, the Kikuyu, constituting 22 percent of the total population. There is no dominant majority. Indonesia has about three hundred ethnolinguistic groups, but the Javanese make up about 45 percent of the population and thus have virtually complete control of political power.[6] China has fifty-six minorities groups that are officially recognized by the state, but the Han constitute 92 percent of the population, and there has been a centuries-old process of sinicization, of assimilating minority people into the Han Chinese way of life.

These demographic differences are reflected in each nation's ethnic theme park. At Bomas and Xishuangbanna, there are ethnic and minority villages, respectively; at Taman Mini there are twenty-six pavilions, each representing one of Indonesia's administrative provinces, a unit based on locality and not ethnicity, and each pavilion contains ethnic houses typical of the region. The provinces were created by the colonial Dutch, and after independence they remained the units of political administration, but their use in Taman Mini may also express the Indonesian state's desire to de-emphasize ethnicity. In Indonesia the issue of ethnicity is so politically charged, with

34. Minority dance at Xishuangbanna National Minorities Park

a history of rivalries, conflict, and separatist movements, that there is the ever-present possibility that the state will break apart. Indonesia, a far-flung island nation is in a more politically precarious position than Kenya, where no one group is dominant, and China, where the Han are overwhelmingly dominant. In Indonesia the majority Javanese, with 45 percent of the population, are concentrated on the island of Java, but other ethnic groups have numerical superiority on the outer islands, where the oil supply and other valuable natural resources are located.

In Bomas of Kenya the aim is to show that all ethnic groups are equal; in Java the park reflects "Javanese overlordship" (S. Errington 1998, 216); in Xishuangbanna the minority villages present only the non-Han minorities residing in the province (fig. 34). There is no Han village; the Han are the tourists. But it is more complicated than that. In a provocative thesis Sara Davis (1999) shows that most of those who perform minority culture in Xishuangbanna are actually Han. They are playing a part, acting as minorities, and most tourists do not know it. Thus the Chinese Han tourists are, in effect, consuming themselves and, at the same time, their own romanticized image of minority peoples. The Xishuangbanna case problematizes the issue—Who are the tourists and who are the toured; who is the guest and who is the host?

Han domestic tourists to Xishuangbanna, mostly men, view non-Han minorities as feminized exotic Others whose women are sexually promiscuous, erotically titillating, and available (Davis 1999, 50; Hyde 2001; Schein 2000, 70–71). This gendered image of the minority female body is reflected at the Xishuangbanna theme park in many ways: the ethnic houses feature attractive young women who are openly flirtatious, women of the Hani minority group give massages, a transvestite performs at a show of minority dances, sex tours to Burma are available as a one-day side trip, and there are mock marriages and sexual banter between performers and tourists. I participated in a mock wedding with a Yao woman (fig. 35), and after the ceremony, as I was carrying my "bride" into the bedroom, my wife, seated in the audience and getting into the spirit of the event, called out, "Don't close that bedroom door!" Someone provided an immediate translation, and everyone laughed. Similar commentary is common in the other ethnic houses.

In Jinghong, where the park is located, there are restaurants featuring Tai minority dancing, and some of the performers are also sex workers (Davis

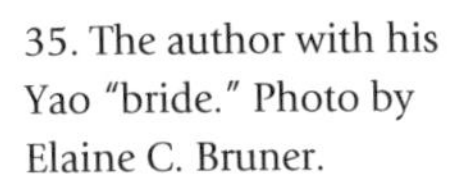

35. The author with his Yao "bride." Photo by Elaine C. Bruner.

1999, 54). Sandra Hyde writes that Jinghong has "become a city of sex tourism" (2001, 144).[7] These overt expressions of sexuality are not present at either Bomas or Taman Mini, but ethnic displays there are sometimes gendered. At Taman Mini, the performers at the Irian Jaya house are bare-chested, robust males, while those at the Balinese display are graceful, beautiful women.

These three ethnic parks may be seen on a continuum moving from Bomas to Taman Mini to Xishuangbanna, as the largest ethnic group constitutes 22 percent of the population in Kenya, 45 percent in Indonesia, and 92 percent in China. I do not want to oversimplify or to imply an invariable one-to-one correspondence between proportion of population and political power; nor do I want to neglect the pattern of ethnic relations within each nation, but the concept of social demography is helpful in the cases discussed here and does highlight the relative power of the majority. There are numerous implications. For example, the accusation of internal colonialism has been applied less to the Kikuyu of Kenya, more so to the Javanese of Indonesia, and most to the Han Chinese. Although there is some animosity about possible Kikuyu dominance and considerable explicit resentment of how the Javanese exercise power, what the minority groups in Kenya and Indonesia face cannot compare to the experience of the non-Han in China, where the cultural absorption of minorities due to the process of sinicization is overpowering. The key difference is that minority ethnic groups in Kenya and Indonesia do not become Kikuyu or Javanese, but in China minorities do become Han.

A case could be made that Han tourists perceive minority peoples in ways similar to those ascribed to Western tourists in Third World countries, in that they reproduce a colonial vision (Nash 1977), enact a differential power relationship, see the Other as feminine (Babcock 1990a), and desire in fantasy or actuality to penetrate the lower-status female body. In Xishuangbanna most of the tourism business is owned by the Han, and only a small portion of the income from tourism remains with minority people, which adds the dimension of economic exploitation. To the extent that Han (or Javanese) domestic tourists behave as foreign ones, the stark opposition between domestic and foreign tourism is blurred, suggesting that there is a need to move beyond a reductionistic dualism to take account not only of the nation's social demography and power differentials, but also its historically constituted and changing patterns of ethnic relations. To paraphrase Kathleen Adams (1998, 77), it would be a "mistake," however, to view Han domestic tourism as simply an adaptation of Western forms of travel. Even the application of the term *internal colonialism* to Indonesia or China may not be entirely appropriate as it simplifies the ethnic dynamics of complex nation states and transports the entire baggage of a bygone colonial era to a setting where it may not be entirely applicable. In China the denigration of minorities, the assumptions about barbarians on the border, predates colonialism. Likewise, the Javanese were the most numerous and powerful group in Indonesia well before the first European colonialists arrived.

The distinction between foreign and domestic tourism is sometimes clear, but in other instances it becomes fuzzy. Sidney Cheung (1999), in his study of Hong Kong heritage trails, shows that Chinese tourists from the mainland, outsiders who number over two million annually, come to Hong Kong seeking modernity and current fashion, not heritage or tradition, while domestic Chinese tourists from Hong Kong itself visit heritage sites in order to recuperate their own authentic past and historic Hong Kong identity. Adams (1998) writes that among domestic Indonesian visitors to Tana Toradja, the Toba Batak and other Christian mountain peoples have very different reactions from those of the Bugis or the Javanese Muslims. What is clearly needed is a more nuanced differentiation between kinds of domestic tourists, based not on a global typology but on the specifics of the local site and the ethnic and social segmentations within the larger national and international community.

Despite these caveats, however, there are very real differences between foreign and domestic tourism. The objectives of travel, the motivations of the tourists, and the nature of the performances constructed are often different. Ethnic parks frequented by local people tend to be deprecated by foreign tourists, by local intellectuals, and even by some anthropologists (see chapter 2).

On the 1999 trip my wife and I made to Xishuangbanna our local tour guide had not even scheduled a visit to the National Minorities Park because, he said, we would not like it as the park was too crowded with Chinese tourists, featured fake reconstructed villages, and was not real. The Lonely Planet guide to South-West China, the bible of the backpackers, has this description of a similar ethnic complex, the Yunnan Nationalities Village in Kunming: "As for the villages, while they show you what the minorities' architecture and costumes look like, it's impossible to get any feel for how these people really live. Add in the hordes of gawking tourists, and the place feels a bit more like a zoo. If you're at all averse to tourist-board fabrications of ethnic cultures, give the place a miss and spend an extra day in Xishuangbanna [the region] or Dehong, where you can see the real thing" (Mayhew and Huhti 1998, 344). This is not from some upscale tour agency but from the main source of advice to the independent young travelers intent on going it alone to experience the "real" China. While serving as a tour guide for affluent American tourists to Taman Mini, I learned that they had a similar negative reaction to the commercialism of that park.

The visitor to Xishuangbanna who follows the advice of the Lonely Planet guidebook, however, finds in its capital city of Jinghong not only a theme park, but also a plethora of constructed ethnic displays for tourists. Davis (1999) tells of meeting a German backpacker in Jinghong who informed her that there is "no real Tai culture" left in Xishuangbanna, (although Davis found enough Tai culture to write a dissertation about it), and he advised her to go to Laos to find the real Tai. This hopeless search for the real is simply a variant of the myth of the vanishing primitive, where the real thing was only to be found in the past—"you should have been here ten years ago"—or it is just around the corner, in a more distant region, in Laos. This is an impossible quest, but an inherent part of tourist discourse. Even though student backpackers disassociate themselves from mass tourists, they may be just another variant of foreign tourists seeking the authentic primitive (see chapter 2).

Anthropologists specializing in foreign tourism are all too familiar with such themes as the real and the fake, the language of authenticity, the pursuit of the true primitive, and the aversion to other tourists. In Xishuangbanna, the itinerary and the experience of the tour were different for foreign and domestic tourists, as they traveled different routes. Ethnic tourism for most foreigners means seeing the authentic native. Tourism producers and the tourism industry are very much aware of the desires of foreign tourists, and they design their sites accordingly, hiding the processes of production and masking the artifice of the display.

Authenticity may not be a significant issue for many domestic tourists who visit ethnic theme parks (Hitchcock 1995, 22; Adams 1998, 82), and they do not object to pastiche, juxtapositions, Western manufactured objects, and modern constructions. Domestic tourists are more interested in recreation than authenticity, and there is no need to conceal how the tourist attraction was produced or to suppress manufactured and newly constructed objects. Taman Mini, for example, has a cable car, Disney-like castles, an army museum, an insect museum, an orchard garden, a bird park, and an IMAX movie theater; Bomas has picnic areas and a swimming pool; Xishuangbanna has extravagant displays for mostly male tourists. Ethnic parks for domestic tourists are more playful, are more entertaining, and have more fun activities than the ethnic performances created for foreigners.

Taman Mini

There is an important literature on Taman Mini by Kathleen Adams (1998), Shelly Errington (1998), Michael Hitchcock (1998), John Pemberton (1994a), Michel Picard (1993), and Robert Wood (1997). Pemberton and Errington have done the most extensive work, but all the scholars have their own projects and all contribute in different ways to our understanding of the park and of Indonesia. Rather than summarize this literature, I focus here on three prominent points: that Taman Mini fosters nation building and nationalism, that it is ahistorical and timeless, and that it displays a limited cultural inventory.

Errington (1998) says that Taman Mini is "a political text of nationalist self-representation" (201) whose aim is to "construct nationhood" (194), and that the park "gives visible form to the Indonesian nation-state's self-imagining" (196). Pemberton quotes President Suharto's statement at the dedication ceremony in 1975 that Taman Mini is "a Park that depicts Our People, a Park that makes us proud to be Indonesians" (1994a, 244). Mrs. Suharto declared, "The main purpose of Taman Mini is to consolidate the cohesion and the unity of the nation" (Adams 1998, 84–85). Adams writes further about "Indonesia's promotion of domestic tourism as a means of solidifying national identity" (1998, 79) and says that the government developed domestic tourism in part "as a nation-building strategy" (77). Picard (1993) and others make similar statements. The Taman Mini web site (Taman Mini 2001) says that the park generates "feelings of pride and love of country."

Errington (1998) also writes that the ethnic "houses emblematize the typical, generic, and timeless architecture of Indonesia's constituent ethnic groups" (199) and that the aim is to "represent the eternal essence of the 'typical' " (200). Pemberton says that Taman Mini "erased the difference between past, present, and future, and thus flattened time—and with it, histories," so that what we have is a "continuously presented present" (245). He calls attention to Taman Mini's "special ahistoricism" (246).

Not only Pemberton and Errington, but also Picard (1997, 197), Hitchcock (1995), and Robert Wood (1997) have commented on how ethnicity is expressed stereotypically in museum displays and tourist sites. Summarizing this literature for Southeast Asia, Erik Cohen writes that what are displayed are "the relatively superficial, external and therefore non-threatening . . . manifestations of ethnicity that are precisely those most accessible to visiting tourists; costumes, arts and crafts, dances and similar performances. Ethnic identity tends thereby to be reduced to a folkloristic display" (2001, 45). R. S. Kipp (1993, 1), cited by Andrew Causey (1998, 104), notes that ethnicity in tourism and in museums is represented by "house types and ceremonial clothing." Thus, in the literature, Taman Mini is seen as being about nationalism, is presented as ahistorical, and displays limited aspects of culture. A key statement about Taman Mini was made by Benedict Anderson, one of the most outstanding Indonesian scholars, who wrote that the traditional houses at Taman Mini are "icons of ethnicity" and that "concrete and immediate life is drained from" those houses (1990, 182). As an important argument in this book is about the emergence of culture, constructivism, human agency, and ethnic creativity, Taman Mini might not seem to be a promising place for me to work, but it proved to be so. As I present the following data about my experience at Taman Mini, I hasten to add that although I have visited the park many times, I did not do systematic field research there.[8]

Having done ethnography in North Sumatra over a period of years since 1957 (see chapter 9), I went directly to that Taman Mini pavilion, which has a replica of a Toba Batak house—rectangular, elaborately carved, raised on stilts, with a distinctive swayback thatched roof (fig. 36). Although Taman Mini advertises itself as Indonesia in miniature, the Toba house is gigantic, far larger than any traditional house I have ever seen in the homeland in Sumatra. Inside the house were male and female mannequins displayed in full ceremonial dress (fig. 37).

The house also had a gift shop that carried a volume on *Batak Tarombo*. The Toba Batak word *tarombo* refers to patrilineal genealogies organized into clans and lineages, and it is important because descent, as well as affinal ties, tells which kinship terms the Toba Batak use with one another. Hence, *tarombo* defines relationships; it is not a relic of the past but a charter for the present. Toba Batak strangers will do what they call *martarombo*, to genealogize, to go through lines of descent and affinity to determine how they are related. A *tarombo* may go back twenty or more generations to clan ancestors, and there are genealogical specialists who have memorized many descent lines as well as stories about notable ancestors.

On the wall of the house at Taman Mini was the Toba Batak phrase *"horas tondi madingin, pir tondi matogu"* which speaks literally to the soul of a person, calls the spirits, is recited on important ritual occasions, and reflects the basics of Batak animistic cosmology. In a display case was a *tunggal panaluan*, a five-foot carved staff used by Batak medicine men, or gurus, which, as the showcase description said, could resist danger and disaster, and had "mysterious powers." The names were in the Toba Batak language but the display explanations were in Indonesian and English. These phrases and items were not superficial and stereotypical, but were culturally specific, symbolically charged, and emotionally significant, if not to the casual visitor, at least to the Toba Batak or to the anthropologist familiar with Batak *adat* (their social and ceremonial system) and culture. If the aim of the state was to channel ethnic display to the arts, where it would be neutralized (Acciaioli 1985; Picard 1997), then that strategy was not entirely successful.[9]

A series of dioramas at Taman Mini presented highlights of Toba Batak history. The first was about Dr. Nommensen, a German from the Rheinische

36. The Toba Batak house at Taman Mini

37. Mannequins in ceremonial dress in the Toba Batak house

Mission Society who arrived in the mountain villages of Tapanuli in North Sumatra in 1864. He established a mission church that subsequently converted most of the then pagan Toba Batak to Christianity, although many animistic and folk beliefs remain to this day. Another diorama was about Singamangaraja XII, a legendary Toba Batak spiritual and political leader who fought the Dutch until his forces were defeated by the colonial army in 1907. He is a revered Batak and national hero (Cunningham 1989). The next diorama portrayed an early plantation in Deli on the east coast of Sumatra, showing Dutch overseers with whips among the Chinese and Indian laborers. I asked one of the visitors about the whips, as it seemed a severe representation of what I had understood to be contract labor, but he informed me that conditions on the plantations were like slavery, or at least that is what they were taught in their history classes. The plantation system was restricted to the coast and never reached the interior homeland of the Batak people. These dioramas were not timeless and ahistorical but rather were depictions of significant chapters in the local history of North Sumatra.

On one visit to the Toba Batak house I saw a class of roughly thirty children, from the ages of about six to the early teens, learning the traditional dances of North Sumatra, including Toba Batak dances (fig. 38). These were well-dressed urban children, most in slacks and T-shirts, whose parents had enrolled them in a dance club. One of the mothers who had accompanied her child to the dance class informed me that the club had been advertised in Jakarta newspapers and that subsequently word had spread through the local community. The practice sessions were held in the Toba Batak traditional house in Taman Mini, which had become a kind of community center. On the second floor of the house, where the classes were held, all around the edges of the room were the dioramas, display cases, and traditional costumes, so that the old Batak culture provided a frame for the new dance culture being performed by the urban children in the center of the room. It was as if the lifeless mannequins in ceremonial dress were silently watching the children in T-shirts learning present-day versions of their traditional dances.

When I visited March 27, 1986, I saw that a stage had been constructed in front of the Toba Batak house. A group of musicians to one side was playing traditional music, and chairs for the audience were facing the stage. The master of ceremonies appeared, and, speaking in the Indonesian language, he called attention to issues of ethnicity: he announced that although he was Javanese, he was serving as announcer for the province of North Sumatra, which showed, he said, that this was the new Indonesia. Then a number of North Sumatran dances and songs were performed. One of the songs, performed by

38. Dance class at the Toba Batak house

a Toba Batak trio, was a Toba Batak *marga,* or clan, song, and in response a segment of the audience whom I recognized as Toba Batak on the basis of previous conversations stood and applauded.

Next I witnessed the most surprising event I had ever seen at Taman Mini. There was a fashion show with tall slim Javanese models wearing modern Batak clothing designed by Edward Hutabarat (fig. 39). A Toba Batak who lives in Jakarta, Hutabarat had made his reputation selling contemporary designer clothing that creatively employs traditional Toba Batak motifs and patterns. Many of the designs are based on the Batak *ulos,* a sacred cloth given on ceremonial occasions by the wife-giving lineage to their wife receivers, part of the ritual exchange enacted at Toba Batak weddings and funerals. Hutabarat sells his creations to the Jakarta elite in upscale department stores as well as in his own boutique. I had been told that his clothing is very expensive, and my uninformed opinion is that his designs are indeed striking. It was a scene—with the models sashaying down the runway—more reminiscent of Milan or Paris than Jakarta. At the end of the show the smiling designer, a Batak Giorgio Armani, came on stage, surrounded by Javanese models, to receive the applause of an appreciative audience (fig. 40). After the show I said hello to Hutabarat in Batak, and he replied, in English, that it made him very happy to hear his own language spoken.

Discussion

What is taking place in the Toba house is not the construction of Indonesian nationalism but a celebration of Toba Batak ethnic identity within the confines of Taman Mini. If Taman Mini is the official version of Indonesia, the state's image of itself, then the display and activities within the Batak house are sites of local production within the larger production. The expression of Toba Batak identity is an instance of human agency and creativity within the limits of how it is possible to publicly express ethnicity in the Indonesian nation state. Indeed, while the Taman Mini Web site acknowledges that what the park depicts are the roots of Indonesia, it indicates that it also showcases

39. Models on the runway during the Batak fashion show

40. The designer Hutabarat with models

"the products of creative activities or innovations that arise within the communities of the respective regions" (Taman Mini 2001).

There is a stunning contrast between the mannequins in ceremonial Batak attire inside the house, enclosed in a glass display case, lifeless and mute, and the mannequins outside the house, the statuesque professional models wearing contemporary Batak designer clothing, very much alive, strutting down the runway, performing with attitude. Pemberton (1994a, 254) compares the museum's diorama of Javanese wedding costumes with the performance of the "authentic" Javanese royal wedding ceremony at Taman Mini in 1983 between Suharto's daughter Siti Hediati and Major Prabowo Subianto. Just as the Javanese perform their contemporary culture at Taman Mini, so do the Toba Batak, although admittedly on a less grand scale.

I do not view what occurs within the Toba house as Toba Batak resistance to Javanese or Indonesian hegemony, for that would be to reduce an expression of living culture to one dimension, as if political opposition were the primary motivation. One ethnic group may behave in opposition to another, but to place all ethnic behaviors under the label of resistance is a simplification. Nor do I think that Toba Batak have to make a choice between their own identity and Indonesian nationalism. They are proud members of an ethnic minority who choose not to renounce their identity and *adat,* but they also remain loyal citizens of the nation state (E. Bruner 1972). They are Batak and Indonesian at the same time. It is now widely accepted within anthropology that expressions of local ethnic culture are not simply traditional, as opposed to expressions of national Indonesian culture that are considered modern, because both are contemporary expressions in the same present. Chapter 9 is about contemporary Toba Batak culture and discusses this issue in more depth.

Again, contrary to what scholars such as Benedict Anderson have suggested, that "concrete and immediate life is drained from" the houses (1990, 182), ethnic culture and identity is not fixed and frozen at Taman Mini; it is alive and well. Clifford Geertz writes, "The so-called 'museum' or 'culture park' view of heritage as something that has only to be preserved and tended, only to be kept pristine, isolated from the alterations going on all around it, is not only utopian, it is mischievous. In trying to freeze a living tradition in the name of authenticity you produce the worst sorts of inauthenticity—decadence, not purity" (1996). A *tarombo,* a musical instrument, a costume, a *tunggal panaluan,* a dance class, and designer clothing are all Toba Batak culture items even though some are historically prior in that they originated earlier in time, and their contemporary expression is just that, contemporary. Historically older forms of culture are shown within the Batak house, but such recently created forms as fashion shows are also performed and are examples of emergent Toba Batak culture in the process of formation.

I see my data from Taman Mini as complementary to the work of other scholars, not in opposition to it, and I recognize that the other scholars had different research objectives. Pemberton and Errington show how the Indonesian ethnic park is a model not only of the nation state but also of the Indic state, with Java at the center of power, hegemonic over the other ethnic groups of Indonesia located on the outer islands of the archipelago, on the periphery. Pemberton demonstrates how a simulacrum becomes more than the original; this is a tenet of postmodernism.

My work builds on the scholarship of others, but there are differences. Pemberton and Errington take a more top-down, text-based view of Taman Mini, in contrast to my own bottom-up, ethnographic approach. While they focus on Indonesia as a Java-centric nation-state, my view and my knowledge base are derived more from the periphery. My conceptual orientation, which is not new (see E. Bruner 1984b; Turner and Bruner 1986), is to show how ethnic culture from the periphery at Taman Mini is perpetually being born again. I talk to performers and visitors, and I observe what actually happens in the Batak house and see it as social practice. To put a larger frame on it, this chapter moves toward a critique of recent poststructuralist and cultural studies approaches, many derived from the early Foucault, emphasizing texts, the discourse, hegemony, episteme, and other top-down, totalizing formulations.[10] I agree with Marshall Sahlins, who, quoting Giambatista Vico, writes that "the very first principle of the new anthropological science would have to be 'respect the specificity [and, I would add, the creativity] of the cultural object' " (2000, 31).

The new cultural forms enacted at Taman Mini do not originate there, but rather arise from within the larger Jakarta and North Sumatran urban Toba Batak communities. There is a thriving Toba Batak social and ceremonial life in Jakarta, Medan, and other cities; Claude Lévi-Strauss could have written his *Elementary Structures of Kinship* (1949/1969) by studying Toba Batak weddings in the city, for it has everything the French structuralist would have needed—patrilineal lineages and clans, affinal alliances, the circulation of women, perpetual gift exchange, debts that can never be repaid—every element of an asymmetrical marriage system (Bovill 1985, chapter 9).

It is ironic, however, that Toba Batak identity is stronger in Taman Mini and in the urban centers of Indonesia than in the homeland, in the rural mountain villages of North Sumatra. When I lived in a Toba Batak village in the Tapanuli highlands, the primary sources of identification were patrilineage and place, genealogy and locality. When Batak met in the countryside they would ask, What is your lineage and where are you from? Everyone in the mountain villages was a Toba Batak and their ethnicity was taken for granted. But in the modern sector, in cities, government offices, the army, large businesses, and Taman Mini, with their mixture of many different peoples, ethnic affiliation becomes more problematic and hence significant (E. Bruner 1961). This is a process that started with the ebb and flow of peoples and cultures in the precolonial period and intensified with nationalism and colonialism—as Benedict Anderson (1983), Pemberton (1994b), Bernard Cohn (1996), and others have demonstrated—as European powers regrouped tribal segments into larger ethnic units and even constructed ethnicities for purposes of colonial administration. The process has continued to the present in the government of Indonesia, especially with the migration of peoples from everywhere in the archipelago who come together in the city and in many new contexts. Toba Batak identity is a modern product.

The Toba Batak domestic tourists at Taman Mini are simultaneously the tourists and the toured; they are both the visitors and the performers. In Xishuangbanna, the Han tourists do not realize that the supposedly minority performers are also Han (Davis 1999, 52); at Taman Mini ethnic identity is not disguised, but is known and openly expressed. It is different again at Bomas of Kenya, where there is one national performance troupe consisting of members of many different tribes, who perform the dances of any ethnic group in Kenya. There is no single national dance troupe at Taman Mini.

There are implications of these data for an anthropology of tourism. Two of the major concepts developed within tourism studies, Dean MacCannell's (1976) concept of authenticity and John Urry's (1990) concept of the tourist gaze are either irrelevant in this case or must be radically revised. In MacCannell's view, modern tourists are dissatisfied with their lives and seek authenticity elsewhere, in another place or another time. The Toba Batak, however, know who they are and do not doubt the realness, genuineness, or credibility of their lives and their culture. They do not go to Taman Mini seeking authenticity elsewhere but rather for a reaffirmation of an authenticity already known and experienced. Nor do they go to Taman Mini with Urry's tourist gaze, the key to which is experiences that are "out of the ordinary" or "different from those typically encountered in everyday life" or "constructed through difference" (1990, 1). While the setting of Taman Mini may be different and extraordinary, what the Toba Batak see there is what they know they are. They do not discover the Other but rather witness a performance of themselves in a different context.

If the Toba Batak plan to visit the exhibits of other provinces and to enter other ethnic houses in Taman Mini, such as those of the Javanese or the

Minangkabau, where they will encounter displays of peoples with a different language and culture, how do they approach these pavilions? The urban Toba Batak who most likely to go to an ethnic theme park in Jakarta encounter members of other Indonesian ethnic groups on a daily basis in their ordinary lives in the city.

Of the two million Toba Batak, Usman Pelly has estimated, about seven hundred thousand have migrated from their rural homeland in Sumatra (chapter 9), mostly to the cities.[11] They do not constitute a majority in any urban center in which they are located. Further, as Christians in an Islamic nation, as a people from the outer islands, and as an ethnic group with the reputation for being *kasar,* or rough, especially in relation to the *halus,* or refined Javanese, the Toba Batak have necessarily developed coping skills that enable them to adapt to the cosmopolitan multiethnic cities of Indonesia. They enact their Toba Batak culture among themselves—at home, in rituals, in church—and disguise or mute many such expressions in public. They eat *sangsang,* a pork dish mixed with the blood of the pig, at important ceremonial occasions, but they do not slaughter the pig in front of their Moslem neighbors.

In the urban centers of the archipelago, the Toba Batak relate to people of other ethnic groups in school, at work, in the neighborhood, and as family, because some intermarry. They already know the Javanese or the Minangkabau before they enter the exhibition pavilions at Taman Mini. They may not know these other cultures in great depth, and they may not possess holistic ethnographic knowledge, but they know enough to get along, to engage in social interaction. They have honed their relational proficiency so they can accurately predict the reactions of others and act accordingly. Anthony Wallace called this knowledge "the organization of diversity" (1970, 23); it is the basis of interaction in many complex systems.

What about young Toba Batak born in Javanese cities who may never have been to Sumatra and who may not even speak the Batak language? What is the significance of the Toba Batak house at Taman Mini to them? Do they understand the meaning of a *tarombo,* a magical *tunggal panaluan,* the Batak animistic phrase *"horas tondi madingin, pir tondi matogu,"* Batak medicine men, and the historical dioramas? Aside from my work in the villages, I have studied Toba Batak life in urban centers in Medan in North Sumatra and in two cities in Java—Jakarta and Bandung—and I have participated in Toba sacred rituals in all three cities. My last visit, in 1997, is discussed in the next chapter. My findings are that young people, even some village children, might disclaim knowledge of the *adat* and express a lack of interest, but that after they are married, and more so after they have children, their interest is awakened as they enter for the first time the Batak social and ceremonial system as fully adult members. This is still so in modern cities (Bovill 1985).

What are the mechanisms of meaning making at Taman Mini, especially as the items in the Toba house seem so fragmentary? Small clues—a historical diorama, a song, a sacred object in a dead display case, an *ulos* design—operate by indexical meaning to evoke memories of a total cultural heritage and a vital ethnic identity. Anthropologists within the past few decades have made significant advances in our understanding of memory,[12] which is not simply a recall of isolated fragments and traces from the past but is an active process, or in Harley Bartlett's terms, "imaginative reconstruction" (Sutton 2001, 9). Marcel Proust, who understood these processes well, wrote about the power "of unsubstantial fragments to reveal the vast structure" (1982, 50–51, quoted in Sutton 2001, 84). A single item encodes broad meaning and serves as a mnemonic device cuing memories of events, family, and home. Implicit meanings are unpacked and multidimensional experiences recalled.

These cognitive processes are universal but are especially significant for Batak visitors viewing representations of their culture at Taman Mini. Batak migrants in Jakarta are well aware that the source of their culture is in North Sumatra. The original mountain village of every Toba Batak is called *bona ni pasogit,* literally the place of the ancestors, the homeland, a sacred location, one of origin and memory. Many urban dwellers return to their home area in Sumatra for important ceremonies; others leave instructions that when they die they want their bodies buried in their *bona ni pasogit* (chapter 9). Even second and third generation urban Batak identify themselves by the name of their *bona ni pasogit,* as it is the source of their lineage. Items evocative of home bring forth this larger complex of meaning and longing.

The same clues may not even be seen by outsiders or foreign tourists, who have no idea of their meaning, and they may be dismissed by anthropologists writing on ethnic theme parks, as superficial, lifeless, or folkloristic, as icons or mere commodifications. The clues may have no significance whatsoever for Javanese or other Indonesians, whose interactions with Batak people are frequently influenced by generalized Indonesian stereotypes of the crude Christians from the mountain highlands of Sumatra. The Toba Batak do understand that much is missing from the display of themselves at Taman Mini, but they look beyond the facade, fill in the blanks, and understand the symbolism, because they know the whole (Fernandez 1986). They accept responsibility for their own interpretation of themselves (MacCannell 2001), and hence they move far beyond the Indonesian government's official reading of Taman Mini.

The government and the various ethnic groups of Indonesia do not share the same conception of the nation. Anthropologists are already familiar with the distinction between the nation as an objective concept and the nation as a symbolic construction, as an imagined community. My point is simpler—

that the idea of the nation, real or imagined, is perceived differently by those in distinct structural positions. The government view of Indonesia is, as Errington and Pemberton correctly point out, the Javanese view of Indonesia, one reflected in Taman Mini. It is a model of the Indic kingdom, a state with the Javanese at the sacred center, in control, a source of power, deserving of respect and deference, on the inside and looking outward at the less refined peoples on the margins of empire on the periphery. But this is not the way the Toba Batak peoples of the outer islands view Indonesia. They acknowledge Javanese political power and numerical majority, and even that the Javanese are more refined, but they do not acknowledge Javanese superiority. They tend to see the Javanese as simply one among the many ethnic groups of Indonesia, and they do not share the view that Indonesia is modeled on the Indic state. Their concern is that because of Javanese control, the resources of the nation are not distributed equally but remain concentrated on the island of Java, or in the pockets of Javanese politicians and the military.

Shelly Errington writes that although Taman Mini constructs a model of the nation, it is a "fantasized image," or, as she puts it in Clifford Geertz's terms, it is not a "model of" Indonesia but a "model for" (1998, 222). Lévi-Strauss might regard Taman Mini as if it were a myth that is designed to resolve a contradiction between an ideal image of the nation and the reality of what that nation actually is. The state mythology is one of ethnic harmony, of unity in diversity, despite Javanese political domination and the ethnic conflict and tensions experienced in daily life. Taman Mini might be seen in Marxist terms as creating false consciousness, where the Javanese governing elite promote an ideology of ethnic egalitarianism as a means of controlling the masses. Shelly Errington, Kathleen Adams, Robert Wood (1997, 15), and others write that Taman Mini, as well as Indonesian museums and tourist attractions, do not always succeed in achieving their political objectives; they contend that there is invariably a discrepancy between the producers' intentions and audience reception.

These perspectives by Clifford Geertz, Lévi-Strauss, and Marx are useful, but I suggest that they apply more to Taman Mini as viewed from above. This chapter builds upon top-down, totalizing analyses but takes a bottom-up, ethnographic approach, giving more prominence to ethnic agency. From below, from inside the house, what is presented to the Batak domestic tourists is experienced as life, not as image. The Toba Batak fashion show is more alive, real, and immediate than the museum mannequins in traditional attire, giving a glimpse of contemporary social life and practice within the Toba Batak house.

9

Reincorporations

Return to Sumatra, 1957, 1997

IN 1957 my wife and I began fieldwork in Indonesia in a Toba Batak mountain village in North Sumatra.[1] We returned to the village in 1971, and then again in 1997, four decades after our initial visit (cf. C. Geertz 1995). In this chapter I reflect on the revisits, emphasizing less how the villagers have changed (they are more prosperous) or on how I have changed (I am older), and more on how anthropology has changed in the past forty years and how this disciplinary development has led me to rethink ethnographic fieldwork and to reevaluate my own role as ethnographer. In my reflections on these sequential experiences and the changes engendered—in the villagers, in myself, and in anthropology—I find the latter most important because it is in the vocabulary of the discipline that anthropologists find the language to think about and to describe the ethnographic encounter. I refer not just to the theory and method of fieldwork, but also to the stories anthropologists tell themselves about the field and to the conventional wisdom of the era about field experience.

Specifically, I raise the question of how to do ethnography in a transnational global world, a current inquiry of the 1990s (Appadurai 1996; Gilroy 1993; Gupta and Ferguson, eds., 1997; Hannerz 1996; Lavie and Swedenburg 1996; Robbins and Bamford 1997). In Sherry Ortner's (1997, 2003) study of her 1958 high school graduating class from Newark, New Jersey, whose members have spread out all over the United States, she writes about doing fieldwork in the postcommunity, her term for a one-time local community that has been radically delocalized. In his study of West African street vendors in New York, Paul Stoller (1997) similarly discusses the problem of doing ethnography in what he calls transnational spaces. In my own work on tourism I have developed the concept of the touristic borderzone, a performative space within which tourists and locals meet (chapter 7).

All three of these concepts (the postcommunity, transnational space, and the touristic borderzone) problematize the notion of locality, and all three studies select sites for ethnography in which the movement of peoples is prominent. All three propose conceptualizations similar to the contact zone proposed by Mary Louise Pratt (1992), the Third Space described by Homi Bhabha (1994), and the Tex-Mex border theory developed by Gloria Anzaldúa (1987), Coco Fusco (1995), and Guillermo Gómez-Peña (1996). These theoretical notions are different from the model of multisited ethnography proposed by George Marcus (1995), which emphasizes discontinuous spaces rather than a third space or borderzone. They are also different from Arjun Appadurai's model of flows or scapes, which, as Marcus (1997, 102) points out, is cartographic imagery. Despite areas of overlap, there are significant differences between the various transnational approaches. Tourism is inherently multisited as the tourists travel along their itinerary from one site to another, but once they have arrived at a new location, they find themselves in the borderzone, a performance space.

Tourism is the quintessential transnational topic for anthropological inquiry, as the studies in this book illustrate. But what do these recent conceptualizations of transnational spaces have to do with ethnography in a mountain village in Southeast Asia, seemingly the most stable of settings? The Toba Batak are a classic case of a people residing in small hamlets and practicing wet rice agriculture, with a social system that includes patrilineal descent and asymmetrical cross-cousin marriage. What do the Toba Batak have to do with borderzones? All of the residents of the villages in North Sumatra are of the same ethnic group, almost all are Christian, and all are related to one another through lineage or affinal ties.

I claim that transnationalism and globalization are as significant in the most traditional anthropological locality, a highland Sumatran village, as they are in a study of a high school graduating class from New Jersey, of West African street vendors in New York, or of international tourism. It is not necessary to seek novel settings in order to study what Appadurai (1997) calls the postlocal. Whereas I label the study of a high school class, street vendors, or tourism as novel or exotic, other writers would consider the Toba Batak an archetype of exotic peoples. As anthropologists know, what is called exotic depends on one's perspective. In any case, I doubt that there are any spaces in today's world that are not in some sense transnational, or to phrase it more cautiously, that could not profitably be approached from a transnational perspective.

A further question arises: were the changes I noticed in 1997 more the result of how the world had changed in the previous four decades or the result of how anthropological theory had changed? Was the perspective I employed in 1957 appropriate to that era and the transnational vision appropriate for 1997? I raise these questions with the understanding that social theory both reflects and is constitutive of changes in the world.

In this chapter I bring to focus some of the shifts in the discipline over the past forty years, and define what revisiting a field site means nowadays. I argue for a more culturally and symbolically sensitive transnationalism, one that takes account of the people's own understanding of a revisit and of global forces. I do not regard earlier work as totally discontinuous with the present or as fatally compromised politically, or as subversive of truth. I argue that we should examine traditional village studies as well as more recent topics of study, such as tourism, with the same ethnographic frame of reference. Finally, I chart where we were and where we are going.

The First Visit

Let me remind the reader where anthropology—or at least where I—began forty years ago. Recently, prompted by Ortner's 1997 reference to Robert Redfield's 1955 work on the "little community," I took the latter book down from my library shelf and was surprised to find on the title page this long forgotten note: "To Edward Bruner, with warm regards and appreciation for your help. Robert Redfield." While I was a graduate student at the University of Chicago, I had apparently contributed in some small degree to Redfield's work on the concept of the little community. Redfield states that the little community, typically a village, is a natural unit that presents itself as common sense and that has four characteristics: it is distinctive, small, homogeneous, and self-sufficient (1955, 4). Redfield did not problematize the concept of the village but took it as a given, and each of his four characteristics has been questioned by contemporary anthropological theory.

In the mid-1950s Redfield, Julian Steward, and others were also working on how the village related to the nation and to the larger civilization of which it was a part. These researchers extended the scope of anthropology beyond the local, although they did not yet have the concept of transnationalism or borderzones. Their inquiry accepted the village as one unit and the nation or the civilization as another unit, and they sought the relationship between them. Graduate students at the University of Chicago in the 1950s were becoming critical of community approaches, particularly if the village or the local unit was depicted as isolated, functionally integrated, and self-enclosed. Subsequently, many anthropologists working in Indonesia and elsewhere further developed and extended the postlocal beyond-the-village tradition. For millennia Indonesia has been in interaction with Chinese, Indic, Islamic, and European civilizations. After independence from the Netherlands in 1949, extensive population movements occurred throughout the archipelago, including rapid migration to the cities. Ethnographers of Indonesia have thus long studied the effects of outside influences on the country, the position of the ethnic group within the nation-state, and processes of urbanization. Nevertheless, it was impossible to fully escape the prevailing wisdom of the era, especially for an aspiring young ethnographer in the 1950s, and a village community was the generally accepted place to begin field study.

I recall the moment in 1957 when I first saw the village in which my wife and I were to work. Lumban Panggabean, located in Tampahan, Lintong ni Huta, near the market town of Balige, is one of thousands of small hamlets (*huta*) in the North Tapanuli highlands along the Bukit Barisan mountain range, the homeland of the Toba Batak (fig. 41). I had been searching for a field site when a distinguished elder invited me to study his village and offered his house during my study. Except for a Dutch priest and a German missionary doctor, no other Westerners lived in the region. As I approached the village, I looked at the massive sloping roofs of the highly decorated rectangular houses built on stilts. I saw people farming with water buffalo in gently curved, terraced rice fields. Small groups of people sat on rattan mats talking to one another. I passed sarong-clad women nursing babies, and a swarm of children followed my every footstep. The scene was idyllic and rural, set against the backdrop of the mist-enshrouded volcanoes that surround Toba Lake. For a boy from New York City who had lived in apartments all his life, it seemed a perfect place to begin. I said to myself, "This is it. This is my little community."

Then, as now, I was aware of the romanticism that pervaded my view not only of the village but also of my role as ethnographer, although I did not then realize the colonialism implicit in my beliefs. My mother-in-law, who had not yet forgiven her daughter for marrying an anthropologist, was particularly concerned about what she saw as the dangers of our 1957 trip to Sumatra. I tried to reassure her by pointing out where Indonesia was located on a map, but she exclaimed, "My God, it's the end of the world." Her comment only served to strengthen my romantic view of myself as heroic adventurer.

During research for my 1954 dissertation, I had used English to communicate with the Native Americans whom I studied, and many of my professors at Chicago believed that I would never become a real anthropologist until I worked in a foreign land, using a foreign language. Meyer Fortes, who had

41. The author in the village in 1957. Photo by Elaine C. Bruner.

come to Chicago from Cambridge as a visiting professor, told me this explicitly and urged me to go overseas. After the 1957–1958 field experience in Indonesia, I felt that I had met the discipline's expectations of foreign fieldwork and had become, more or less, real.

In 1957 my intention was to remain in Tapanuli for the full fifteen-month field period, but unanticipated circumstances changed that plan. My wife and I were listening to the radio when, to our surprise, we received a Voice of America broadcast from the Philippines reporting that because of the impending civil war, all U.S. women and children had already been evacuated from North Sumatra. I looked at my wife and she at me, and we had no response but to laugh, an anxious, nervous laughter. We knew of the political troubles and had heard rumors of impending armed conflict. The villagers, showing concern for our safety, had placed a U.S. flag on our house, I suppose to indicate that we were not Dutch. The villagers also assigned an adolescent boy to stand guard at night to protect us. This was a heavy burden for the villagers to bear, as they not only had concern for their own safety, but knew it would not be easy for unarmed villagers to protect two Americans from a military attack. They informed us that should trouble develop in the village, they would escape to the jungle. Not only would they bring us with them, they were prepared to share their food. I did not relish going into the jungle, especially as I was already being treated for amoebic dysentery.

My concern heightened when growing numbers of rebel troops appeared in our area, carrying military equipment clearly marked as the property of the United States. It is now known that this equipment was courtesy of the Central Intelligence Agency, which supported the rebellion as part of the worldwide Cold War fight against communism. Thus, in 1957 transnational forces were clearly visible in the towns of the Batak highlands as global powers aimed to overthrow the Sukarno regime and its communist supporters, who were then governing Indonesia.

After hearing that the elite Javanese Suliwangi division from the central government was approaching from the coast, my wife and I sought out the local military commander, Major Sahala Hutabarat, to ask if he was prepared to fight the government forces from his base in the highlands. He told us that he had known of our research and had been following its progress. He then shared with us his experience in the United States, where he had trained at Fort Benning, Georgia, and told us he was prepared to fight. My wife and I made plans to leave Lumban Panggabean the next day. We started on the road to the coast only to find that we were driving into a tank battle, so we returned to the village and sold our car to the rebels, then traveled by boat on Lake Toba to avoid the fighting. Once ashore, we rode a bus to the coastal city of Medan. In Medan, the U.S. consul informed us that he had made plans for our evacuation, but we decided to stay. Clifford and Hildred Geertz, whom I had visited in Jakarta in 1957, had a similar experience with the rebellion at about the same time in Central Sumatra, in Padang. They escaped to Jakarta, he with malaria and she with hepatitis, and then moved on to do their research in Bali (C. Geertz 1995). Such was ethnography in Indonesia in the 1950s.

Medan had a large Toba Batak migrant population, and I continued my studies of Batak culture in this urban location. I had not intended to study urbanization, but the exigencies of the war situation led me to do so. The transition from a village to an urban research setting was made somewhat easier by the fact that my wife had been adopted in the village as a daughter of the local lineage of the Simandjuntak clan. As her husband, I had become a brother-in-law to the patrilineage. These relationships gave both my wife and me a kinship position as a wife receiver (*boru*) of the Simandjuntak clan.[2] When we arrived in Medan, the urban Batak recognized these fictive kinship ties, and we began work with our lineage and affinal relatives and branched out from there (E. Bruner 1961, 1963, 1974a, 1984a).

We visited Lumban Panggabean briefly in 1971 (E. Bruner 1974b), but then some twenty-six years passed before we returned to Sumatra again. Preparing for the 1997 visit, I was concerned that after such a long period of time, forty years since the initial field trip, the people with whom we had lived would no longer remember us, or those we had known would have died. Nor did I trust my own memory, as Toba Batak villagers I had known as teenagers would now be middle aged, and I was not sure I would recognize them. Conceptually, returning to an old field site is like going to a high school reunion, revisiting after a temporal gap of decades to see people you remember only as they once were, which raises questions about then and now, about age and memory (Ikeda 1999). Although we had made many other trips to Indonesia, our Indonesian and Toba Batak language skills were at best rusty, and we did not know if we could communicate with the villagers. I must admit that I was also concerned about my health, for at the age of seventy-two, I was not entirely sure if I still had the stamina for even a brief period of fieldwork. I had other doubts as well. Maybe the idea of a revisit was too much of an anthropological dream, a fantasy about a return to "our" village, where I had performed the rite of passage from fledgling neophyte to established fieldworker.

The Encounter

When we returned to Sumatra in 1997, we took advantage of both established Batak kinship and anthropological professional ties. We also employed electronic means of communication to contact educated, cosmopolitan people in Sumatra who knew the local Toba Batak world.

I first contacted a daughter of the Simandjuntak lineage. I had known her in 1957 when she was a child and in 1971 when she was a university medical student. She now lived in Washington, DC, where her Batak husband was employed at the Indonesian Embassy. Her father, Arnold Simandjuntak, now deceased, was brother to the elder who had originally invited us to the village in 1957. Both the former medical student and my wife were Simandjuntak daughters from Lumban Panggabean, which gave us the right to ask for her help. I communicated with her by telephone and e-mail to explain the purpose of my planned visit. She telephoned her mother in Medan, who in turn asked her brother to go to the village on his motorbike and inform the villagers of our impending visit. We had known her mother, Mrs. Arnold Simandjuntak, in 1957–1958. Her old age and high social standing allowed her to act authoritatively on her deceased husband's behalf. I then communicated by e-mail and fax with Mangasa Silitonga and Usman Pelly, both PhDs from the University of Illinois who were living and teaching in Medan.

Mangasa, a linguist, had been my research assistant in 1971, and I had been a member of Usman's dissertation committee in the Illinois anthropology department. They greatly facilitated our visit.

The day after we arrived in Medan, on February 21, 1997, a traditional Toba Batak ritual (*adat*) was held in our honor at the home of Mrs. Simandjuntak. It was attended by our adoptive kin living in Medan, including both Simandjuntak lineage members and their affines who were descended from the founder of the village of Lumban Panggabean. The ceremony was characterized by the eating of *sangsang,* Batak singing and dancing, the delivery of ritual speeches, and the presentation of a sacred cloth (*ulos*) that symbolizes the blessing for health, prosperity, and generativity and is given by the lineage members (*hula hula*) to their wife-receiving affines (*boru*). I had attended such *adat* ceremonies in the past (E. Bruner 1974b), and while this version was shortened and there was a more playful tone to the proceedings than I had previously experienced, the ceremony still contained the essential elements. One person who was about to make a ritual speech in the ceremony jokingly asked what language should be used, Toba Batak, Indonesian, English, or French. My wife, who loves old Batak songs, left her assigned place in the ceremony to join the Simandjuntaks, who were singing together as a group. In some rounds she became a featured soloist, a role I have never seen her play at any social gathering in Illinois.

Our son-in-law and daughter accompanied us to Indonesia, and the Batak were especially delighted to meet our daughter—our eldest child—to whom we had given a Batak middle name, Riana (joyous one). The Batak subsequently referred to us as Ama ni Ria and Nai Ria, father and mother of Ria(na). At the welcoming ceremony, our son-in-law and daughter were also given an *ulos* cloth and a blessing to encourage spiritual powers to give her the gift of fertility (fig. 42). My daughter, then age thirty-seven, had hoped for children for some years. The Simandjuntaks wished her seventeen sons and sixteen daughters, a traditional saying. Four months after receiving the sacred blessing of the Toba Batak, my daughter became pregnant. It must have been a powerful blessing because she gave birth to twin sons.

The Medan reception was warmer than we had anticipated. We learned that we had become something of a legend, as stories were told of how I had slipped from a terraced edge and had fallen into the rice fields in 1957 and of how my wife spoke Toba Batak with the coarse accent of a village woman. On the wall in the living room of one home, we found a framed picture of my wife and me that had been taken in 1971 (fig. 43).

At the Medan ceremony I met Dr. Sinaga who, like me, had married a daughter of the Simandjuntak lineage; this made us members of the same

42. Jane and Blair Valentine, the author's daughter and son-in-law, receiving the sacred *ulos* blessing

43. Framed picture of the author and his wife taken in 1971, on the wall of a Batak home

kinship category. Dr. Sinaga was a medical doctor who also had received a PhD in biochemistry from a university in Holland and held a prominent position at a large teaching hospital in Medan. He was an imposing figure who spoke in many languages with wit and insight. In the presence of Dr. Sinaga, it was difficult to maintain my romantic vision of the Toba Batak Other, any residual notion of the Batak as primitive, or any sense of the ethnographer as a person of privilege relative to the "natives." The power inequalities of 1957 between the wealthy and prestigious visiting American scientist and the poor uneducated natives had been leveled by 1997. Of course, given the postmodern critique in anthropology in the years between our visits, I was already predisposed to give up these colonialist notions; indeed, I had contributed to the critique (E. Bruner, ed., 1984; Turner and Bruner 1986).

What is at issue here is the distinction between the anthropologist and the native, the scientist and the primitive, old anthropological binaries that I had accepted so readily in 1957. In discussing the preparations for our return to Sumatra in this chapter, I described first our fictive kinship relations through the Simandjuntak lineage and then professional anthropological ties through two Illinois PhDs. From a Western perspective, the kinship and the professional might seem quite distinct, as oppositions, the old and the new, gemeinschaft and gesellschaft, but these oppositions merged during the visit to Sumatra. The kinship ties led to the performance of a "traditional" Toba Batak welcoming ritual, but the playful tone and the presence of Dr. Sinaga, a thoroughly modern man, disrupted the association between kinship and tradition.

On the professional side, my former assistant, Professor Mangasa Silitonga, himself a Toba Batak, held what he called a party for us that included not only Batak dancing and ceremonial food such as *sangsang,* but also an old-style Batak orchestra using classic instruments to perform the most traditional of Batak ritual music (*gondang*), designed to recall the ancestral spirits. This was not the recuperation of tradition in performance art, but rather was the enactment of living Toba Batak culture, 1990s style. In some respects, the party Professor Silitonga held for us was even more old Batak, given the form of the dancing and the music, than the kinship-based ceremony held at the home of Mrs. Simandjuntak. The weary oppositions between anthropologist and native, traditional and modern were indeed problematized on our return to Sumatra.

Our entourage arrived in Lumban Panggabean the next day in two Toyota sport-utility vehicles. We found that almost the entire village population had been waiting for us, including representatives of each of the community's thirty-five families. My wife and I had come with two drivers, my daughter and son-in-law, and three Simandjuntaks who had appeared from nowhere to accompany us from the city.

As we entered the village, Batak women hugged my wife (fig. 44), while men and women shook my hand, including those who were too young to have known us on previous visits but had heard about us since. Villagers told and retold stories and recalled memorable moments from our earlier visits, some of which I had forgotten. The group crowded together in the local coffee shop (*warung*), a gathering place and sometimes a meeting hall. We then resumed the exchange of gifts, a practice characteristic of Batak society, that we had begun together forty years before. In 1957, the villagers had welcomed us into their lives, adopted my wife as their daughter, patiently facilitated our research, answered our questions, and generously provided their blessing and protection. When we left the village in 1958, they had given us as gifts some

44. Elaine Bruner entering the village in 1997

45. The author distributing money gifts. Photo by Blair O. Valentine.

of their sacred lineage heirlooms, including priceless old carvings and bark books, which I had in turn donated as part of a collection to the Peabody Museum at Yale University, where I was on the faculty. These old Batak heirlooms were very meaningful to us, but we felt they should be in the public domain for all to see.

In 1997 in our role as wife receivers it was appropriate to make cash gifts (fig. 45) to my wife's lineage. We gave each of the thirty-five families an envelope containing twenty thousand rupiah (then about U.S. $10). Among the Batak themselves, affines make cash gifts to their wife-giving lineage. The Batak kinship pattern is one of exchange, with the wife receivers in perpetual debt for the supreme gift of a wife and of offspring to perpetuate the family line. These are debts that can never be repaid, which precipitates exchanges among kin groups that may continue for generations.

The village that once had no running water, indoor toilets, or electricity had all of these and even television in 1997. In the coffee shop people could gather and drink a Coca-Cola or a beer and watch television. CNN no less. They could watch and discuss the O.J. Simpson trial, the movements in the New York Stock Exchange, the latest Mideast conflict, and events in the Balkans. In this isolated village in Sumatra—at the end of the world, to use my mother-in-law's phrase—people could watch the same news that I viewed in my Illinois living room at approximately the same time.

CNN may well be the exemplary transnational medium, as Lila Abu-Lughod points out, although I disagree with her statement that television and transnational influences render "more and more problematic a concept of cultures as localized communities of people suspended in shared webs of meaning" (1997, 123). It is true that Toba Batak culture is no longer localized, but I do not agree with the second part. Batak people are indeed enmeshed in shared webs of meaning, as may be seen from their vibrant kinship network, even if they are dispersed. I will say more about shared meanings in the next section.

Monuments and Migration

Another new development in Lumban Panggabean has been the construction of massive cement monuments along the road (fig. 46) marking the graves of prominent and wealthy men of the village and with a place for the remains of their wives. It was striking to me that early in their lives all these

46. Recent Toba Batak gravesites in the village

men had left the village to make their fortunes elsewhere in Indonesia, usually in cities. They had lived their adult lives in a modern international world, and only after death had they returned permanently to their highland village. The graves gave a symbolic presence to men who were otherwise absent and were a daily reminder to villagers that the route to a celebrated afterlife, a goal in the Batak cosmological system, lies in leaving the village. Such monumental gravesites are to be found in other villages as well throughout the Tapanuli highlands.

One elaborate monument was dedicated to Sia Marinus Simandjuntak, Ompu Tagururadja, the respected elder who had invited us to study Lumban Panggabean and to stay in his house in 1957. He died at the age of ninety. As I stood by his grave, I recalled the times forty years ago when we had met every morning over tea and papaya to discuss Batak culture. S. M., as he was called, had been a prominent journalist in his early years, an ardent nationalist, and later the *bupati,* the highest government administrative officer for the district of North Tapanuli. My mentor and teacher had moved back and forth between village and city, and we were fortunate that he had been in residence in the village for the period of our fieldwork. He had a good anthropological mind and enjoyed discussing the complexities and ambiguities of Toba Batak life and culture. My wife and I both cried at his gravesite.

All monuments, by their nature, serve to bring the past into the present. Among the Toba Batak, the gravesites are built in the villages, but they are not constructed just anywhere. The specific location selected is thought to be the ancestral homeland of that particular deceased person. It is sacred territory, the *bona ni pasogit,* literally the place of the ancestors. The gravesite is hallowed, magical ground, a site of origin, a place to give offerings to one's ancestors and to ask for their blessing. For these reasons, gravesites are not ordinarily constructed in areas outside Tapanuli.

Elaborate mortuary practices involving the reburial of the bones of important ancestors have long been a part of Toba Batak culture, probably going back to megalithic times (Bartlett 1934). At a first funeral a man is usually buried in the earth. Later there may be reburials with ever-larger grave monuments until finally the bones may be exhumed and placed in a cement structure. In the past, the decision of whether a man was considered to be a venerated ancestor was made by his patrilineal descendants, who organized and paid for the reburial ceremony. In a sense, reburial was a testimony as much to the power and status of the descendants as to the power and status of the ancestor himself.

In addition to individual tombs, in recent decades there have been constructed in the highlands enormous monuments (*tugu*) to clan ancestors,

47. The monument dedicated to the founder of the Simandjuntak clan

some going back fifteen generations (fig. 47). They may contain space not only for the ancestor and his spouse, but also for his sons and their wives. As all clan descendants have the right to attend the mortuary ritual commemorating the building of the *tugu,* these ceremonies may draw thousands of people and last many days. Monuments are expensive to build and the associated rites are costly. The villagers themselves cannot afford them; they are paid for with urban money—by clan members who have become successful in modern Indonesia or abroad and who participate in clan rituals as a tribute to themselves, their descendants, and their clan ancestors.

It is ironic that in these monumental gravesites, these massive structures, the bones of the deceased are literally fixed in concrete, immobilized. Yet the graves themselves are symbols of mobility, of dispersal, of movement by the deceased or his descendants elsewhere, to the centers of Indonesian modernity. It is only the urban rich who can afford to build them. These grave monuments of such great durability attempt to fix the past, to immobilize in concrete the shared culture of the Toba Batak (E. Bruner 1987).

In the case of Lumban Panggabean and other villages, however, the recent grave structures were planned for and in some cases paid for and designed by the wealthy men later buried within them. Each one is different, as each man assures for himself that he will be remembered after his death. These monuments occupy prominent locations, and in Lumban Panggabean they are visible every time one enters or leaves the village. The row of monuments can be seen from the windows or verandas of some houses, and they are close to the coffeehouse, the village meeting place. No one in the village can escape the daily reminder that the route to success in life and in death is migration.

Almost all of the young Toba Batak with whom I spoke in 1957 and 1997, both men and women, wanted to leave the village. Those who migrate seek education, employment, and a better life in the larger society, while those who remain have few choices other than to labor in the rice fields, as the Batak say, like water buffalo. The Batak maintain that education is the golden plow, although education offers different hopes for men and women. Men have greater employment opportunities, whereas women aspire to marry men who have left or will leave the village.

Compared with highland Tapanuli and its few employment possibilities, Indonesia's urban sector was enjoying an expanding economy and high annual growth rates until the political turmoil of 1998. Urban centers provide abundant opportunities for the entrepreneurial Batak, while development and progress are hardly visible in the villages. During the Dutch colonial era migration was discouraged as a matter of colonial policy, and only after Indonesian Independence in late 1949 did large-scale migration become possible. In the half-century since 1950, hundreds of thousands of Toba Batak have left the highland villages. Usman Pelly, a demographic anthropologist, estimates that there are about two million Toba Batak, of whom seven hundred thousand have migrated outside of the Tapanuli highlands, and that of these about three hundred thousand reside in the city of Medan (personal communication, September 8, 1997). The overwhelming majority of those who leave maintain their Batak identity and their Batak clan name, which immediately identifies their ethnicity to other Indonesians; participate in their local variant of Batak ritual practice; and return to the village for important ceremonies. There are, of course, extensive changes in the culture of those who have left, as well as in that of those who remain in the village. Still, almost all Toba Batak continue to maintain an ever-evolving but distinctive Toba Batak social and ceremonial system wherever they reside.

Rituals of Reincorporation

I have described two sets of rituals as if they were independent. First I described the Batak ceremonies of blessing and gift exchange, in which my family participated, and then I described the rituals for deceased migrants who have constructed gravesites and monuments in the highlands. I theorize that there is a connection between these two seemingly discrete ceremonial practices, and I do so from the villager's perspective, taking into account Batak symbolics. My thesis is that both sets of rituals serve to domesticate difference and are an example of the production of locality (Appadurai 1996).

The rituals involving my family incorporated us into the Toba Batak sociocultural system. As foreign travelers we became "Batakized" and were given a position within a living kinship system so that every time we address another member of the lineage or indeed any Simandjuntak, we and they use the appropriate kin terms. My description of these rituals may serve another purpose as well, that of constructing myself as an ethnographer and of situating myself as an active researcher within the anthropological community.

Wealthy migrants who build monumental graves in the highlands do so in part to make a claim to their success in the larger society and to display their wealth and power. From the villagers' point of view, though, mortuary rituals and the monuments serve to reincorporate powerful Batak migrants into village society. Despite their prominence in transnational, cosmopolitan settings, where they may have been international businessmen, high government officials, or generals in the army, they return at death to their village of origin to rest in the soil of their ancestors. What for the migrants is a symbol of prestige then becomes for the villagers a symbol of domestication and reincorporation within the local village world. For the villagers both sets of rituals—the rituals for my family and the rituals for the migrants—make the strange familiar and the global local. They are the means by which Batak culture renews itself and comes alive again, incorporating poor village farmers, wealthy migrants, and foreign anthropologists into one shared web of meaning.

What happens to those who resist incorporation and refuse to play by Toba Batak rules? Anthropologists and returning migrants are predisposed to accept the Batak system and to allow themselves to be enmeshed in a shared web of meaning, but what of members of different ethnic groups, say the Javanese, Minangkabau, or Indonesian Chinese? Urban Batak may relate to these groups on a daily basis as colleagues, neighbors, shopkeepers, schoolmates, or government officials. In these interactions Batak cannot simply extend or adapt their social system because at some point, at the point of conjuncture (Sahlins 1981), people experience irreconcilable differences and inherent contradictions.

Indonesia is ethnically diverse; there are three hundred ethnolinguistic groups in the archipelago. Within their own ethnic group, and especially in their ethnically homogeneous rural areas, the Toba Batak practice Batak culture by Batak rules. In the city Batak learn the new rules of an emerging Indonesian urban culture. The Toba Batak compartmentalize and adapt.

Toward other Batak, in village or city, they behave one way—speaking the Batak language, using Batak rules and kinship terms. With Indonesians of other ethnic groups they speak Indonesian and live by the rules and practices of Indonesian city life (see E. Bruner 1973b and 1974a). Of course, the boundaries are not impenetrable; there is seepage along the ethnic borders, and Batak relations with non-Batak have transformed the Batak system in village and city alike.

Discussion

When I look back to my Batak papers based on my field work of 1957–1958 and the 1970s, I see that the major research focus was an analysis of the transformations in the Toba sociocultural system in different locations and contexts. I studied how the system changed in the village, in the coastal city of Medan, and in Bandung and Jakarta, two cities in Java. In this early fieldwork, I was a mobile ethnographer, following my subject matter, doing multisited ethnography (Marcus 1995) informed by traveling theory (Clifford 1997a). Appadurai (1996), too, might have been delighted to know how brilliant the Toba people were in producing locality. Let me explain.

When Batak people first arrive in a new city, they form a ceremonial and mutual aid society consisting of members of all the different Batak subgroups, not only Toba, but also Karo, Simelungun, Pakpak, Angkola, and Mandailing. This happened in Bandung in the 1950s (E. Bruner 1972). As the population increases, the Toba Batak form their own separate ethnic organization, then divide into units of related partrilineal clans, and then further segment into single-clan associations (*dongan samarga*). With even further growth, each clan association subdivides into regionally based clan segments. For example, the Tobing clan may form four district groups for the northern, southern, eastern, and western parts of a city. These divisions reproduce the system of lineage segmentation and adapt it to an urban environment. An interesting feature is that the patrilineal segmentation goes to the clan level, and then further division occurs along territorial lines. Some large clans now have thirty or more territorially based clan segments in one city. The associations help with weddings and funerals, facilitate the *adat,* provide emergency aid, give scholarships to promising students, and form a network to assist new migrants as they adjust to the city and find employment.

Thus, the Toba Batak reproduce their social ceremonial system with adaptations, thereby producing locality wherever they may reside. They place a map of lineage segments and affinal relations as an overlay on their new territory. I learned this only by following the Batak migration routes and studying permutations in the Toba Batak social and cosmological system.

It would, perhaps, be more accurate to say that rather than following the Batak people, I was following an anthropological problem, that of continuity and transformation in the Batak sociocultural system. The Batak utilize the principles of the patrilineal asymmetrical system not out of some innate cultural imperative, as if somehow "tradition" mechanically reproduces itself, but in response to the situation in which the Batak find themselves in urban Indonesia and in the nation-state.

Abu-Lughod (1991) says that anthropologists should be "writing against culture," that is, against culture as a homogeneous, shared set of meanings. The phrase *writing against culture* conveys Abu-Lughod's notion of culture as a contested and partial arena of struggle and captures current disciplinary thinking. I have advocated this position as well in this book. Abu-Lughod's stance is a reaction against the concept of culture as integrated, functionally consistent, and static. Taking a longer view, though, I maintain that culture can be conceptualized as both contested and shared, in part because in the contestation there is sharing. If the parties to a conflict have nothing in common, they have no grounds to disagree. My position is that anthropologists should be writing not against culture, but against our own anthropological preconceptions of what constitutes culture and where it is located. Aspects of culture that ethnographers leave out are often the ones they take for granted or the ones they somehow deem inappropriate for their ethnographic account.

Anthropological perceptions of what should be included in the study of a culture do change over time. The profession is now well aware that pre–World War II ethnographers failed to situate their accounts in the larger patterns of colonialism and political domination within which they were embedded. In his famous introduction to the frequently cited and criticized *The Nuer* (1940), E. E. Evans-Pritchard at least provided some information on the context of British rule, although he never could have envisioned the extent of the subsequent anthropological critique of colonialism.

In his classic 1935 study of the Crow, Robert Lowie presented a view of culture that was based on a narrative structure, widely shared in the discipline at the time, that led him to describe not Crow practice—what he actually observed in the field—but rather a historical composite. He included aspects of Crow culture that had completely disappeared, such as buffalo hunting and the nomadic warrior life, and he omitted aspects of Crow culture that were still current, such as the relationship of the tribe to the federal government. His characterization of the Crow was based on a prior theoretical vision of what should properly be included in an ethnographic description, and the reader cannot know from his account how the Crow actually lived in the 1920s. Ethnographers know this now, and there have been many critiques of salvage ethnography. The relevant questions for this chapter become: What was my 1957 prior vision? What were my unexamined, taken-for-granted narratives about fieldwork, anthropology, and myself as ethnographer? More significantly, what might the discipline's current prior visions and narratives be?

Clifford Geertz (1973) once wrote that anthropologists do not study villages, they study in villages. I would amend that now, and Geertz might agree (see 1995, 53): anthropologists should no longer study in villages, and if we do, then our view of the village we study in should be radically altered. As I have shown, the set of beliefs and practices that exists within the physical confines of a Toba Batak village would now be a very incomplete characterization of contemporary, real-time Toba Batak culture because so much of that culture is located elsewhere and takes place outside of the village, in sites all over Indonesia and the world at large. The village population is demographically skewed, as a disproportionate number of widows, children, and old people live there. A study restricted to one site thus risks neglecting the flow of knowledge, money, symbols, people, and goods to and from other sites, Appadurai's "scapes." Further, the thoughts of those inside the village include a consciousness of the outside: thoughts of their relatives in diverse locations, stories migrants tell when they return to the village, schemes for escape from the labor of work in the rice fields (fig. 48), knowledge of economic opportunities elsewhere, and images depicted on television and in film and

48. The mud of the rice fields from which village youth want to escape

other media. To take the village as the unit of analysis and then to see forces as impinging from the outside is no solution because many of these forces already exist within the village and within the consciousness of the villagers.

The postmodern critique has perhaps transformed most anthropologists' attitude toward ethnography; certainly my own view has changed. In 1957 I was more confident about the discipline and more secure about my role as ethnographer. Everything seemed clearer in those years, and anthropology appeared more stable. In retrospect, however, I see that anthropology was somewhat rigid and limited in the scope of what could be studied. I enjoy the freedom postmodern innovations bring to my investigations: freedom to follow my humanistic inclinations; to discuss the politics of fieldwork; to revel in the inherent ambiguities of the situation; to seek the ironic inconsistencies of life; to view the subject matter historically and processually; to bring more play and openness into field research; to grapple with the global interconnectedness of the world; to study new topics such as tourism, which did not appear to be serious enough for the anthropology of the 1950s; and to write reflexively, as in this chapter. I applaud the new transnational work of Ortner, Stoller, Abu-Lughod, Appadurai, and Marcus, and they would probably agree that the profession needs to take account of transnationalism in all anthropological settings.

Sherry Ortner's 1958 high school class was together in one locality, engaged in face-to-face relations, only during the school years, for after graduation the members of the class dispersed. There was 100 percent geographic mobility, and class members and their spouses came together most prominently in reunions. In Ortner's terms, they are a postcommunity. In Paul Stoller's case of the West African street vendors, the members of different African nations and ethnic groups migrate to New York City for varying periods of time, and while they are there, they form an occupational subgroup in one of the most ethnically diverse cities in the world. For Stoller, they occupy a transnational space. In my work on tourism, the tourists come from distant places and the natives come out of their communities to coexist in a specially constructed locality, a performance space that I call a touristic borderzone, from which the tourists return to their hotels and the locals to their homes and families, each to their own spaces.

The Batak village remains a fixed, bounded locality, but the ways of the outside world now reside within the village and within the minds of the villagers. For nearly fifty years a stream of villagers has been migrating while maintaining an identification with their place of origin; some migrants even retain ownership of their village homes and rice fields. This was already clear to some extent in 1957 but was stunningly apparent by 1997. The Batak as a group constitute a postlocal community, one that is radically delocalized, but the culture of the Toba Batak continues to emerge in many diverse transnational spaces, and there is continuous interaction among geographically dispersed ethnic and kin group members. Just as Ortner's class has a center in the high school and Stoller's street vendors have centers in Senegal or other West African nations, so too do the Batak have a center (*bona ni pasogit*) in their home village. Batak identify themselves as members of that village even if they were born elsewhere and have never been there. The village represents for them the sacred origin of their spirit (*tondi*), and of their lineage, kin, and ancestors.

Some recent conceptualizations (Clifford 1997a) privilege travel, mobility, and movement, but I would contend that Clifford's formulation must be tempered by an ethnographic understanding of the specific cultural symbolics involved and of the people's own sense of travel, mobility, locality, and place. These topics can best be studied by fieldwork and by the methods of ethnography. The particular strength of anthropological science compared to other disciplines is precisely that it can produce a more culturally and symbolically sensitive transnationalism.

Appadurai writes that "the task of ethnography now becomes the unraveling of a conundrum: what is the nature of locality as a lived experience in a globalized, deterritorialized world?" (1996, 52). However, locality, in this case the Toba Batak village, has no monolithic meaning as "lived experience." Researchers cannot assume that a bounded space such as a village has its own intrinsic meaning. For most younger Batak, the village is a place from which to escape, a site of lifelong drudgery, poverty, and, for some, a symbol of their failure to position themselves so as to experience the excitement and opportunities available in the larger world. For some wealthy urban elders, it is a place to be buried, to return to in the afterlife, to be forever with the ancestors. For yet other sophisticated Batak living in transnational spaces, the village becomes an imaginary place, a sacred center, a site of memory that they glorify in nostalgic and even romantic terms, much as this ethnographer first did in 1957.

ACKNOWLEDGMENTS AND CREDITS

EVERY AUTHOR BUILDS upon the shoulders of others, but three people have been central in helping me with this volume. My wife, Elaine C. Bruner, my constant companion, to whom this book is dedicated, has done fieldwork, gathered data, and made insightful contributions on every research project described here. We are a team. She has enjoyed doing the ethnography of tourism as much as I have. Barbara Kirshenblatt-Gimblett, a coauthor and colleague, was especially skillful in encouraging me to finish this book. We had fun working together and still do. Alma Gottlieb has given most of the chapters in this book a close reading, and her suggestions and support over the years have been invaluable. These are three exceptional women. Sally Price and Barbara Babcock have read the entire manuscript, and I thank them for their excellent and thoughtful comments. Victor Turner came into my life about 1980 and was an inspiration during a period of close collaboration.

Since 1988 I have taught a seminar on tourism at the University of Illinois and at the Chinese University of Hong Kong, and student input has been critical in the development of the ideas presented in these studies. Bridget Mullin worked as a research assistant in the preparation of this volume. The introduction, chapter two, and chapter eight were presented in the University of Illinois sociocultural workshop; for their comments at the workshop I thank Matti Bunzl, Clark Cunningham, Timothy Daniels, Brenda Farnell, Richard Freeman, Bill Kelleher, Janet Keller, Alejandro Lugo, Bruno Nettl, Andrew Orta, David Plath, Helaine Silverman, Nicole Tami, Arlene Torres, and Joy Sather-Wagstaff. It is a blessing to have congenial colleagues who take an interest in my work. David Brent encouraged this project from the beginning, and Meg Cox was a caring copy editor. My children, Jane and Dan, have accompanied me on some of my trips to Bali and Kenya and were not only a personal delight but proved to be inveterate travelers. I took all of the photographs in this book except where specified otherwise. Previously published chapters have been edited and revised, and details about their previous publication are noted below; all have been reprinted with the permission of the publishers.

Chapter 1 appeared as an article coauthored with Barbara Kirshenblatt-Gimblett, "Maasai on the Lawn: Tourist Realism in East Africa," *Cultural Anthropology* 9, no. 2 (1994): 435–70. Stanley Ambrose, Alan H. Jacobs, Michel Picard, and Aidan Southall helped with incisive comments. Chapter 2 appeared as "The Maasai and the Lion King:

Authenticity, Nationalism, and Globalization in African Tourism," *American Ethnologist* 28, no. 4 (2001): 881–908. An early version was presented at a conference on tourism in September 1999 at the Department of Anthropology, Yunnan University, Kunming, People's Republic of China. Chapter 3 appeared as "Tourism in Ghana: The Representation of Slavery and the Return of the Black Diaspora," *American Anthropologist* 98, no. 2 (1996): 290–304. I hesitated to write about this topic, given its sensitivity and my own subject position, but after reading early drafts of this chapter, African American colleagues and specialists in African American studies felt the data were useful and encouraged me to publish. Kal Alston, Alice Deck, Faye V. Harrison, Emily Osborn, Richard Price, Enid Schildkrout, and especially my colleague in Ghana, Kofi Agyeman, made important contributions to the study.

Chapter 4 appeared as "Lincoln's New Salem as a Contested Site," *Museum Anthropology* 17, no. 3 (1993): 14–25. The National Endowment for the Humanities Summer Stipend, the Hewlett grant program, and the University of Illinois Research Board and Center for the Study of Cultural Values and Ethics provided financial support for my research at New Salem. Christina Hardway was my assistant on the project. I thank Richard S. Taylor for facilitating my work at New Salem, for his friendship, and for many exciting discussions. Robert Johannsen, Jean-Philippe Mathy, Norman Denzin, Daphne Berdahl and the students in my 1992 tourism seminar made perceptive comments. Chapter 5 appeared as "Abraham Lincoln as Authentic Reproduction: A Critique of Postmodernism," *American Anthropologist* 96, no. 2 (1994): 397–415. Earlier versions were presented at the anthropology departments of the Universities of Wisconsin, Chicago, and Virginia, as well as at "Le Tourisme International entre Tradition et Modernité," a conference held at Carrefour Universitaire Méditerranéen, Nice, in 1992. Chapter 6 appeared as an article coauthored with Phyllis Gorfain, "Dialogic Narration and the Paradoxes of Masada," pp. 56–79 in *Text, Play, and Story: The Construction and Reconstruction of Self and Society*, ed. Edward M. Bruner, 1983 Proceedings of the American Ethnological Society (Washington, DC: American Anthropological Society, 1984). The order of the coauthors' names is alphabetical and indicates no precedence in authorship. Nina Auerbach, Dan Ben-Amos, Peter Garrett, Jack Glazier, Linda Taranik Grimm, Guneli Gun, Don Handelman, Benjamin Hrushovsky, Keiko Ikeda, Diana Grossman Kahn, Cary Nelson, Isaac Neuman, William Schroeder, Stephen Sniderman, Victor Turner, Ana Cara Walker, Sandra Zagarell, and Yael Zerubavel made helpful comments.

Chapter 7 appeared as "Tourism in the Balinese Borderzone," pp. 157–79 in *Displacement, Diaspora, and Geographies of Identity*, ed. Smadar Lavie and Ted Swedenburg (Durham, NC: Duke University Press, 1996). An earlier draft was presented at "Tourism and the Change of Life Styles," a conference held at Instytut Turystyki, Warsaw, Poland, in 1988; at the Department of Performance Studies, New York University; and at the anthropology departments of SUNY Buffalo and Rice University. Insightful suggestions were made by Barbara Kirshenblatt-Gimblett, Richard Schechner, Dennis and Barbara Tedlock, Bruce Jackson, George Marcus, and Hildred Geertz. Chapter 8 has not been previously published. I am indebted to Kathleen Adams for her comments. Chapter 9 appeared as "Return to Sumatra: 1957, 1997," *American Ethnologist* 26, no. 2 (1999): 461–77, and has been presented at a seminar at the Chinese University of Hong Kong.

NOTES

Introduction

1. I could have paid my own way and gone on the tour simply as another tourist, which I did do elsewhere, but that was expensive, and it was more difficult to gather data. The tourists were more likely to ask questions, to offer their impressions, and to express their feelings directly to the tour guide than to another tourist. The best presentation of the methodological problem of gathering data on a highly mobile population of tourists is Graburn (2002), although he does not discuss the strategy of the anthropologist becoming a guide.

2. The agency paid me two hundred dollars per tourist, plus expenses. For the 1986 and the 1987 tours I earned a total of about four thousand dollars, but as my wife always accompanies me on my ethnological field trips and we had to pay her expenses both times, we actually lost money.

3. I also wanted photographs of tourist-Indonesian interactions for my research and for class lectures.

4. It was not exactly a disaster as I had served as a guide-lecturer four times in Indonesia, for three different agencies, and once in Thailand-Burma, and I had accomplished my research objectives in this role. Thereafter, I turned to other approaches in my studies of tourism. In addition to serving as guide, I did traditional field work in all the tourist destinations described in this book by staying in one place, sometimes for many months, to study the local performers and producers, as well as how the tourists moved through the sites.

5. The term *postmodernism* is used in so many different ways that it needs clarification. I reject those radical postmodern positions that are antiscience, that claim that nothing exists outside the text, and that neglect the materiality of the physical world. I see no conflict between postmodernism and science, and indeed I see myself as doing anthropological postmodern science. External reality does not present itself as an objective given but always in a context that must be interpreted by persons located in particular subject positions in a given historical era. My views, I believe, are not radical but foundational, and they have been widely accepted within cultural anthropology.

6. One critique of Kirshenblatt-Gimblett's (1998) book *Destination Culture* is that it relies so much on recontextualization, in which cultural heritage is seen as being taken from one context and given a second life in another, as a material object would be taken from an indigenous ritual and then placed in a museum display. My position is more radically constructivist in that for me, every time heritage or tradition is enacted it is given new life, irrespective of where that enactment takes place, as a continuous ongoing process.

7. One participant on the Indonesian trip remarked that he would never go on one of those tours that that cover Asia in a few weeks, moving from Hong Kong, to Singapore, to

Bangkok, to Bali with a brief three days in each locality. He claimed that by spending three weeks in one country our group was able to explore Indonesia in depth. In three weeks!

8. Over the past few decades there clearly has been increasing scholarly interest in tourism, as may be seen from the number of published books and the number of panels devoted to the topic at scientific meetings. Recent works on tourism include Abram, Waldren, and Macleod 1997; Boissevain 1996; Castaneda 1996; Causey 2003; Chambers 1999; Cohen 1996, 2004b; Coleman and Crang 2002; Crick 1994; Dahles 2001; Dann 1996, 2002; Desmond 1999; Franklin 2003; Gmelch 2004; Handler and Gable 1997; Harrison 2003; Kirshenblatt-Gimblett 1998; Lanfant, Allcock, and Bruner 1995; Lavie and Swedenburg 1996; Löfgren 1999; Nash 1996; Ness 2003; Oakes 1998; Phillips and Steiner 1999; Picard 1996; Picard and Wood 1997; Rojek and Urry 1997; Schein 2000; Selwyn 1996; Tan, Cheung, and Yang 2001; Teo, Chang, and Ho 2001; Yamashita 2003. I have published on tourism in such professional journals as the *American Anthropologist, American Ethnologist,* and *Cultural Anthropology* with the explicit purpose of contributing to the acceptance of tourism studies within anthropology. My focus has been on American upscale packaged tours, on ethnographic tourism. I recognize that this is just one form of tourism; there are regional and national differences in tourist objectives and outcomes.

9. Barbara Kirshenblatt-Gimblett says in Franklin 2001 (p. 212) that "Ed Bruner turned me on to tourism as a research subject." Equally, Barbara turned me on to the concept of performance and to the analysis of staged events as units of study.

10. Although I had already read Bakhtin, it was Phyllis Gorfain who suggested a more systematic application of his ideas to the study of Masada (chapter 6).

11. In this volume, when I use the words *native, Third World, traditional,* and *indigenous,* they should be understood as though they were in quotes. In anthropological discourse such words can have negative and sometimes derogatory connotations, but in tourist discourse and in tourist advertising, they are used frequently and unreflexively.

12. My trip was made possible by the generosity of the donors, Ann and Paul Krouse, and the University of Illinois Foundation.

13. The key idea in Gottlieb's paper, the importance of social class in tourism, has still not been adequately explored.

14. University of Illinois student Nicole Tami and New York University student Margaret A. Vail, are investigating independent travelers in Kenya and Bolivia for their dissertation research. Tami reports that there are more occasions for interactions with locals as independent travelers negotiate directly for lodging, meals, and guides, and hence there are more opportunities for stories of adventure and chance encounters. Vail (1995) notes that because of their lack of funds and their mode of travel, backpackers are not in a position to accumulate souvenirs, so what they bring home are memories and travel stories. See Cohen 2004a for a nuanced discussion of the many forms of backpacking. Also see Richards and Wilson 2004.

15. There was of course no independent way of verifying the personal information that was offered. On tour, among strangers, individuals may construct a false identity, or at least a biased one. Because of their temporary fleeting nature, journeys provide an opportunity for self construction more in the realm of fantasy and play than in actuality.

16. That tourism creates home while away in an alternating pattern is a very different concept from Adrian Franklin's argument that the distinction between the everyday and the touristic has become "entirely blurred" and that the two are now "indistinguishable" (2003, 5). In his view, the condition of the current world is such that our experience becomes increasingly touristic because of globalization, new consumption patterns, and migrant com-

munities in major cities (see also Urry 2004). Tourism for Franklin is a metaphor of the postmodern condition; tourism for me is less a contemporary sensibility than a mode of travel.

17. Many other scholars write about tourist narratives; see especially the provocative work by Jamieson (2002), Löfgren (1999), and Vail (1995).

18. In the late 1970s, during a period when Marxism was prominent in the social sciences, there were a number of studies interpreting tourism as neocolonialism (e.g. Greenwood 1977, Nash 1977). Tourism was seen in negative terms as corrupting local cultures and leading to exploitation and commoditization. In this frame, capitalism was the culprit, a malevolent outside force penetrating indigenous society. These analyses were associated with an economic cost-benefit framework that measured the good versus the bad in tourism. In recent decades, tourism scholars have turned to more interpretive and global perspectives, or to a more sophisticated neo-Marxism. Assessing the effects of tourism on the host society, however, is still an important research issue. I have argued elsewhere that tourism changes the locals more than it does the tourists (E. Bruner1991).

19. This is true not only of tourism, but also of other travels, including those of missionaries, colonialists, traders, and journalists. Colonial Bali, for example, is just as much an invention, with its own metanarratives, as is tourist Bali (Boon 1977, Lansing 1991).

20. Nicole Tami has suggested that in addition to the trip as lived, experienced, and told, there is a fourth dimension, the trip as imagined. This is an intriguing idea. It is most applicable before travel begins, as part of the pretour narrative process, but it goes beyond this into the consciousness and imagination of the traveler. The trip as imagined may simply replicate what is presented in the standard tour agency brochures, which frequently tell the tourists what they should think and how they should feel, but individual travelers may construct their own pretour narratives. Nicole writes "I thought about my father who begins to prepare for a vacation at least a year in advance by scouting guidebooks, novels, and the internet for information about the place he intends to visit" (personal communication, July 5, 2003). The trip as imagined certainly speaks to the agency of tourists and to how travelers personalize their journey.

21. I am indebted to Barbara Babcock for this idea.

22. Julia Harrison (2003) has written a book based entirely on posttour tellings. Anthropological posttour narratives are contained in anthropologists' professional writings and presentations (E. Bruner 1986b).

23. It is worth noting that the best theorists, who have influenced me and have contributed the most to research on tourism, heritage, and travel, such as Dean MacCannell (1976, 1992), John Urry (1990), Erik Cohen (1996), Barbara Kirshenblatt-Gimblett (1998), and James Clifford (1997a), are not ethnographers. They certainly know anthropology, but MacCannell, Urry, and Cohen are sociologists; Kirshenblatt-Gimblett is a folklorist; and Clifford is an historian. Established anthropologists, such as Richard Handler and Eric Gable (1997), and Richard and Sally Price (1992, 1994), who deal with tourism and related issues do solid ethnography, and I am particularly encouraged by the newer ethnographic work on tourism by Orvar Löfgren (1999) for its delightful sensitivity and by Ruth Phillips and Christopher Steiner (1999) for its insights on tourist arts, as well as by Heidi Dahles (2001), Andrew Causey (2003), and Sally Ann Ness (2003).

Chapter One

1. In the literature, *Maasai* is sometimes spelled with the double *a* and sometimes, as in *Masai,* with a single *a*. Except where the single *a* spelling has become part of a proper name, as in *Masai Mara,* we will use the double *a* spelling derived from the language group

Maa, which is current scholarly practice (Spear and Waller 1993). Aside from the Maasai, other Maa-speaking peoples include the Samburu, the Njemps, and the Arusha. Both Maasai and Samburu people perform at Mayers Ranch. In this chapter we sometimes use the term *Maasai* to refer to both Maasai and Samburu performers.

2. See E. Bruner 1993a; Clifford 1992; Crick 1989; Graburn and Jafari 1991; D. Harrison 1992; Hitchcock, King, and Parnwell 1993; Pratt 1992; Smith 1977/1989; Smith and Eadington 1992.

3. There are about 400,000 Maasai in Kenya; fewer than a hundred are employed at Mayers Ranch.

4. The Maasai term is *murran* or *ilmurran,* but at Mayers they use the term *moran.*

5. Jane's comment was prophetic: the tourist performance at Mayers Ranch was closed down by the government a few years after she posed the question. As Jane said at the time, tribalism and colonialism were anachronisms, and as events unfolded they proved to be too anachronistic for modern-day Kenya. The issue is discussed in the next chapter, which deals with Maasai tourism in a more comparative and historical framework. The closing of Mayers Ranch, however, does not diminish the scholarly importance of our analysis of the performance as it existed in 1984.

6. The data for this chapter was gathered in 1984, so all references to "now" or "at this time" refer to that time period.

7. In February 1984 the exchange rate was U.S. $1 = 13.78 Kenyan shillings.

8. There are Maa-speaking peoples who are agriculturalists and others who are hunters, despite the popular understanding of the Maasai as dedicated pastoralists. Pastoralism remains an ideal, but economic choices depend on ecological and climatic conditions, and the diet varies accordingly.

9. Important sources on the Maasai age-set system include Jacobs 1965, Galaty 1977, and Spencer 1988 and 1993.

10. We do not claim that these photos are scientific representations or that they are in any sense superior to photographs taken by the tourists.

11. Tourist realism at Mayers Ranch should be distinguished from Lisa's master narrative about tourist productions as representations of an authentic culture, as described in the introduction. The two concepts differ. *Tourist realism* refers to a process of production leading to an end product of naturalism, while *metanarrative* refers to a story that places a frame around all cultural performances, which in Lisa's case are unexamined replicas of life in the ethnographic present. Tourist realism is a conscious construction, as indicated by Jane's efforts to make the Maasai look "smart" and "natural." Both Jane and the Maasai are well aware of the continuing effort required to achieve realism, as in the process Jane changes the way the Maasai dress, behave, and present themselves. Jane's expertise is in how she shapes a particular production. Lisa's expertise is in how she shapes a tour itinerary that she purchases for her agency. Lisa does not strive to change a performance, as she does not have specialized knowledge about local cultures; nor does she raise issues of realism or authenticity, which for her remain essentially taken for granted. What Jane and Lisa share, however, is the hope that the tourists will be satisfied with the performance, as both are selling a product. Jane and Lisa do have different roles in the tourist enterprise, in that Jane is a theater producer whereas Lisa is a theater impresario. Related issues are further considered in the next chapter.

12. The picture is not equivalent to MacCannell's front stage, as discussed in the introduction. The phrase *the picture,* based on a photographic metaphor, is a folk concept, an

indigenous term that developed at Mayers and refers specifically to the performance there. The front stage is a sociological concept that implies a back stage that is thought to be more real and true. There are many activities at Mayers Ranch, such as the flower export business, that are not included in the picture and that the tourists do not attempt to explore, so that they do not constitute a back stage in MacCannell's sense.

13. Alan Jacobs, personal communication, September 15, 1986.

Chapter Two

1. Although the subject matter is different, the methodology is not unlike that employed by James Clifford (1997a) in his paper "Four Northwest Coast Indian Museums."

2. Adams 1998, Cheung 1999, and Hughes-Freeland 1993 are exceptions.

3. My "questioning gaze" was inspired by Dean MacCannell's (2001) concept of the "second gaze," which he developed in opposition to Urry's (1990) "tourist gaze." I agree with most of MacCannell's critique of John Urry. See also Kasfir 1999.

4. Barbara Kirshenblatt-Gimblett and I did fieldwork together in 1984 at Mayers Ranch, the results of which we published, and at Bomas, the results of which we did not publish. I returned to Kenya in 1995 and 1999 to revisit old sites, gather new data, and initiate fieldwork on Maasai tourism on the Mara, including the Sundowner. For the past fifteen years, Kirshenblatt-Gimblett has influenced my work on the Maasai and on tourism.

5. Members of the tour group had to obtain visas, but their passports were collected by the Intrav tour guides, who handled all the immigration and customs arrangements.

6. Bomas of Kenya was initiated by the government in 1971 and opened in 1973 under the Kenya Tourist Development Corporation, a part of the Ministry of Tourism and Wildlife.

7. As there are forty-two ethnic groups in Kenya, but only eleven traditional villages at Bomas, many groups are left out, although some that are not represented in the villages are represented in the performance. There is no representation of such minorities as the resident Indian population.

8. At the time of my visit, Bomas charged a Kenyan citizen about one-third the amount paid by a foreign tourist, and for a resident child it charged only about one-third of the amount paid by a Kenyan adult, making it financially feasible for many Kenyans to come to Bomas for a family outing with their children.

9. The African Classic Tours brochure for 1986 states:

> Here in East Africa, we can still view the world as our primitive ancestors saw it, in its natural state, without the influences of modern civilization. . . . Here are the living remains of prehistoric human cultures, people who still live by hunting and gathering: nomadic peoples living in small family groups. Here we can view the daily struggle for survival . . . and see people and wildlife living, for the most part, unaffected by our rapidly changing society.

10. All quotes are from the brochure for the Intrav "On Safari in Africa" trip, February 2 to 25, 1999.

11. I must acknowledge the ambiguity of my subject position especially at the Sundowner, for I oscillated between being a tourist and being an ethnographer (see chapter 7). All ethnographers occasionally experience a similar oscillation between being there as a participant in another culture and merging into the ongoing activity, and attending to the demands of being a scholar, striving for the distance and objectivity necessary to write for an anthropological audience. I have felt this tension in my work on tourism more than in other ethnographic endeavors.

12. I am indebted to Mulu Muia, Duncan Muriuki, and to Jean Kidula for helpful information on the musical scene in Kenya. The data here was gathered by modern electronic means, e-mail and the Internet. Bomas, Kichwa Tembo Tented Camp, and Them Mushrooms all have their own Web sites.

13. I do not know the relationship between the use of *hakuna matata* in "Jambo Bwana" and its use in the Elton John–Tim Rice song. Neither the lyrics nor the music are the same, but the phrase is equally prominent in both songs.

14. Them Mushrooms also are known for reggae and for their fusion of reggae with local musical traditions. They are credited with the first recording of a reggae song in East Africa, in 1981 with CBS Kenya Records. Their inspiration was Jamaican reggae musician Bob Marley (Them Mushrooms 2000). Reggae also has a political meaning connected to the Rastafarians.

15. Megan Wood (1999) reports that funds flow inequitably to the Maasai chiefs and politicians, and there have been many accusations of corruption. Dhyani Berger (1996) discusses these inequities, offers solutions, and shows how the Maasai are being integrated into the tourism industry in Kenya. Kiros Lekaris, Stanley Ole Mpakany, Meegesh Nadallah, and Gerald Ole Selembo have helped me to better understand how the Maasai on the Mara do profit economically from safari tourism.

16. I thank Eric Gable for many of the ideas in this paragraph.

Chapter Three

1. My larger aim is to study the global transnational process of tourism in its local manifestations. Methodologically, this chapter takes Elmina as the local site for analysis, examining the castle both as a performance and as a physical structure.

2. I was in Ghana in June and again in September 1994, for a total of approximately six weeks, as part of a USAID contract administered by MUCIA (Midwest Universities Consortium for International Activities) through the Tourism Center at the University of Minnesota. I acknowledge that this was a short time for fieldwork, but I had considerable help in the field. J. B. Lomo-Mainoo and Ben Anane-Nsiah of the Ghana Tourist Board were my local hosts. I assembled a research team consisting of Dominic Kofi Agyeman of the Sociology Department at the University of Cape Coast; his assistant, Henry D. K. Baye; my wife, Elaine C. Bruner; and Joanna Mensah and John Akofi-Holison, university students and residents of Elmina. Our team interviewed members of many segments of the Elmina community, including government officials, traditional chiefs, the queen of the fishmongers, the chief fisherman, the priest and priestess of Benya shrine, the heads of asafo companies (military organizations), the chair of the bakatue (festival) planning committee, owners of bars and hotels catering to tourists, tour guides, and ordinary citizens. In addition, we set up six focus groups in Elmina consisting of fifty-nine individuals ranging in age from fifteen to seventy, about equally divided between men and women. The focus group discussions were conducted in the Fanti language, transcribed, and then translated into English. As fieldwork was conducted in 1994, all references to "now" refer to that time period.

3. The romantic notions are there, but Angelou, Harris, and other African American writers who return to Africa also describe their disillusionment with the poverty, sickness, heat, and hardship of modern Africa.

4. Imahküs Robinson gave me a typed copy of her article dated January 1994, but I was unable to obtain the newspaper citation.

5. I do not claim that the Robinsons represent the voice of all African Americans who

travel to Ghana, but the couple are prominent in local discourse, they establish relationships with African American visitors, and they are articulate spokespersons for one stream of diaspora thought.

6. The question of whether or not to paint the castles was discussed in the local newspapers, and I raised the issue with the Council of Chiefs of Edina (Elmina) at a meeting in the House of Chiefs. The chiefs were in favor of Elmina Castle being painted, but without covering up the faces of the atrocities of the slave trade.

7. See Appiah 1990 for an analysis of the many meanings of *racism*.

8. "We Shall Overcome" and the Negro National Anthem, as well as "Kum Ba Yah" and the reggae version of "Hakuna Matata" performed by the Maasai at the Sundowner (chapter 2), are essentially American songs, or American-influenced songs, that are presented for foreign tourists in Africa.

9. Faye V. Harrison, in her review of this chapter, made some comments so relevant to issues discussed here that I obtained her permission to quote her directly, rather than to simply paraphrase her words. She writes as follows:

> The independent and quite controversial film, *Sankofa,* produced and directed by Ethiopian filmmaker and Howard University professor Haile Gerima, begins its storyline in one of Ghana's "slave castles" with a tour group being shown the dungeons. A beautiful (blond wig–wearing) black fashion model who's being photographed on the outside of the castle becomes curious when she sees the tourist group descend into a dark tunnel, so she follows them. Her path takes her across time into the 17th or 18th century. The film accomplishes what the Robinsons' performance does, except in much more graphic terms and imagery! I remember coming out of the theater needing to be debriefed for my return to 20th-century everyday life. The intensified anger and hostility I felt toward racial oppression stimulated me to think and talk through complexities and nuances that the film erased. In light of "Tourism in Ghana," what's interesting about the film is that it was produced largely for an African American audience, but the director and scriptwriter were African as were many of the cultural agents who made the project feasible. This is an instance when a diasporic return home was the result of a transcultural and transnational collaboration. The film could not have been produced without the meeting in the borderlands conjoining the diaspora and continent.

Harrison's comment is in the theoretical tradition of Paul Gilroy (1993), to which we shall turn later in this chapter. Relevant also is the difference between texts produced by writers and intellectuals and ethnographic data gathered from ordinary citizens.

10. The silence about slavery in Ghanaian public discourse may reflect shame and embarrassment, even guilt, about the Ghanaian role in the slave trade. Liz Sly reports that in December 1994 "a group of Ghanaian chiefs performed a ceremony of atonement for their ancestors' role in slavery for a group of visiting African-Americans" (1995).

11. This formulation may be so jarring to an American sensibility because it speaks of wealthy African Americans who return to Ghana almost as if they were like European immigrants who became successful in the New World and returned for a visit to the old country to display their newfound prosperity. It blurs the distinction so crucial to the American experience between slavery and migration, between forced migration for involuntary servitude and a voluntary journey to seek a better life. The Ghanaian formulation leads us to further problematize the concept of travel and traveling theory (Clifford 1989).

12. For the larger context of the politics of the representation of race at Colonial Williamsburg, see Gable, Handler, and Lawson, 1992.

13. Charisse Jones reports that within the last decade many African Americans have "begun to re-examine slavery—reflecting upon it in film and music, remembering it through ritual and ceremony, assessing its legacy from universities to neighborhood study groups." Particular expressions are enumerated that document the "transition from feelings of shame and denial about slavery to an embrace of that painful past" (1995). Jones writes that there has been an increase in performances about slavery within the U.S. black community. My point, however, may still be valid—that America has not yet come to terms with slavery as a national rather than simply as a black or ethnic tragedy, and that we have not yet fully acknowledged the necessity for a truly national catharsis. As I write these words, the O. J. Simpson trial and the Million Man March have precipitated renewed discussion of race relations in America, but I ask, How can America come to terms with racism if we don't yet have ways of representing and talking about the single most significant experience in black American history, the experience of slavery?

14. As part of the tourism development project, a team from the Smithsonian Institution produced the exhibits at the West African Museum at Cape Coast Castle, and their challenge was to balance the conflicting political currents to which they were exposed. According to observer Enid Schildkrout, who is a specialist on Ghana as well as a museum professional, the voice of the diaspora "dominated the script of the exhibition" at the expense of the voice of the Ghanaians (personal communication, 1995).

15. I do not have firm statistical data on the precise incidence of crime against tourists in Elmina.

16. Ruth Behar (1993) reports similar findings.

17. The Maasai at the tourist attractions described in chapters 1 and 2 are paid performers, and it is mutually understood that tourists have the right to take pictures of them. If a tourist were to take photographs of the Maasai on the reserve without permission, there might well be similar objections.

18. Sophisticated agencies like Intrav (chapter 2) are especially skilled in masking the commercial nature of their tour itinerary.

19. Recent economic studies on Ghana include Mikell 1989 and Clark 1994.

20. The institution of chieftaincy, of course, is influenced by many factors other than tourism development, for example, local politics and economics.

Chapter Four

1. See Benedict 1983; J. Anderson 1984, chapter 6; Stocking 1985; Blatti 1987; Kirshenblatt-Gimblett and Bruner 1989; Clifford 1988; Handler and Saxton 1988; Fischer 1989; Dorst 1989; Karp and Lavine 1991; and Gable, Handler, and Lawson 1992.

2. There are, of course, alternate Lincoln stories and even anti-Lincoln narratives. For example, during the civil rights movement of the 1960s, the notion that Lincoln had freed the slaves was considered at best premature, for the struggle was not yet over, and Lincoln was labeled a white supremacist (Oates 1984).

3. This hypothesis is more explicit in some tellings than in others. See Thomas 1954, where it is very explicit.

4. For a more complete account of the development of the restored New Salem, see Taylor and Johnson 1993.

5. Two recent reinterpretations (Simon 1990 and Wilson 1990) suggest that Ann Rutledge was more important in Lincoln's life than is currently assumed. Simon's point is that although Herndon distorted the record about Mary Todd, this does not mean he was misinformed about Ann Rutledge. Simon is convinced that Abe loved Ann, but the new

mystery is whether Ann reciprocated his feelings—whether she loved Abraham Lincoln. In recent feminist scholarship there is also a renewed interest in putting the record straight about Mary Todd Lincoln (see Neely and McMurtry 1986; Schreiner 1987; Baker 1987; Van Der Heuvel 1988).

6. See Woodward 1987. The replies and rejoinders were "Gore Vidal's 'Lincoln'?: An Exchange," *New York Review of Books* 35, no. 7 (April 28, 1988); and "Vidal's 'Lincoln': An Exchange," *New York Review of Books* 35, no. 13 (August 18, 1988).

7. In 1990 the Christmas celebration at New Salem was not held, in part because in previous years the tourists had been disappointed that there were no colored lights and no decorated trees; hence the celebration did not visibly conform to their twentieth-century expectations of what Christmas should look like.

8. These multiple purposes, to portray the transformation of Abraham Lincoln at New Salem, to show life in an 1830s prairie village, and to protect the environment for recreational use, have always been part of New Salem, but this does not mean that the various purposes do not come into conflict.

9. There are many more constituencies than those discussed in this chapter, including Lincoln buffs, antique collectors, the local business community, schoolchildren, and Boy Scouts. The Lincoln Pilgrimage is the largest annual gathering of the Boy Scouts of America.

Chapter Five

1. Relevant literature on authenticity includes Trilling 1972; MacCannell 1976; Handler 1986; Appadurai, ed., 1986; Cohen 1988; Morris 1988; and Handler and Saxton 1988.

2. At the suggestion of the students in my seminar on tourism, we took a field trip to New Salem in April 1988 to explore some of the theories we were reading about. It was my first visit. I became fascinated with the site. I returned later that season, then worked on New Salem full time during the summers of 1989 and 1990, with financial support for the fieldwork from the National Endowment for the Humanities summer stipend program and the University of Illinois Research Board. I spent part of the time in the library doing historical research on New Salem and the early Abraham Lincoln and devoted the remaining time to participation, observation, and interviewing at New Salem.

3. Relevant literature on reconstructed villages, historic sites, theme parks, and museums includes M. Wallace 1981; J. Anderson 1984; Schechner 1985; Lowenthal 1985; Dorst 1989; Karp and Lavine 1991; Gable, Handler, and Lawson 1992; and Willis 1993. The definitive work on American heritage sites is Handler and Gable 1997.

4. The Onstot house, which was moved from New Salem to Petersburg and then, with the site reconstruction, back to New Salem, is an original. The interpretive guides at New Salem point this out to the visitors.

5. This paragraph relies on Taylor and Johnson (1993), historians at the Illinois Historic Preservation Agency, the branch of state government in charge of the interpretive program at New Salem.

6. I make no claim that there are only four meanings of authenticity, only that these four emerged in my fieldwork. There are other shades of meaning (see the *Oxford English Dictionary*). If one says, for example, that an object is a counterfeit or a forgery, it implies that the object is not authentic but was falsely or mistakenly presented as an original. *Authenticity* in this sense means that the object actually is what it professes to be.

7. After I presented my findings to the superintendent at New Salem, he said that he had never thought about some of the issues raised in my study, but that the issues now made sense to him. This is what I mean by penetrating the taken-for-granted.

8. *Mrs. Hinsley* is a pseudonym.

9. My criticisms here are of the assumptions in Handler (1986) and Handler and Saxton (1988), not of those in Handler and Linnekin (1984) and not of the Colonial Williamsburg research (Handler and Gable 1997). I criticize MacCannell 1976, not MacCannell 1992. Nevertheless, after this material was published, both Handler and MacCannell let me know that they disagreed with my criticisms. Gable and Handler (1996) is a rebuttal of some of the major theses of this chapter. I leave it for the reader to decide. Needless to say, Handler, Gable, and MacCannell are among the leading scholars in tourism research.

10. Criticisms of this position in the tourism literature include Van den Abbeele 1980; Goldberg 1983; Cohen 1988; Morris 1988; and E. Bruner 1989, 1991.

11. Gable and Handler (1993) have made a similar observation about Colonial Williamsburg.

12. Exceptions are Schechner 1985 and Cohen 1988.

Chapter Six

1. The authors of this chapter, anthropologist Edward M. Bruner and folklorist Phyllis Gorfain, are not Middle East specialists and do not read Hebrew. Fortunately many of the primary texts, such as Josephus 1936 and Yadin 1966, have been translated into English, and we have relied on such excellent secondary sources as Yudkin 1971, Shargel 1979, and Zerubavel 1980.

2. New Salem, described in chapters 4 and 5, illustrates many instances of dialogic narration—between the popular and the historical, the mythic Lincoln and the scholarly Lincoln, the Lincoln story and the emphasis on crafts. In the widest sense, tourist tales and master narratives are always in dialogic interplay with the particular sites that embody a story.

3. This was clearly evident in chapter 3 on Elmina Castle in Ghana.

4. We are indebted to Hayden White for this phrasing.

5. The way different sites included in a tour itinerary engage in a dialogic process with one another is worthy of more attention in the tourism literature. The phenomenon has been relatively neglected in this volume. My impression is that on some tours the various sites tend to tell the same story and reinforce each other, but on other tours the stories told at the sites may be in conflict, may emphasize different aspects of the master tourist tale, or may be in dialogue with each other.

6. That the Israelis conduct a national debate and inquiry through the idiom of the Masada story is not an original idea; many others have stressed this important concept (e.g., Alter 1973; Zerubavel 1980; Ben-Yehuda 1995). Our emphasis is on the way these uses of the story constitute a dialogic discourse in narration and on how that process can be generalized.

Chapter Seven

1. Specialists might argue about the precise date when tourism began in Bali, but by the time the KPM steamship line initiated weekly service in 1924 and opened the Bali Hotel in 1928, there was international tourism.

2. See Picard 1992 and Vickers 1989. The same exuberant phrases have been found in the travel brochures for Bali from the 1930s to the 1990s.

3. Other groups—for example, participants in national liberation movements—may also seek an essentialized precolonial purity.

4. I use the term *postcolonial* in the sense of "after the colonial era," but I realize that the term is problematic.

5. This was in 1986, not during the 1987 tour described in the introduction.

6. For the Balinese, ceremonial attire at a temple festival is less an expression of individual identity and more a matter of respect toward others, especially the gods and demons who inhabit the ritual world. The Balinese would expect an ethnographer to dress respectfully.

7. I did return to Bali the next month, and Hilly helped me gather data on Balinese tourism.

8. This is best documented in Picard 1992.

9. The decision about which indigenous dances to perform for tourists has long been a problem for the Balinese (Picard 1996) because some dances are considered inappropriate for display to tourists, Westerners have influenced Balinese dance for more than a half-century, some dances are more interesting to tourists, and dance forms have changed over time. Further, different segments of Balinese society produce dances performances for tourists, introducing even more variation. This is a general predicament in tourism.

10. This thesis was presented at the annual meetings of the American Folklore Society in Cincinnati in 1985 by Barbara Kirshenblatt-Gimblett and myself in a paper titled "Tourist Productions and the Semiotics of Authenticity." See also the seminal work of Boon (1977), the scholarly work of Picard (1990), and the popular book by Vickers (1989).

11. I wish to thank Edi Sedyawati for her help in understanding the Ramayana. I am also indebted to I Made Bandem for his help with Balinese performances.

12. The local Javanese guide in Yogya complained in 1987 that there were now so many tourists at the Prambanan temple for the Ramayana performance that the Javanese could no longer attend. He had missed the point completely—that the Ramayana was constructed precisely for a tourist audience—and had thus blurred the distinction between performances for tourists and performances for Javanese.

13. From the performers' point of view, the enactment of the Ramayana was more a rite of modernity that generated cash income in a market economy.

14. Compare the performances at Mayers Ranch and Bomas of Kenya (chapter 2).

15. In 1986, after the tourists had left, I saw a Ramayana ballet that was performed as part of a large, multiple-day temple ceremony; it was another example of how a dance created for tourists becomes part of Balinese ceremony. The Ramayana, however, was held on the day after the major temple ritual. Such occurrences are commonplace in Bali.

Chapter Eight

1. See Benedict 1983 (43–45) for an early account, as well as Coombes 1994 and di Leonardo 1998.

2. Some parks are private commercial enterprises.

3. In a perceptive discussion of the Polynesian Cultural Center, an ethnic theme park in Hawaii, Andrew Ross (1994) recognizes the special aspects of his case: that it is owned by a religious group, the Church of Jesus Christ of Latter-Day Saints (Mormons); that most of the Polynesian performers are students from the nearby branch of Brigham Young University; that the Polynesians depicted are people of different countries and ethnicities; and most crucially, that most of the tourists at the Polynesian Cultural Center are visitors from outside the islands, the comparative significance of which Ross may not appreciate. In worldwide perspective, the Polynesian theme park is indeed unique.

4. Field notes, March 1986.

5. Personal communication, Han Hua Xing, vice director of the Xishuangbanna Tourism Bureau, personal communication, September 26, 1999.

6. There is no firm demographic data for Indonesia; I have used best estimates.

7. Although my remarks are accurate for ethnic/minority tourism in Xishuangbanna, the overall relationship between the Han and the minorities in China has a long and very complex history beyond the scope of this chapter and my competence. Minorities do possess a moral spiritual authority, and government policy now empowers minority peoples in many ways.

8. The data presented here were gathered in March 1986. Wendy Soebadio and Ezra Chosen, then anthropology students from the University of Indonesia, provided helpful research assistance. Subsequently, both received M.A. degrees in anthropology from the University of Illinois.

9. Kathleen Adams (personal communication, November 15, 2000) reports that the Toradja, like the Toba Batak, feel a deep connection to the displays of themselves at Taman Mini, and they discuss which local Toradja carvers worked on the Toradja *adat* house at Taman Mini. The same attachment may be true of the Karo Batak house (Kipp 1993).

10. See especially Foucault 1973.

11. Personal communication, September 8, 1997.

12. Janet Keller has helped me understand the cognitive processes involved; David Sutton (2001) has a particularly good review of the literature; see also Connerton 1989 and Shore 1996.

Chapter Nine

1. My wife, Elaine C. Bruner, an educator and counselor, has been a partner in all of my field trips, beginning in 1948 with my first undergraduate field experience as part of Clyde Kluckhohn's project among the Ramah Navajo. For our work in Sumatra she learned to speak both Indonesian and Toba Batak, and she fully participated in village life, focusing on the women and children.

2. Shortly after our arrival in the village, the Batak had explained that if my wife was adopted as a daughter, we could have a small ceremony for which I would have to contribute only one pig, but that if I was adopted as a son of the clan, it would require a large ritual for which I would have to donate at least one water buffalo. They presented their option as if they were saving me money, and only subsequently did I realize that when my wife was adopted we became wife receivers and hence were placed in a subservient position in the kinship system.

REFERENCES

Abram, Simone, Jacqueline Waldren, and Donald V. L. Macleod, eds.
1997 *Tourists and Tourism: Identifying with People and Places.* Oxford: Berg.
Abu-Lughod, Lila
1991 "Writing against Culture." Pp. 137–62 in *Recapturing Anthropology: Working in the Present,* ed. Richard G. Fox. Santa Fe, NM: School of American Research Press.
1997 "The Interpretation of Culture(s) after Television." *Representations* 59:109–34.
Acciaioli, Greg
1985 "Culture as Arts: From Practice to Spectacle in Indonesia." *Canberra Anthropology* 8 (nos.1, 2): 148–74.
Adams, Kathleen M.
1998 "Domestic Tourism and Nation-Building in South Sulawesi." *Indonesia and the Malay World* 26 (75): 77–96.
Adorno, Theodor W.
1984 *Aesthetic Theory.* London: Routledge and Kegan Paul.
Alter, Robert
1973 "The Masada Complex." *Commentary* 56:19–24.
Anagnost, Ann
1993 "The Nationscape: Movement in the Field of Vision." *Positions* 1 (3): 585–606.
Anderson, Benedict R. O'G.
1983 *Imagined Communities: Reflections on the Origin and Spread of Nationalism.* London: Verso.
1990 "Cartoons and Monuments: The Evolution of Political Communication under the New Order." Pp. 152–93 in *Language and Power: Exploring Political Cultures in Indonesia.* Ithaca, NY: Cornell University Press.
Anderson, Jay
1984 *Time Machines: The World of Living History.* Nashville: American Association for State and Local History.
Angelou, Maya
1986 *All God's Children Need Traveling Shoes.* New York: Vintage.
Anzaldúa, Gloria
1987 *Borderlands/La Frontera, The New Mestiza.* San Francisco: Spinsters/Aunt Lute Foundation.
Appadurai, Arjun
1988 "Putting Hierarchy in Its Place." *Cultural Anthropology* 3 (1): 37–50.
1991 "Global Ethnoscapes: Notes and Queries for a Transnational Anthropology." Pp. 191–210 in *Recapturing Anthropology: Working in the Present,* ed. Richard G. Fox. Santa Fe, NM: School of American Research Press.
1996 *Modernity at Large.* Minneapolis: University of Minnesota Press.

1997 "Discussion: Fieldwork in the Era of Globalization." *Anthropology and Humanism* 22 (1): 115–18.

———, ed.

1986 *The Social Life of Things: Commodities in Cultural Perspective.* Cambridge, UK: Cambridge University Press.

Appiah, Kwame Anthony

1990 "Racisms." Pp. 3–17 in *Anatomy of Racism,* ed. David Theo Goldberg. Minneapolis: University of Minnesota Press.

1992 *In My Father's House: Africa in the Philosophy of Culture.* New York: Oxford University Press.

Arendt, Hannah

1958 *The Human Condition.* Chicago: The University of Chicago Press.

Asad, Talal

1975 *Anthropology and the Colonial Encounter.* London: Ithaca Press.

Atherton, Lewis B.

1939 *The Pioneer Merchant in Mid-America.* New York: Da Capo Press.

Babcock, Barbara A.

1980 "Reflexivity: Definitions and Discriminations." *Semiotica* 30 (1/2): 1–14.

1990a "By Way of Introduction." In *Inventing the Southwest.* Special issue, *Journal of the Southwest* 32 (4): 383–99.

1990b " 'A New Mexican Rebecca': Imaging Pueblo Women." In *Inventing the Southwest.* Special issue, *Journal of the Southwest* 32 (4): 400–437.

1999 *Subject to Writing: The Victor Turner Prize and the Anthropological Text.* Special issue. *Anthropology and Humanism* 24 (2): 91–173.

Baker, Jean H.

1987 *Mary Todd Lincoln: A Biography.* New York: Norton.

Bakhtin, M. M.

1981 "Discourse in the Novel." In *The Dialogic Imagination,* ed. Michael Holquist. Austin: University of Texas Press.

Bandem, I. Made, and F. de Boer

1981 *Kaja and Kelod: Balinese Dance in Transition.* Kuala Lumpur: Oxford University Press.

Barthes, Roland

1981 *Camera Lucida: Reflections on Photography.* Trans. R. Howard. New York: Hill and Wang.

Bartlett, Harley Harris

1934 *The Sacred Edifices of the Batak of Sumatra.* Ann Arbor: University of Michigan Press.

Basler, Roy P.

1935 *The Lincoln Legend: A Study of Changing Conceptions.* Boston: Houghton Mifflin.

Bateson, Gregory

1972 *Steps to an Ecology of Mind.* New York: Ballantine Books.

Baudrillard, Jean

1983 *Simulations.* New York: Semiotext(e).

1988 *America.* London: Verso.

Baum, Vicki

1937 *A Tale From Bali.* Singapore: Oxford University Press.

Bauman, Richard
1992 "Performance." Pp. 41–49 in *Folklore, Cultural Performances, and Popular Entertainments*, ed. Richard Bauman. New York: Oxford University Press.
Behar, Ruth
1993 *Translated Woman: Crossing the Border with Esperanza's Story*. Boston: Beacon.
Belo, Jane
1960 *Trance in Bali*. New York: Columbia University Press.
Benedict, Burton
1983 *The Anthropology of World's Fairs: San Francisco's Panama Pacific International Exposition of 1915*. With contributions by Marjorie M. Dobkin, Gary Brechin, Elizabeth N. Armstrong, and George Starr. London: Scolar Press.
Benjamin, Walter
1969 *Illuminations*. Ed. Hannah Arendt, trans. H. Zohn. New York: Schocken.
Ben-Yehuda, Nichman
1995 *The Masada Myth: Collective Memory and Mythmaking in Israel*. Madison: University of Wisconsin Press.
Berger, Dhyani J.
1996 "The Challenge of Integrating Maasai Tradition with Tourism." Pp. 175–97 in *People and Tourism in Fragile Environments*, ed. Martin F. Price. Chichester, UK: John Wiley and Sons.
Berntsen, John L.
1979 "Economic Variations among Maa-Speaking Peoples." In *Ecology and History in East Africa*, ed. Bethwell A. Ogot. Nairobi: Kenya Literature Bureau.
Bhabha, Homi K.
1994 *The Location of Culture*. London: Routledge.
Blatti, Jo, ed.
1987 *Past Meets Present: Essays about Historic Interpretation and Public Audiences*. Washington DC: Smithsonian Institution Press.
Bodnar, John
1992 *Remaking America: Public Memory, Commemoration, and Patriotism in the Twentieth Century*. Princeton: Princeton University Press.
Boissevain, Jeremy, ed.
1996 *Coping with Tourists: European Reaction to Mass Tourism*. Providence: Berghahn.
Bomas of Kenya
2000 Bomas of Kenya Limited. Electronic document, http://www.africaonline.co.ke/bomaskenya/profile.html, now available at http://www.accesskenya.info/new_bomas.asp and http://kenyan.8m.com/kencu/institut.htm.
Boon, James
1977 *The Anthropological Romance of Bali, 1597–1972: Dynamic Perspectives in Marriage and Caste, Politics and Religion*. New York: Cambridge University Press.
1990 *Affinities and Extremes: Crisscrossing the Bittersweet Ethnology of East Indies History, Hindu-Balinese Culture, and Indo-European Allure*. Chicago: University of Chicago Press.
Boorstin, Daniel
1961 *The Image: A Guide to Pseudo-Events in America*. New York: Harper.

Borofsky, Robert
1987 *Making History: Pukapukan and Anthropological Constructions of Knowledge.* Cambridge, UK: Cambridge University Press.
Bourdieu, Pierre
1984 *Distinction: A Social Critique of the Judgment of Taste.* Cambridge, MA: Harvard University Press.
Bovill, Kathryn
1985 "Toba Batak Marriage and Alliance: Family Decisions in an Urban Context." PhD diss., University of Illinois.
Bruner, Edward M
1955 "Two Processes of Change in Mandan-Hidatsa Kinship Terminology." *American Anthropologist* 57 (4): 840–50. Reprinted in *Kinship and Social Structure,* ed. Nelson H. Graburn. New York: Harper and Row, 1971.
1956a "Cultural Transmission and Cultural Change." *Southwestern Journal of Anthropology* 12 (2): 191–99.
1956b "Primary Group Experience and the Processes of Acculturation." *American Anthropologist* 59 (4): 605–23.
1961 "Urbanization and Ethnic Identity in North Sumatra." *American Anthropologist* 63 (3): 508–21.
1963 "Medan: The Role of Kinship in an Indonesian City." Pp. 1–12 in *Pacific Port Towns and Cities,* ed. Alexander Spoehr. Honolulu: Bishop Museum Press.
1972 "Batak Ethnic Associations in Three Indonesian Cities." *Southwestern Journal of Anthropology* 28 (3): 207–29.
1973a "The Missing Tins of Chicken: A Symbolic Interactionist Approach to Culture Change." *Ethos* 1 (2): 219–38.
1973b "Kin and Non-Kin." Pp. 373–92 in *Urban Anthropology: Cross-Cultural Studies in Urbanization,* ed. Aidan Southall. Oxford, UK: Oxford University Press.
1974a "The Expression of Ethnicity in Indonesia." Pp. 251–80 in *Urban Ethnicity,* ed. Abner Cohen. ASA Monograph 12. London: Tavistock.
1974b *Indonesian Homecoming: A Case Study in the Analysis of Ritual.* Module Publication 54. Reading, MA: Addison-Wesley.
1984a "The Symbolics of Urban Migration." Pp. 64–76 in *The Prospects for Plural Societies,* ed. David Maybury-Lewis. Washington, DC: American Anthropological Association.
1984b "The Opening Up of Anthropology." Pp. 1–16 in *Text, Play, and Story: The Construction and Reconstruction of Self and Society,* ed. Edward M. Bruner. 1983 Proceedings of the American Ethnological Society. Washington, DC: American Anthropological Association.
1986a "Experience and Its Expressions." Pp. 3–30 in *The Anthropology of Experience,* ed. Victor Turner and Edward M. Bruner. Urbana: University of Illinois Press.
1986b "Ethnography as Narrative." Pp. 139–55 in *The Anthropology of Experience,* ed. Victor Turner and Edward M. Bruner. Urbana: University of Illinois Press.
1987 "Megaliths, Migration, and the Segmented Self." Pp. 133–49 in *Cultures and Societies of North Sumatra,* ed. R. Carle. Verffentlichungen des Seminars fr Indonesische und Sdseeprachen der Universitt Hamburg, 19. Berlin/Hamburg: Dietrich Reimer Verlag.
1989 "On Cannibals, Tourists, and Ethnographers." *Cultural Anthropology* 4:438–45.

1991 "The Transformation of Self in Tourism." *Annals of Tourism Research* 18 (2): 238–50.

1993a "Epilogue: Creative Persona and the Problem of Authenticity." In *Creativity/Anthropology*, ed. Smadar Lavie, Kirin Narayan, and Renato Rosaldo. Ithaca, NY: Cornell University Press.

1993b "Lincoln's New Salem as a Contested Site." In *Museums and Tourism*, ed. Edward M. Bruner, special issue of *Museum Anthropology* 17 (3): 14–25.

1994 "Abraham Lincoln as Authentic Reproduction: A Critique of Postmodernism." *American Anthropologist* 96:397–415.

1995 "The Ethnographer/Tourist in Indonesia." Pp. 224–41 in *International Tourism: Identity and Change*, ed. Marie-Françoise Lanfant, John B. Allcock, and Edward M. Bruner. London: Sage.

1996a "Tourism in Ghana: The Representation of Slavery and the Return of the Black Diaspora." *American Anthropologist* 98 (2): 290–304.

1996b "Tourism in the Balinese Borderzone." Pp. 157–79 in *Displacement, Diaspora, and Geographies of Identity*, ed. Smadar Lavie and Ted Swedenburg. Durham, NC: Duke University Press.

1999 "Return to Sumatra: 1957, 1997." *American Ethnologist* 26 (2): 461–77.

2001 "The Maasai and the Lion King: Authenticity, Nationalism, and Globalization in African Tourism." *American Ethnologist* 28 (4): 881–908.

2002 "The Representation of African Pastoralists: A Commentary." *Visual Anthropology* 15:387–92.

———, ed.

1984 *Text, Play, and Story: The Construction and Reconstruction of Self and Society*. 1983 Proceedings of the American Ethnological Society. Washington, DC: American Anthropological Association.

1993 *Museums and Tourism*. Theme issue, *Museum Anthropology* 17 (3).

Bruner, Edward M., and Barbara Kirshenblatt-Gimblett

1994 "Maasai on the Lawn: Tourist Realism in East Africa." *Cultural Anthropology* 9 (2): 435–70.

Bruner, Edward M., and Phyllis Gorfain

1984 "Dialogic Narration and the Paradoxes of Masada." Pp.56–79 in *Text, Play, and Story: The Construction and Reconstruction of Self and Society*, ed. Edward M. Bruner. 1983 Proceedings of the American Ethnological Society. Washington, DC: American Anthropological Association.

Bruner, Jerome

1986 *Actual Minds, Possible Worlds*. Cambridge, MA: Harvard University Press.

2003 *Making Stories: Law, Literature, Life*. Cambridge, MA: Harvard University Press.

Buck-Morss, Susan

1987 "Semiotic Boundaries and the Politics of Meaning: Modernity on Tour—A Village in Transition." Pp. 200–236 in *New Ways of Knowing: The Sciences, Society, and Reconstructive Knowledge*, ed. Marcus G. Raskin and Herbert J. Bernstein. Totowa, NJ: Rowman and Littlefield.

Carrington, Tim

1994 "Ray of Hope: Amid Africa's Agony, One Nation, Ghana, Shows Modest Gains." *Wall Street Journal*, January 26.

Castañeda, Quetzil E.
1996 *In the Museum of Maya Culture: Touring Chichen Itza.* Minneapolis: University of Minnesota Press.
Causey, Andrew
1998 "Ulos or Saham? Presentations of Toba Batak Culture in Tourism Promotions." *Indonesia and the Malay World* 26 (75): 97–105.
2003 *Hard Bargaining in Sumatra: Western Travelers and Toba Bataks in the Marketplace of Souvenirs.* Honolulu: University of Hawai'i Press.
Chambers, Erve
1999 *Native Tours: The Anthropology of Travel and Tourism.* Prospect Heights, IL: Waveland.
Chatman, Seymour
1978 *Story and Discourse.* Ithaca, NY: Cornell University Press.
Cheung, Sidney C. H.
1999 "The Meanings of a Heritage Trail in Hong Kong." *Annals of Tourism Research* 26 (3): 570–88.
Chilungu, Simeon W.
1985 "Kenya: Recent Developments and Challenges." *Cultural Survival Quarterly* 9 (3): 15–17.
Clark, Gracia
1994 *Onions Are My Husband: Survival and Accumulation by West African Market Women.* Chicago: University of Chicago Press.
Clifford, James
1986 "On Ethnographic Allegory." Pp. 98–121 in *Writing Culture: The Poetics and Politics of Ethnography,* ed. James Clifford and George E. Marcus. Berkeley: University of California Press.
1988 *The Predicament of Culture.* Cambridge, MA: Harvard University Press.
1989 "Notes on Travel and Theory." *Inscriptions* 5:177–88.
1992 "Traveling Cultures." Pp. 96–116 in *Cultural Studies,* ed. Lawrence Grossberg, Cary Nelson, and Paula Treichler. New York: Routledge.
1994 "Diasporas." *Cultural Anthropology* 9:302–38.
1997a *Routes: Travel and Transformation in the Late Twentieth Century.* Cambridge, MA: Harvard University Press.
1997b "Four Northwest Coast Museums: Travel Reflections." Pp. 107–45 in *Routes: Travel and Transformation in the Late Twentieth Century.* Cambridge, MA: Harvard University Press.
Clifford, James, and George E. Marcus, eds.
1986 *Writing Culture: The Poetics and Politics of Ethnography.* Berkeley: University of California Press.
Cohen, Erik
1974 "Who Is a Tourist? A Conceptual Clarification." *The Sociological Review* 22 (4): 527–55.
1979 "A Phenomenology of Tourist Experiences." *Sociology* 13 (2): 179–201.
1985a "Tourist Guides: Pathfinders, Mediators, and Animators." *Annals of Tourism Research* 12 (1): 5–29.
1985b "Tourism as Play." *Religion* 15:291–304.
1988 "Authenticity and Commoditization in Tourism." *Annals of Tourism Research* 15:371–86.

1996 *Thai Tourism.* Bangkok: White Lotus.

2001 "Ethnic Tourism in Southeast Asia." Pp. 27–53 in *Tourism, Anthropology, and China,* ed. Tan Chee-Beng, Sidney C. H. Cheung, and Yang Hui. Bangkok: White Lotus Press.

2004a "Backpacking: Diversity and Change." Pp. 389–405 in *Tourists and Tourism: A Reader,* ed. Sharon Bohn Gmelch. Long Grove, IL: Waveland.

2004b *Contemporary Tourism: Diversity and Change (Collected Articles).* Oxford, UK: Pergamon.

Cohn, Bernard S.

1996 *Colonialism and Its Forms of Knowledge: The British in India.* Princeton, NJ: Princeton University Press.

Coleman, Simon, and Mike Crang, eds.

2002 *Tourism: Between Place and Performance.* New York: Berghahn.

Colie, Rosalie

1966 *Paradoxical Epidemica.* Princeton, NJ: Princeton University Press.

Connerton, Paul

1989 *How Societies Remember.* Cambridge, UK: Cambridge University Press.

Coombes, Annie

1994 *Reinventing Africa: Museums, Imperial Culture and Popular Imagination.* New Haven: Yale University Press.

Crapanzano, Vincent

1986 "Hermes' Dilemma: The Masking of Subversion in Ethnographic Description." Pp. 51–76 in *Writing Culture: The Poetics and Politics of Ethnography,* ed. James Clifford and George E. Marcus. Berkeley: University of California Press.

Crick, Malcolm

1989 "Representations of International Tourism in the Social Sciences: Sun, Sex, Sights, Savings, and Servility." *Annual Review of Anthropology* 18:307–44.

1994 *Resplendent Sites, Discordant Voices: Sri Lankans and International Tourism.* Switzerland: Harwood Academic Publishers.

1995 "The Anthropologist as Tourist: An Identity in Question." Pp. 205–23 in *International Tourism: Identity and Change,* ed. Marie-Françoise Lanfant, John Allcock, and Edward M. Bruner. London: Sage.

Culler, Jonathan D.

1981 "Semiotics of Tourism." *American Journal of Semiotics* 1 (1/2): 127–40.

Cultural Information Service

1981 *A Viewer's Guide to Masada.* An ABC Novel for Television. New York: Cultural Information Service.

Cunningham, Clark E.

1989 "Celebrating a Toba Batak National Hero: An Indonesian Rite of Identity." Pp. 166–200 in *Changing Lives, Changing Rites: Ritual and Social Dynamics in Philippine and Indonesian Uplands,* ed. Susan D. Russell and Clark E. Cunningham. Ann Arbor: Center for South and Southeast Asian Studies, University of Michigan.

Dahles, Heidi

2001 *Tourism, Heritage, and National Culture in Java: Dilemmas of a Local Community.* Richmond, UK: Surrey.

Dann, Graham M. S.

1996 *The Language of Tourism: A Sociolinguistic Perspective.* Wallingford, UK: CABI Publishing.

———, ed.
2002 *The Tourist as a Metaphor of the Social World.* Wallingford, UK: CABI Publishing.

Davis, Sara Leila Margaret
1999 "Singers of Sipsongbanna: Folklore and Authenticity in Contemporary China." PhD diss., University of Pennsylvania.

de Certeau, Michel
1984 *The Practice of Everyday Life.* Trans. Steven Rendall. Berkeley: University of California Press.

Derrida, Jacques
1974 *Of Grammatology.* Baltimore: Johns Hopkins University Press.
1980 "Law of Genre." *Critical Inquiry* 7:55–81.

Desmond, Jane C.
1999 *Staging Tourism: Bodies on Display from Waikiki to Sea World.* Chicago: University of Chicago Press.

di Leonardo, Micaela
1998 *Exotics at Home: Anthropologies, Others, American Modernity.* Chicago: Chicago University Press.

Dinesen, Isak
1938 *Out of Africa.* New York: Random House.

Dominguez, Virginia R.
1986 "The Marketing of Heritage." *American Ethnologist* 13 (3): 546–55.

Donald, David
1948 *Lincoln's Herndon.* New York: Knopf.

Dorst, John D.
1989 *The Written Suburb: An American Site, An Ethnographic Dilemma.* Philadelphia: University of Pennsylvania Press.

Durkheim, Emile
1915 *The Elementary Forms of the Religious Life.* London: Allen and Unwin.

Ebron, Paulla A.
1998 "Enchanted Memories of Regional Difference in African American Culture." *American Anthropologist* 100 (1): 94–105.

Eco, Umberto
1986 "Travels in Hyperreality." Pp. 3–58 in *Travels in Hyperreality: Essays.* San Diego: Harcourt Brace Jovanovich.

Edensor, Tim
2001 "Performing Tourism, Staging Tourism." *Tourist Studies* 1 (1): 59–81.

Eggan, Fred
1954 "Social Anthropology and the Method of Controlled Comparison." *American Anthropologist* 56 (5): 743–63.

Empson, William
1950 *Some Versions of Pastoral.* New York: New Directions.

Errington, Frederick, and Deborah Gewertz
1989 "Tourism and Anthropology in a Post-Modern World." *Oceania* 60:37–54.

Errington, Shelly
1998 *The Death of Authentic Primitive Art and Other Tales of Progress.* Berkeley: University of California Press.

Evans-Pritchard, E. E.
1940 *The Nuer.* New York: Oxford University Press.
Fabian, Johannes
1990 *Power and Performance: Ethnographic Explorations through Proverbial Wisdom and Theater in Shaba, Zaire.* Madison: University of Wisconsin Press.
Farnell, Brenda
1999 "Moving Bodies, Acting Selves." *Annual Review of Anthropology* 28:341–73.
Feifer, Maxine
1985 *Going Places.* London: Macmillan.
Fernandez, James W.
1986 "The Argument of Images and the Experience of Returning to the Whole." Pp. 159–87 in *The Anthropology of Experience,* ed. Victor Turner and Edward M. Bruner. Urbana: University of Illinois Press.
Fischer, Michael M. J.
1989 "Museums and Festivals: Notes on the Poetics and Politics of Representation Conference, The Smithsonian Institution, September 26–28, 1988, Ivan Karp and Steven Levine, Organizers." *Cultural Anthropology* 4 (2): 204–21.
Franklin, Adrian
2001 "Performing Live: An Interview with Barbara Kirshenblatt-Gimblett, 19 April 2001, New York City." *Tourist Studies* 1 (3): 211–32.
2003 *Tourism: An Introduction.* London: Sage.
Foucault, Michel
1973 *The Order of Things: An Archaeology of the Human Sciences.* New York: Vintage.
1978 *The History of Sexuality.* New York: Pantheon.
1979 *Discipline and Punish: The Birth of the Prison.* Translated by Alan Sheridan. New York: Vintage.
1980 *Power/Knowledge: Selected Interviews and Other Writings, 1972–1977.* New York: Pantheon.
Fusco, Coco
1989 "The Border Art Workshop/Taller de Arte Fronterizo, Interview with Guillermo Gómez-Peña and Emily Hicks." *Third Text* 7:53–76.
1995 *English Is Broken Here: Notes on Cultural Fusion in the Americas.* New York: New Press.
Gable, Eric, and Richard Handler
1993 "Colonialist Anthropology at Colonial Williamsburg." *Museum Anthropology* 17 (3): 26–31.
1996 "After Authenticity at an American Heritage Site." *American Anthropologist* 98 (3): 568–78.
Gable, Eric, Richard Handler, and Anna Lawson
1992 "On the Uses of Relativism: Fact, Conjecture, and Black and White Histories at Colonial Williamsburg." *American Ethnologist* 19 (4): 791–805.
Galaty, John G.
1977 "In the Pastoral Image: The Dialectic of Maasai Identity." PhD diss., University of Chicago.
1983 "Ceremony and Society: The Poetics of Maasai Ritual." *Man* 18 (2): 361–82.
Gann, Ernest K.
1981 *Masada.* New York: Jove.

Geertz, Clifford
1966 "Religion as a Cultural System." In *Anthropological Approaches to the Study of Religion,* ed. M. Banton. London: Tavistock.
1973 *The Interpretation of Cultures.* New York: Basic.
1983 *Local Knowledge: Further Essays in Interpretive Anthropology.* New York: Basic.
1986 "Making Experience, Authoring Selves." Pp. 373–80 in *The Anthropology of Experience,* ed. Victor Turner and Edward M. Bruner. Urbana: University of Illinois Press.
1988 *Works and Lives: The Anthropologist as Author.* Stanford: Stanford University Press.
1995 *After the Fact: Two Countries, Four Decades, One Anthropologist.* Cambridge, MA: Harvard University Press.
1996 "Cultural Diplomacy." Keynote address, conference on Tourism and Heritage Management. Yogyakarta, Indonesia, October 1996.
Geertz, Hildred
1994 *Images of Power: Balinese Paintings Made for Gregory Bateson and Margaret Mead.* Honolulu: University of Hawai'i Press.
Genette, Gerard
1980 *Narrative Discourse.* Trans. Jane E. Lewin. Ithaca, NY: Cornell University Press.
Geschiere, Peter
1997 *The Modernity of Witchcraft: Politics and the Occult in Postcolonial Africa.* Charlottesville: University Press of Virginia.
Gilroy, Paul
1993 *The Black Atlantic: Modernity and Double Consciousness.* Cambridge, MA: Harvard University Press.
Gmelch, Sharon Bohn, ed.
2004 *Tourists and Tourism: A Reader.* Long Grove, IL: Waveland.
Goldberg, A.
1983 "Identity and Experience in Haitian Voodoo Shows." *Annals of Tourism Research* 10 (4): 479–95.
Gómez-Peña, Guillermo
1993 *Warrior for Gringostroika.* Saint Paul, MN: Graywolf Press.
1996 *The New World Border: Prophecies, Poems, and Loqueras for the End of the Century.* San Francisco: City Lights Books.
Gottlieb, Alma
1982 "Americans' Vacations." *Annals of Tourism Research* 9 (2): 165–88.
Graburn, Nelson H. H.
1977 "Tourism: The Sacred Journey." Pp. 17–31 in *Hosts and Guests,* 1st ed., edited by V. Smith. Philadelphia: University of Pennsylvania Press.
1983 "The Anthropology of Tourism." *Annals of Tourism Research* 10 (1): 1–11.
2002 "The Ethnographic Tourist." Pp. 19–39 in *The Tourist as a Metaphor of the Social World,* ed. Graham M. S. Dann. Wallingford, UK: CABI Publishing.
Graburn, Nelson H. H., and Jafar Jafari
1991 "Introduction: Tourism Social Science." *Annals of Tourism Research* 18 (1): 1–11.
Greenhouse, Steven
1988 "At a Resort in Western Zaire, It's Visit the Gorilla Families or the Old Hotels." *New York Times,* May 29.

Greenwood, Davydd J.
1977 "Culture by the Pound: An Anthropological Perspective on Tourism as Cultural Commoditization." Pp. 129–38 in *Hosts and Guests: The Anthropology of Tourism,* 1st ed., edited by V. Smith. Philadelphia: University of Pennsylvania Press.

Gupta, Akhil, and James Ferguson
1992 "Beyond 'Culture': Space, Identity, and the Politics of Difference." *Cultural Anthropology* 7:6–23.

———, eds.
1997 *Anthropological Locations: Boundaries and Grounds of a Field Science.* Berkeley: University of California Press.

Handler, Richard
1986 "Authenticity." *Anthropology Today* 2 (1): 2–4.

Handler, Richard, and Eric Gable
1997 *The New History in an Old Museum: Creating the Past at Colonial Williamsburg.* Durham, NC: Duke University Press.

Handler, Richard, and Jocelyn Linnekin
1984 "Tradition, Genuine or Spurious." *Journal of American Folklore* 97 (385): 273–90.

Handler, Richard, and William Saxton
1988 "Dyssimulation: Reflexivity, Narrative, and the Quest for Authenticity in 'Living.'" *Cultural Anthropology* 3 (3): 242–60.

Hannerz, Ulf
1996 *Transnational Connections.* London: Routledge.

Hanson, Allan
1989 "The Making of the Maori: Cultural Invention and Its Logic." *American Anthropologist* 91 (4): 890–902.

Haraway, Donna
1984 "Teddy Bear Patriarchy: Taxidermy in the Garden of Eden, New York City, 1908–1936." *Social Text* 11:20–64.
1989 *Primate Visions: Gender, Race, and Nature in the World of Modern Science.* New York: Routledge.

Harding, Susan, and Fred Myers, eds.
1994 "Further Inflections: Toward Ethnographies of the Future." Special issue of *Cultural Anthropology* 9 (3).

Harris, Eddy L.
1992 *Native Stranger: A Black American's Journey into the Heart of Africa.* New York: Vintage Books.

Harrison, David, ed.
1992 *Tourism and the Less Developed Countries.* New York: Halsted Press.

Harrison, Julia
2003 *Being a Tourist: Finding Meaning in Pleasure Travel.* Vancouver: UBC Press.

Herndon, William H., and Jesse William Weik
1889 *Herndon's Lincoln: The Story of a Great Life.* Chicago: Belford, Clarke.

Herrnstein-Smith, Barbara
1980 "Narrative Versions, Narrative Theories." *Critical Inquiry* 7:213–36.

Hertz, Emanuel
1940 *The Hidden Lincoln: From the Letters and Papers of William Herndon.* New York: Viking Books.

Hicks, Emily

1991 *Border Writing: The Multidimensional Text.* Minneapolis: University of Minnesota Press.

Hitchcock, Michael

1995 "The Indonesian Cultural Village Museum and Its Forbears." *Journal of Museum Ethnography* 7:17–24.

1998 "Tourism, Taman Mini, and National Identity." *Indonesia and the Malay World* 26 (75): 124–35.

Hitchcock, Michael, Victor T. King, and Michael J. G. Parnwell, eds.

1993 *Tourism in South-East Asia.* London: Routledge.

Hobsbawn, Eric, and Terence Ranger, eds.

1983 *The Invention of Tradition.* Cambridge, UK: Cambridge University Press.

Horne, Donald

1992 *The Intelligent Tourist.* McMahons Point, NSW: Margaret Gee.

Howells, William Dean

1960 *Life of Abraham Lincoln.* Bloomington: Indiana University Press.

Hubert, H., and M. Mauss

1898/1964 *Sacrifice: Its Nature and Functions,* trans. W. D. Halls. Chicago: University of Chicago Press.

Hughes-Freeland, Felicia

1993 "Packaging Dreams: Javanese Perceptions of Tourism and Performance." Pp. 138–54 in *Tourism in South-East Asia,* ed. Michael Hitchcock, Victor T. King, and Michael J. G. Parnwell. London: Routledge.

Huxtable, Ada Louise

1992 "Inventing American Reality." *The New York Review of Books,* December 3, pp.24–29.

Hyde, Sandra Teresa

2001 "Sex Tourism Practices on the Periphery: Eroticizing Ethnicity and Pathologizing Sex on the Lancang." Pp. 143–64 in *China Urban: Ethnographies of Contemporary Culture,* ed. Nancy N. Chen, Constance D. Clark, and Suzanne Z. Gottschang. Durham, NC: Duke University Press.

Hymes, Dell

1975 "Folklore's Nature and the Sun's Myth." *Journal of American Folklore* 88:345–69.

———, ed.

1972 *Reinventing Anthropology.* New York: Vintage.

Ikeda, Keiko

1999 *A Room Full of Mirrors: High School Reunions in Middle America.* Stanford, CA: Stanford University Press.

Jacknis, Ira

1988 "Margaret Mead and Gregory Bateson in Bali: Their Use of Photography and Film." *Cultural Anthropology* 3 (2): 160–77.

Jackson, Michael

2002 *The Politics of Storytelling: Violence, Transgression, and Intersubjectivity.* Copenhagen: Museum Tusculanum Press.

Jacobs, Alan H.

1965 "The Traditional Political Organization of the Pastoral Masai." D.Phil. thesis, Department of Anthropology, Oxford University.

Jamieson, Kristina Lynn
2002 "In the Isle of the Beholder: Traversing Place, Exploring Representations and Experiences of Cook Islands Tourism." PhD diss., Australian National University.

Janofsky, Michael
1994 "Mock Auction of Slaves Outrages Some Blacks." *New York Times*, October 8.

Johannsen, Robert W.
1989 *The Frontier, the Union, and Stephen A. Douglas*. Urbana: University of Illinois Press.

Jones, Charisse
1995 "Bringing Slavery's Long Shadow to the Light." *New York Times*, April 2.

Josephus, Flavius
1936 *The Works of Flavius Josephus*. Philadelphia: Porter & Coates.

Jules-Rosette, Bennetta, and Edward M. Bruner
1994 "Tourism as Process." *Annals of Tourism Research* 21 (2): 404–406.

Kahn, Miriam
2000 "Tahiti Intertwined: Ancestral Land, Tourist Postcard, and Nuclear Test Site." *American Anthropologist* 102 (1): 7–26.

Karp, Ivan, and Steven Lavine, eds.
1991 *Exhibiting Culture: The Poetics and Politics of Museum Display*. Washington, DC: Smithsonian Institution Press.

Kasfir, Sidney Littlefield
1999 "Samburu Souvenirs: Representations of a Land in Amber." Pp. 66–82 in *Unpacking Culture: Art and Commodity in Colonial and Postcolonial Worlds*, ed. Ruth B. Phillips and Christopher B. Steiner. Berkeley: University of California Press.

Kichwa Tembo
2000 Kichwa Tembo Tented Camp. Electronic document, http://www.ccafrica.com/destinations/Kenya/Kichwa/.

Kipp, R. S.
1993 *Dissociated Identities: Ethnicity, Religion, and Class in an Indonesian Society*. Ann Arbor: University of Michigan Press.

Kirshenblatt-Gimblett, Barbara
1998 *Destination Culture: Tourism, Museums, and Heritage*. Berkeley: University of California Press.

Kirshenblatt-Gimblett, Barbara, and Edward M. Bruner
1985 "Tourist Productions and the Semiotics of Authenticity." Paper presented at the meetings of the American Folklore Society. Cincinnati, Ohio.
1989 "Tourism." Pp. 249–53 in *International Encyclopedia of Communications*, vol. 4. New York: Oxford University Press.

Klumpp, Donna
1987 "Maasai Art and Society: Age and Sex, Time and Space, Cash and Cattle." PhD diss., Columbia University.

Knowles, Joan N., and D. P. Collett
1989 "Nature as Myth, Symbol, and Action: Notes towards a Historical Understanding of Development and Conservation in Kenyan Maasailand." *Africa* 59 (4): 433–60.

Kwedar, Melinda F., John A. Patterson, and James R. Allen
1980 *Interpreting 1830s Storekeeping in New Salem, Illinois.* Report submitted to the National Endowment for the Humanities, July 1.
Lanfant, Marie-Françoise
1989 "International Tourism Resists the Crisis." In *Leisure and Life-Style: A Comparative Analysis of Free Time,* ed. A. Olszewska and K. Roberts. London: Sage.
Lanfant, Marie-Françoise, John Allcock, and Edward M. Bruner, eds.
1995 *International Tourism: Identity and Change.* London: Sage.
Lansing, Stephen
1991 *Priests and Programmers: Technologies of Power in the Engineered Landscape.* Princeton, NJ: Princeton University Press.
Lavie, Smadar, Kirin Narayan, and Renato Rosaldo, eds.
1993 *Creativity/Anthropology.* Ithaca, NY: Cornell University Press.
Lavie, Smadar, and Ted Swedenburg, eds.
1996 *Displacement, Diaspora, and Geographies of Identity.* Durham, NC: Duke University Press.
Lévi-Strauss, Claude
1967 *Structural Anthropology.* Trans. Claire Jacobson and Brooke Grundfest Schoepf. New York: Anchor.
1949/1969 *The Elementary Structures of Kinship.* London: Eyre and Spottiswood.
Lewis, Lloyd
1957 *Myths after Lincoln.* New York: Grosset and Dunlap.
Leys, Colin
1975 *Underdevelopment in Kenya: The Political Economy of Neo-Colonialism.* London: Heinemann.
Livneh, Micha, and Ze'ev Meshel
ca. 1970 *Masada.* Jerusalem: National Parks Authority.
Löfgren, Orvar
1999 *On Holiday: A History of Vacationing.* Berkeley: University of California Press.
Lowenthal, Richard
1985 *The Past is a Foreign Country.* Cambridge, UK: Cambridge University Press.
Lowie, Robert
1935 *The Crow Indians.* New York: Farrar and Rinehart.
Luthin, Reinhard H.
1960 *The Real Abraham Lincoln.* Englewood Cliffs, NJ: Prentice-Hall
Lyotard, Jean-Francois
1979 *The Postmodern Condition: A Report on Knowledge.* Minneapolis: University of Minnesota Press.
MacCannell, Dean
1976 *The Tourist: A New Theory of the Leisure Class.* New York: Schocken.
1992 *Empty Meeting Grounds: The Tourist Papers.* London: Routledge.
2001 "Tourist Agency." *Tourist Studies* 1(1): 23–37.
Macnaghten, Phil, and John Urry, eds.
2001 *Bodies of Nature.* London: Sage.
Marcus, George E.
1994 "General Comments." *Cultural Anthropology* 9:423–28.
1995 "Ethnography in/of the World System: The Emergence of Multi-Sited Ethnography." *Annual Review of Anthropology* 24:95–117.

1997 "The Uses of Complicity in the Changing Mise-en-Scène of Anthropological Fieldwork." *Representations* 59:85–108.

Marcus, George E., and Michael M. J. Fischer

1986 *Anthropology as Cultural Critique: An Experimental Moment in the Human Sciences.* Chicago: University of Chicago Press.

Marx, Karl, and Frederick Engels

1947 *The German Ideology.* Edited and with an introduction by C. J. Arthur. New York: International Publishers.

Mathur, Saloni

2000 "Living Ethnological Exhibits: The Case of 1886." *Cultural Anthropology* 15 (4): 492–524.

Mattingly, Cheryl

1998 *Healing Dramas and Clinical Plots: The Narrative Structure of Experience.* Cambridge, UK: Cambridge University Press.

Mayhew, Bradley, and Thomas Huhti

1998 *South-West China.* Hawthorn, Australia: Lonely Planet Publications.

McClary, Janice McIlvaine

1985 "A Glimpse of Eden on Safari in Zaire." *New York Times,* August 11.

Mikell, Gwendolyn

1989 *Cocoa and Chaos in Ghana.* New York: Paragon.

Mintz, S. M.

1977 "Infant, Victim, and Tourist: The Anthropologist in the Field." *Johns Hopkins Magazine* 27:54–60.

Morris, Meaghan

1988 "At Henry Parkes Motel." *Cultural Studies* 2 (1): 1–47.

1995 "Life as Tourist Object." Pp. 177–91 in *International Tourism: Identity and Change,* ed. Marie-Françoise Lanfant, John B. Allcock, and Edward M. Bruner. London: Sage.

Mullaney, Steven

1983 "Strange Things, Gross Terms, Curious Customs: The Rehearsal of Cultures in the Late Renaissance." *Representations* 3:40–67.

Mulvey, Laura

1989 *Visual and Other Pleasures.* Bloomington: Indiana University Press.

Nash, Dennison

1977 "Tourism as a Form of Imperialism." Pp. 33–47 in *Hosts and Guests: The Anthropology of Tourism,* 1st ed., edited by V. Smith. Philadelphia: University of Pennsylvania Press.

1996 *The Anthropology of Tourism.* Oxford, UK: Pergamon.

Neely, Mark E., Jr.

1982 *The Abraham Lincoln Encyclopedia.* New York: McGraw-Hill.

Neely, Mark E., Jr., and R. Gerald McMurtry

1986 *The Insanity File: A Case of Mary Todd Lincoln.* Carbondale: Southern Illinois University Press.

Ness, Sally Ann

2003 *Where Asia Smiles: An Ethnography of Philippine Tourism.* Philadelphia: University of Pennsylvania Press.

Oakes, Tim

1998 *Tourism and Modernity in China.* London: Routledge.

Oates, Stephen B.

1984 *Abraham Lincoln: The Man Behind the Myths.* New York: Harper and Row.

Okumu, John J.

1975 "The Problem of Tribalism in Kenya." Pp. 181–202 in *Race and Ethnicity in Africa,* ed. Pierre L. van den Berghe. Nairobi: East African Publishing Company.

Olsen, Kjell

2002 "Authenticity as a Concept in Tourism Research: The Social Organization of the Experience of Authenticity." *Tourist Studies* 2 (2): 159–82.

Onstot, T. G.

1902 *Pioneers of Menard and Mason Counties.* Forest City, IL: T. G. Onstot.

Ortner, Sherry B.

1984 "Theory in Anthropology since the Sixties." *Comparative Studies of Society and History* 26 (1): 126–66.

1997 "Fieldwork in the Postcommunity." *Anthropology and Humanism* 22 (1): 61–80.

2003 *New Jersey Dreaming: Capital, Culture, and the Class of '58.* Durham, NC: Duke University Press.

Pearce, Philip L.

1982 *The Sociology of Tourist Behavior.* Oxford, UK: Pergamon.

Pemberton, John

1994a "Recollections from 'Beautiful Indonesia' (Somewhere beyond the Postmodern)." *Public Culture* 6 (2): 241–62.

1994b *On the Subject of "Java."* Ithaca, NY: Cornell University Press.

Peoria Journal

1936 "Speed 'Aging' at New Salem," *Peoria Journal,* June 19, p. 4.

Phillips, Ruth B., and Christopher B. Steiner, eds.

1999 *Unpacking Culture: Art and Commodity in Colonial and Postcolonial Worlds.* Berkeley: University of California Press.

Picard, Michel

1990 " 'Cultural Tourism' in Bali: Cultural Performances as Tourist Attractions." *Indonesia* 49:37–74

1992 *Bali: Tourisme culturel et culture touristique.* Paris: Harmattan.

1993 " 'Cultural Tourism' in Bali: National Integration and Regional Differentiation." Pp. 71–98 in *Tourism in South-East Asia,* ed. Michael Hitchcock, Victor T. King, and Michael J. G. Parnwell. London: Routledge.

1996 *Bali: Cultural Tourism and Touristic Culture,* trans. Diana Darling. Singapore: Archipelago Press.

1997 "Tourism, Nation-Building, and Culture." Pp. 181–214 in *Tourism, Ethnicity, and the State in Asian and Pacific Societies,* ed. Michel Picard and Robert E. Wood. Honolulu: University of Hawai'i Press.

Picard, Michel, and Robert E. Wood, eds.

1997 *Tourism, Ethnicity, and the State in Asian and Pacific Societies.* Honolulu: University of Hawai'i Press.

Pratt, Mary Louise

1992 *Imperial Eyes: Travel Writing and Transculturation.* New York: Routledge.

Price, Richard

1983 *First Time: The Historical Vision of an Afro-American People.* Baltimore: Johns Hopkins University Press.

Price, Richard, and Sally Price

1992 *Equatoria.* New York: Routledge.

1994 *On the Mall: Presenting Maroon Tradition-Bearers at the 1992 FAF.* Special Publication of the Folklore Institute, no. 4. Bloomington: Indiana University Press.

Proust, Marcel

1982 *Remembrance of Things Past.* Vol. 1. Translated by C. K. Scott Moncrieff and Terence Kilmartin. New York: Vintage.

Rabkin, Norman

1967 *Shakespeare and the Common Understanding.* New York: Macmillan.

Radcliffe-Brown, A. R.

1952 *Structure and Function in Primitive Society: Essays and Addresses.* Glencoe, IL: The Free Press.

Redfield, Robert

1955 *The Little Community: Viewpoints for the Study of a Human Whole.* Uppsala, Sweden: Almqvist and Wiksells.

Reep, Thomas P.

1927 *Lincoln at New Salem.* Chicago: Old Salem Lincoln League (Petersburg, IL).

Ren, Hai

1998 "Economies of Culture: Theme Parks, Museums, and Capital Accumulation in China, Hong Kong, and Taiwan." PhD diss., University of Washington.

Report of the Proceedings of the Conference on Preservation of Elmina and Cape Coast

1994 "Castles and Fort St. Jago in the Central Region Held in the Cape Coast Castle," May 11–12.

Richards, Greg, and Julie Wilson, eds.

2004 *The Global Nomad: Backpacking Tourism in Theory and Practice.* Clevedon, UK: Channel View Publications.

Ricoeur, Paul

1984 *Time and Narrative.* Vol. 1. Trans K. McLaughlin and D. Pellauer. Chicago: University of Chicago Press.

1985 *Time and Narrative.* Vol. 2. Trans. K. McLaughlin and D. Pellauer. Chicago: University of Chicago Press.

1987 *Time and Narrative.* Vol. 3. Trans. K. Blamey and D. Pellauer. Chicago: University of Chicago Press.

Robbins, Joel, and Sandra Bamford, eds.

1997 "Fieldwork Revisited: Changing Contexts of Ethnographic Practice in the Era of Globalization." Special issue. *Anthropology and Humanism* 22 (1): 3–118.

Rojek, Chris, and John Urry, eds.

1997 *Touring Cultures: Transformations of Travel and Theory.* London: Routledge.

Rosaldo, Renato

1986 "Illongot Hunting as Story and Experience." Pp. 97–138 in *The Anthropology of Experience,* ed. Victor Turner and Edward M. Bruner. Urbana: University of Illinois Press.

1989 *Culture and Truth: The Remaking of Social Analysis.* Boston: Beacon.

Rosenberg, Bruce A.

1974 *Custer and the Epic of Defeat.* University Park: Pennsylvania State University Press.

Ross, Andrew

1994 *The Chicago Gangster Theory of Life: Nature's Debt to Society.* London: Verso.

Ruby, Jay
1980 "Exposing Yourself: Reflexivity, Anthropology, and Film." *Semiotica* 30(1/2): 153–180.

Sahlins, Marshall
1981 *Historical Metaphors and Mythical Realities: Structure in the Early History of the Sandwich Islands Kingdom.* Ann Arbor: University of Michigan Press.
2000 *Culture in Practice: Selected Essays.* New York: Zone Books.

Sandburg, Carl
1954 *Abraham Lincoln: The Prairie Years and the War Years.* San Diego: Harcourt Brace Jovanovich.

Schafer, Roy
1980 "Narration in the Psychoanalytic Dialogue." *Critical Inquiry* 7:29–53.

Schechner, Richard
1985 "Restoration of Behavior." In *Between Theater and Anthropology.* Philadelphia: University of Pennsylvania Press.

Schein, Louisa
2000 *Minority Rules: The Miao and the Feminine in China's Cultural Politics.* Durham, NC: Duke University Press.

Schieffelin, Edward
1992 "Performance and the Cultural Construction of Reality: A New Guinea Example." In *Creativity/Anthropology,* ed. Smadar Lavie, Kirin Narayan, and Renato Rosaldo. Ithaca, NY: Cornell University Press.

Schreiner, Samuel A., Jr.
1987 *The Trials of Mrs. Lincoln: The Harrowing, Never-Before-Told Story of Mary Todd Lincoln's Last and Finest Years.* New York: Donald I. Fine.

Scott, David
1991 "That Event, This Memory: Notes on the Anthropology of African Diaspora in the New World." *Diaspora* 1 (3): 261–84.

Selwyn, Tom, ed.
1996 *The Tourist Image: Myths and Myth Making in Tourism.* Chichester, UK: John Wiley and Sons.

Seminar Sendra Tari Ramayana Nasional
1970 "Laporan, Seminar Tari Ramayana Nasional." N.p.: Panitia Penjelenggara.

Shargel, Baila R.
1979 "The Evolution of the Masada Myth." *Judaism* 28:357–71.

Shore, Brad
1996 *Culture in Mind.* Oxford: Oxford University Press.

Simon, John Y.
1990 "Abraham Lincoln and Ann Rutledge." *Journal of the Abraham Lincoln Association* 11:13–33.

Sinclair, M. Thea, Parvin Alizadeh, and Elizabeth Atieno Adero Onunga
1992 "The Structure of International Tourism and Tourism Development in Kenya." Pp. 47–63 in *Tourism and the Less Developed Countries,* ed. David Harrison. New York: Halsted Press.

Sly, Liz
1995 "Ghana Planning to Restore Castle." *Dallas Morning News,* April 9.

Smith, Valene L.
1977/1989 *Hosts and Guests: The Anthropology of Tourism,* 2nd ed. Philadelphia: University of Pennsylvania Press.
Smith, Valene L., and William Eadington
1992 *Tourism Alternatives: Potentials and Problems in the Development of Tourism.* Philadelphia: University of Pennsylvania Press.
Smith, Valene L., and Stephen R. C. Wanhill, eds.
1986 *Domestic Tourism.* Special issue, *Annals of Tourism Research* 13 (3): 329–479.
Snow, Stephen Eddy
1993 *Performing the Pilgrims: A Study of Ethnohistorical Role-Playing at Plimoth Plantation.* Jackson: University Press of Mississippi.
Sontag, Susan
1973 *On Photography.* New York: Delta.
2003 *Regarding the Pain of Others.* New York: Farrar, Straus and Giroux.
Spear, Thomas
1981 *Kenya's Past: An Introduction to Historical Method in Africa.* Essex: Longman.
Spear, Thomas, and Richard Waller, eds.
1993 *Being Maasai: Ethnicity and Identity in East Africa.* London: James Currey.
Spencer, Paul
1988 *The Maasai of Matapato: A Study of Rituals of Rebellion.* Bloomington: Indiana University Press.
1993 "Becoming Maasai, Being in Time." Pp. 140–56 in *Being Maasai: Ethnicity and Identity in East Africa,* ed. Thomas Spear and Richard Waller. London: James Currey.
Stanley, Nick
1998 *Being Ourselves for You: The Global Display of Cultures.* London: Middlesex University Press.
Stanley, Nick, and King Chung Siu
1995 "The Indonesian Cultural Village Museum and Its Forbears." *Journal of Museum Ethnography* 7:25–40.
Stewart, Kathleen
1988 "Nostalgia—A Polemic." *Cultural Anthropology* 3 (3): 227–41.
Stewart, Susan
1984 *Objects of Desire.* Baltimore: Johns Hopkins University Press.
Stocking, George W., ed.
1985 *Objects and Others: Essays on Museums and Material Culture.* Madison: University of Wisconsin Press.
Stoller, Paul
1997 "Globalizing Method: The Problems of Doing Ethnography in Transnational Spaces." *Anthropology and Humanism* 22 (1): 81–94.
Sutton, David
2001 *Remembrance of Repasts: An Anthropology of Food and Memory.* Oxford, UK: Berg.
Syrkin, Marie
1973 "The Paradox of Masada." *Midstream* 19:66–70.
Taman Mini
2001 Taman Mini. Electronic Document, http://www.taman-mini.co.id/php/viewMenuUtama.php?lokID=4.

Tan, Chee-Beng, Sidney C. H. Cheung, and Yang Hui, eds.
2001 *Tourism, Anthropology, and China.* Bangkok: White Lotus Press.
Taussig, Michael
1993 *Mimesis and Alterity: A Particular History of the Senses.* New York: Routledge.
Taylor, Richard S.
1984 *The New Salem Tradition.* Springfield, IL: Lincoln's New Salem State Park, Illinois Department of Conservation.
Taylor, Richard S., and Mark L. Johnson
1993 "Inventing Lincoln's New Salem: The Reconstruction of a Pioneer Village." Unpublished manuscript.
Tedlock, Barbara
2000 "Ethnography and Ethnographic Representation." Pp. 455–86 in *Handbook of Qualitative Research,* 2nd edition, ed. Norman K. Denzin and Yvonna S. Lincoln. Thousand Oaks: Sage.
Teo, Peggy, T.C. Chang, and K. C. Ho, eds.
2001 *Interconnected Worlds: Tourism in Southeast Asia.* Amsterdam: Pergamon.
Them Mushrooms
2000 Them Mushrooms. Electronic document, http://stockholm.music.museum/mmm/africa/mushroom.html.
Thomas, Benjamin P.
1954 *Lincoln's New Salem.* Carbondale: Southern Illinois University Press.
Trilling, Lionel
1972 *Sincerity and Authenticity.* Cambridge, MA: Harvard University Press.
Trinh, T. Minh-Ha
1985 "Mechanical Eye, Mechanical Ear, and the Lure of Authenticity." *Wide Angle* 6 (2): 58–63.
Trouillot, Michel-Rolph
1995 *Silencing the Past: Power and the Production of History.* Boston: Beacon.
Turner, Victor W.
1969 *The Ritual Process.* Chicago: Aldine.
1982 *From Ritual to Theatre.* New York: Performing Arts Journal Publications.
Turner, Victor W., and Edward M. Bruner, eds.
1986 *The Anthropology of Experience.* Urbana: University of Illinois.
Turner, Victor W., and Edith Turner
1978 *Image and Pilgrimage in Christian Culture.* New York: Columbia University Press.
Urry, John
1990 *The Tourist Gaze.* London: Sage.
1992 "*The Tourist Gaze* Revisited." *American Behavioral Scientist* 36 (2): 172–86.
2000 *Sociology Beyond Societies: Mobilities for the Twenty-First Century.* London: Routledge.
2004 "Tourism, Europe, and Identity." Pp. 433–41 in *Tourists and Tourism: A Reader,* ed. Sharon Bohn Gmelch. Long Grove, IL: Waveland.
Vail, Margaret A.
1995 *Tell Me a Souvenir.* Unpublished manuscript.
Van Dantzig, Albert
1980 *Forts and Castles of Ghana.* Accra, Ghana: Sedco.

Van den Abbeele, Georges
1980 "Sightseers: The Tourist as Theorist." *Diacritics* 10 (December): 2–14.
Van Der Heuvel, Gerry
1988 *The Crowns of Thorns and Glory: Mary Todd Lincoln and Varina Howell Davis: The Two First Ladies of the Civil War.* New York: E. P. Dutton.
Van Gennep, Arnold
1909/1960 *The Rites of Passage,* trans. M. Vizedom and G. Caffee. London: Routledge and Kegan Paul.
Vickers, Adrian
1989 *Bali: A Paradise Created.* Berkeley, CA: Periplus Editions.
Vidal, Gore
1984 *Lincoln: A Novel.* New York: Random House.
Voelkl, Cyndi
1980 "The New Salem Volunteers." *Historic Illinois,* October 1980, pp. 8–9.
Wagner, Roy
1975 *The Invention of Culture.* Englewood Cliffs, NJ: Prentice-Hall.
Wallace, Anthony F.C.
1970 *Culture and Personality.* New York: Random House.
Wallace, Michael
1981 "Visiting the Past: History Museums in the United States." *Radical History Review* 25:63–96.
Waller, Richard
1993 "Conclusions." Pp. 290–302 in *Being Maasai: Ethnicity and Identity in East Africa,* ed. Thomas Spear and Richard Waller. London: James Currey.
Warner, Lloyd W.
1953 *American Life.* Chicago: University of Chicago Press.
Whisnant, David
1983 *All That Is Native and Fine: The Politics of Culture in an Appalachian Region.* Chapel Hill: University of North Carolina Press.
Williams, Raymond
1973 *The Country and the City.* New York: Oxford University Press.
Willis, Susan, ed.
1993 *The World According to Disney.* Special issue. *South Atlantic Quarterly* 92 (1).
Wilson, Douglas L.
1990 "Abraham Lincoln, Ann Rutledge, and the Evidence of Herndon's Informants." *Civil War History* 36 (4): 301–24.
Wood, Megan Epler
1999 "Ecotourism in the Masai Mara: An Interview with Meitamei Ole Dapash." *Cultural Survival* 23 (2): 51–54.
Wood, Robert E.
1997 "Tourism and the State: Ethnic Options and Constructions of Otherness." Pp. 1–34 in *Tourism, Ethnicity, and the State in Asian and Pacific Societies,* ed. Michel Picard and Robert E. Wood. Honolulu: University of Hawai'i Press.
Woodward, C. Vann
1987 "Gilding Lincoln's Lily." *The New York Review of Books* 34, no. 14 (September 24, 1987), 23–26.

Wright, Richard
1954 *Black Power.* New York: Harper and Brothers.
Yadin, Yigael
1966 *Masada: Herod's Fortress and the Zealots Last Stand.* New York: Random House.
Yamashita, Shinji
2003 *Bali and Beyond: Explorations in the Anthropology of Tourism.* Translated by J. S. Eades. New York: Berghahn.
Yudkin, Leon T.
1971 *Isaac Lamdan: A Study in Twentieth-Century Hebrew Poetry.* Ithaca, NY: Cornell University Press.
Zerubavel, Yael
1980 *Last Stand: On the Transformation of Symbols in Modern Israeli Culture.* Ann Arbor, MI: University Microfilms.
Zipes, Jack
1979 *Breaking the Magic Spell: Radical Theories of Folk and Fairy Tales.* Austin: University of Texas Press.

INDEX

Note: Italicized page numbers indicate figures.